CHUCK BERRY

ROCK 'N' ROLL MUSIC

ROCK&ROLL

Reference Series

Tom Schultheiss, Series Editor

ROCK&ROLL

Remembrances Series

Tom Schultheiss, Series Editor

Available only through Pierian Press • P.O. Box 1808 • Ann Arbor, Michigan 48106 • 1-800-678-2435

CHUCK BERRY

ROCK 'N' ROLL MUSIC

Second Edition

by Howard A. DeWitt

With research assistance
and a discography by
Morten Reff

Pierian Press
1985

ISBN 0-87650-171-4
LC 84-61230

Grateful acknowledgement is extended to the following individuals and companies for permission to include photographic materials in this volume:

Billy Asprodites; John Garodkin/Forlaget Mjolner; Larry Hulst; Tore Jensen; Mike Mulhern; Jean Pierre Ravelli; Morten Reff.

Decca International/Decca Record Company Ltd. (David Wedgbury, U.K.); Phonogram International b.v. (E.J. van Eyk, Holland); Sonet Grammofon AB (Dag Haggquist, Sweden); Sugar Hill Records Ltd. (Marshall Chess, U.S.).

Cover design by Carol Jennet
Cover photos: Movie Still Archives, Santa Fe, New Mexico

The Pierian Press
P.O. Box 1808
Ann Arbor, Michigan 48106

CONTENTS

PREFACE

This book is an attempt to assess the importance of Chuck Berry's music against the backdrop of the rise of popular culture in the United States.

Books on rock-and-roll performers are usually either embarrassingly enthusiastic about their subjects, or excessively critical. We have attempted to balance praise and criticism. There is little doubt that Chuck Berry is one of a handful of musicians who helped to create the rock music revolution, but there have been few attempts to relate his personal life to his music. This book attempts to interpret Chuck's music in light of his background, upbringing, and life experiences. We have not sought to analyze his marriage, his personal business dealings, or his relationship with his children. Rather, we have concentrated on the interrelationship of Chuck's personality, music, and creative contribution to American popular culture.

This book is divided into two distinct sections: the first part is a biographical analysis of Chuck's life and recording career. This is followed by a reference section which provides a number of exhaustive discographies and other listings detailing Chuck's worldwide musical impact.

The book also contains quite a large number of rare photographs, and there has been a concerted effort by a number of people to help us present all phases of Chuck's life through pictures. We believe that this is the fullest and most complete book on Chuck Berry published to date. It will not satisfy some journalists and rock critics, but we believe that it is as close as anyone has come to uncovering the roots of Chuck Berry's enormous creative genius.

Howard A. DeWitt
Morten Reff

ACKNOWLEDGMENTS

This book is the result of the efforts of a number of people. The first edition of *Chuck Berry: Rock N Roll Music*, published by Horizon Books in 1981, was the product of a labor of love spanning a quarter of a century. Since 1958, I had collected materials on Chuck's career, and these research files set the stage for the first book. In addition, I had seen Chuck more than thirty times in concert since 1956, and I was able to interview a number of people close to Chuck's career and personal life. Since that initial book, however, I have been inundated with more than 200 letters. It is impossible to thank everyone but, to those of you who sent letters, please accept my profound thanks and keep the materials coming in the mail! To anyone who has more information for future editions, please direct this material to Howard A. DeWitt, PO Box 3083, Fremont, California 94539.

The most important person in recasting this book in its second edition is Morten Reff. In 1981, I received a letter from Morten asking if he could make a few suggestions for the next edition of the book. In a few weeks I received a five pound package with his "few" suggestions. Morten then kindly arranged a series of lectures for me in Norway and Sweden, and he also opened his personal archives for my research on this book. The list of cover records was greatly expanded, and Morten single-handedly revised the discography to include world-wide listings of Chuck Berry records. During the next weeks that I spent with Morten and Anita, I realized how significant Chuck Berry's European fans are in the 1980s. As a result, a chapter was added to the book to commemorate my visit with Morten and Anita. He is not only a good friend, but, in many respects, is this edition's co-author, having provided much information and numerous corrections to many of my ideas.

Equally important to this book has been Jean Pierre Ravelli. All of Mr. Ravelli's suggestions for changes in this volume were communicated through Morten Reff, and Ravelli's criticism of this manuscript was an important aspect of his worth to this project. Mr. Ravelli also provided a number of excellent photos and several suggestions for the discography. John Garodkin was another European who was instrumental in the collection of photos and obscure materials on Chuck's European career. Johann Hasselberg of Flying Hot Music arranged a speaking engagement for me in Lidkoping, Sweden, and Mr. Hasselberg and his parents were too generous with their time and attention. Hasselberg's Flying Hot Music is one of the best rock clubs in Europe, and he was able to provide many insights into Chuck's musical appeal.

Another important Swedish contact on this book was Tommy Holmstrom, the tenor sax player in Promille Hill. He not only arranged my talk about Chuck Berry in Gavle, Sweden, but he housed and fed us during our stay. As an active blues and r and b musician, Tommy is one of Sweden's outstanding young talents. Yet another important Swedish critic was Tommy Lofgren of the Scandinavian Blues Association. Lofgren offered some excellent criticism about the direction of the Chuck Berry book, and he shared his extensive knowledge of blues and rock music with me. The Scandinavian Blues Association, Zetterlunds vag 90 B, s-186 00 Vallentura, Sweden, publishes one of the best blues magazines in the world.

In Germany, Christian Kluver was able to introduce me to Tony Sheridan, who recounted his early days with the Beatles and told some interesting Chuck Berry stories. Horst Fascher also provided a number of significant details about Chuck Berry's European career, and was both a gentleman and an honest and open interviewee. Charles "Dr. Rock" White of Scarborough, England, kindly provided a tape of a Chuck Berry radio show he produced for BBC radio. White, known affectionately to English rock enthusiasts as Dr. Rock, is Bo Diddley's official biographer, and his letter and tape helped immensely.

In Belgium, Willy and Lutgarde Pauwels provided some excellent criticism of the book, and they also introduced me to the better side of Antwerp. Rudy and Noela Vermeiren were also a source of friendly inspiration in Antwerp. Rudy's guitar playing is much like Chuck Berry's, and he is an undiscovered musical talent who provided some interesting times during my European visit. Jacky Huys, the Greil Marcus of Belgian journalism, graciously opened his home and provided some critical, but insightful, comments on American rock music. Jacky is a fine journalist and his collection of essays on rock music, *Cadillac County*, deserves an English publication.

In Liverpool, Bob Wooler, who is truly the fifth Beatle, aided my research into the roots of English rock music. Also, Joe Flannery opened his home and commented on the British rock music scene. Jim and Liz Hughes at the Cavern Mecca, as well as Connie and Eddie, answered a number of my inane questions and provided me with a great deal of material on Chuck Berry's influence upon the Beatles. Charlie Lennon, John's uncle, provided a lengthy interview on Chuck Berry's influence upon John Lennon. Dave Caryl at City Records was another important contact who went out of his way to introduce me to the Liverpool scene.

In London, Barry Miles provided telephone help in finding key research spots, and Adam Komorowski also helped me to find my way through the maze of English sources. Although neither Miles nor Komorowski were directly involved in this book, they offered advice on it. I can only thank them for taking the time.

The Aachen Hotel in Liverpool was also an unexpected source of material, as it was there I met a stranger with a road map to the early English rock music scene. Quinns Hotel in Richmond was another helpful spot, and these sources all were useful in producing the book.

In America, Lee Cotten of Golden Oldies Records in Sacramento, California, provided pictures, records, and historical data for this book. Lee, who was my co-author on a previous book, is one of the most knowledgeable people in rock journalism. Ed "G.N." Diaz was another important source of materials. In addition, Dennis De-Witt and Dean Silverstone provided information on Chuck's career. Professor Herb Schott of Ohlone College was another excellent critic, and Professor B. Lee Cooper of Newberry College provided research and editorial criticism. Although Professor Cooper was not directly involved in the writing, his reviews and research suggestions were important ones. Rodney Masuoka of Honolulu helped to straighten out some of my thoughts late in the preparation of the book, and Joseph "Sonny Knight" Smith helped to recall some of the bright moments of the 1950s in a brief conversation. Tommy Sands recalled some of his early experiences and this helped to shape the atmosphere of the book. Johnny Tillotson provided an in-depth interview on his relationship with Elvis Presley, which also provided some Chuck Berry insights.

There were many more people who were involved in peripheral ways, and I would like to thank Ken Holden, Jim McCue, Rip Lay, Sharon McCormick, Hans Larsen, Chuck Beazley, Carrol Tuttle, Jimmy Beasley, Joe Mendoza, Mark Naftalin, Craig Texera, Nancy and Al Spencer, Guitar Mac, and Bo Diddley for their support and help.

Finally, thanks to my good friend Fred Worth, who read this manuscript in two stages, provided analytical suggestions for improvement, and added a number of interesting facts, and to Tom Schultheiss of Pierian Press, who edited the manuscript and brought everything together in its final form.

My family was an inspiration: my wife, Carolyn, read and critiqued the manuscript five times. She is still my wife, and I can only thank her for being the most understanding woman in the world. Melanie Dawn and Darin Dion DeWitt made this book a joy, as they periodically tore up some of its pages.

INTRODUCTION

In 1955, five rock-and-roll music pioneers changed the direction of American music. Bill Haley and his Comets recorded the national anthem of rock music, *Rock Around the Clock*. Elvis Presley gave a new cultural art form its biggest impetus when he left the small Memphis-based Sun Record label to sign with RCA Victor; soon, Elvis brought rock music into every living room in America when he appeared on Ed Sullivan's Sunday night television show. Three other rock pioneers helped the Big Beat to become a mainstream part of our national culture: Little Richard belted out a brand of fire-eating vocals, complemented by his own special piano style. An unassuming New Orleans musician, Fats Domino, provided the musical antithesis of Little Richard. The fifth and final rock pioneer was Chuck Berry, unique among the Founding Fathers of rock-and-roll music because he was the only one to write both the music and lyrics to his songs. It was Chuck's ability to convey themes of teen-age joy, depression, and other more mundane adolescent concerns which made him the most creative of the early rock pioneers.

It is notable that Berry is the only early rock star who continues to perform in the 1980s. Elvis Presley and Bill Haley died tragic deaths. Little Richard retired to become a minister, and Fats Domino languishes in self-imposed retirement in New Orleans. Yet, Chuck Berry continues to do his famous duck walk, play the old hits, and occasionally reach into his reservoir of performing zeal to bring an audience to a fever pitch. In May, 1981, for example, after traveling all night on a flight from Tokyo, Chuck appeared in a small California town, Dixon, at the May Fair. He began by quietly appearing on stage and, after a pregnant pause during which he looked knowingly at Mark Naftalin seated at the piano, he suddenly launched energetically into his concert. As Chuck began to reel off his string of early hits, the audience started to dance in the aisles. During this show, Naftalin's piano playing was reminiscent of Johnny Johnson's early piano duos with Chuck; it was Naftalin's capable Rhythm and Blues Revue which had prompted Chuck to deliver such as extraordinary concert. There have been many times when Chuck did not have bands of this quality to back him, however. At the 1980 Seattle Blues Festival, Chuck unplugged the guitar of a local bass player who could not play the licks necessary to support his (Berry's) performance. Tom Bergen, lead guitarist of Ravenna and the Magnetics, recalls that Berry was visibly agitated over the lack of good backup music. As a result, he walked over to the bass player and said, "Listen motherfucker, when I stomp my foot, stop playing." When the guitarist failed to heed Chuck's admonition, Berry simply unplugged his instrument for the rest of the set.

The two incidents point up the problems that Chuck Berry faces in the 1980s. He is continually in demand to do local concerts, but the inevitable requests for the same old songs and the reliance on fundamentally inept backup musicians has taken its toll on Chuck's musical career. Also, while he is still a tremendous performer, the well of creative songwriting has seemingly dried up for Chuck Berry. His last period of intense songwriting in 1964 produced *Nadine* and *No Particular Place to Go*, but he has not produced a hit record in more than a decade.

In the 1980s, however, Chuck Berry has finally received some of the recognition which otherwise eluded him throughout his lengthy and distinguished musical career. On October 11, 1982, for example, the Nashville Songwriters Association International Hall of Fame inducted Chuck into its prestigious organization. True to form, Berry was elusive and noncommittal about his continued success in the recording business. Frances Preston of BMI accepted the award for Chuck, and there was no comment in the press on his feelings about this important honor.

What is it that makes Chuck Berry's early music so timeless? The answer to this question lies in the manner in which Berry uses lyrics in his songs. There is no more significant aspect of Berry's career than his ability to employ poetic lyrics to weave images of American social change. In particular, he has pioneered the use of automobile imagery in his tunes. The automobile has been the object of popular songs for years. From Robert Johnson's *Terraplane Blues* to Bruce Springsteen's **The River** album, there has been a dependence upon automobile themes to focus attention upon cultural change. Peter Guralnick's study, *Lost Highway: Journeys and Arrivals of American Musicians*, suggests that popular musicians embody a sense of freedom and willingness to experiment which appeals to rock music fans, who idolize such figures as an expression of their own concerns about society. To the extent that the automobile is also representative of this sense of freedom, then, it has been one of the strongest focuses of the rock music revolution, one recognized and developed by Chuck Berry very early on. There is much more to

Berry's music than a fascination with the automobile, of course. He was also an astute commentator on urban life, changing trends in American culture, and the technological advances in our society. But it was the motorcar which was central to his music. In order to understand his fascination with the automobile, it is necessary to examine some key automobile imagery in his songs.

In *Maybellene*, for example, Chuck challenged the idea that the person with the biggest, fastest cutomized car would invariably capture the attention of the young girl. (There is also a subtheme revolving around the automobile's destruction of a young girl's life. "You've started back doin' the things you used to do," intones Chuck.) In the song, the older man driving the Cadillac Coupe de Ville is the villain, whereas the hero drives a Ford V-8. When the overheated Ford catches the Cadillac at 110 miles an hour, there is a sense of triumph for the young man. It is the triumph of youthful pursuit over the well-heeled owner of the Cadillac which gives Berry's song its final irony for young listeners.

In the song *Come On*, Chuck uses a broken-down automobile to interpret some of the key problems of America's youth. (Surprisingly, this song was largely ignored until the Rolling Stones recorded it.) The theme behind *Come On* is one of lost love and technological change. The automobile becomes the symbol for the modern problems faced by the young man. His car won't start. Having lost his job and being unable to afford a mechanic, the hero laments his victimization by a rapidly changing society. The song epitomizes a common frustration of young people in the 1950s.

Changes in American life in the early 1960s are also reflected in Chuck's *Nadine*. The song portrays the problems of a young man coping in the city without a car; Nadine, who lives uptown, must be pursued using public transportation. The inability to please his fiancee causes the song's hero to lament the urban blight which creates traffic congestion, and he complains that he cannot court his girl properly because of the lack of the "indispensable" automobile. Perhaps Chuck's most interesting car song is *No Money Down*. This tune suggests that while owning a new Cadillac symbolized power, social mobility, freedom, and a sense of status, nevertheless, the car dealer is the person who utlimately determines one's success level by his assessment of a car's value — even a Cadillac. Another brief but interesting use of automobile lyrics is contained in *Too Much Monkey Business*. In this song, a woman attempts to get the hero to settle down. When he is drafted and the army robs him of his freedom, he summarizes his own plight by speaking out against the inferiority of military automobiles. Perhaps the best car song, however, is *No Particular Place to Go*. In 1964, this song put Chuck back on the charts. It was the tale of a young man "cruising and playing the radio" with a young girl seated next to him. A typical recital of the longing for the physical and mental freedom of youth, it also suggested themes of enforced morality and made a plea for economic freedom for young people. When Chuck commented that he was "Riding along . . . still trying to get her belt unloose," he succinctly analyzed the moral dilemmas of the pre-Pill generation.

These songs are just a few examples of how Chuck Berry employed automobile imagery to analyze and mirror important trends in American popular culture. He was also able to use the Greyhound bus in songs such as *Johnny B. Goode, Bye Bye Johnny*, and *The Promised Land*. The young were unemployed and generally unwanted in the affluence of the late 1950s. This created an alienation and a rebellion which paved the way for the protests of the sixties. Through his allusions to the Greyhound bus, Chuck was able to make some important comments on the direction of American life, its fluidity, mobility, and the restlessness which lay beneath the surface. Later, when he wrote and recorded *Dear Dad* in the mid-1960s, he carried his lyrical poetry on youthful alienation into a new generation. It was this ability to interpret the essential attributes of American popular culture which qualify Chuck Berry as a true creative genius. As a result, by carefully analyzing the various stages of his career in the chapters which follow, it should be possible to draw some conclusions about American popular culture in its broader musical aspects, and thus provide an important window into our national consciousness as a whole.

CHAPTER 1

ROCK ROOTS, 1926-1954

On a Wednesday morning at 6:59 a.m., October 18, 1926, Charles Edward Anderson Berry was born on Goode Street in St. Louis, Missouri. Thirty years later, Chuck Berry would write a song entitled *Johnny B. Goode* to celebrate his birthplace. Chuck was born into a solid, middle-class Christian family. His father, Henry Berry, was a carpenter and part-time lay minister. His mother, Martha, was busy with six children and a large house. The Berry family lived in a treelined suburb, Elleardsville, and they were much like the other residents of this sleepy St. Louis community. They worked hard, held family gatherings, celebrated birthdays, and maintained a strong family unit in the midst of the worst depression in American history.

The Berry family was not wealthy, but they were comfortable by the standards of the 1930s. The children were allowed to take music lessons, and the house vibrated with the sounds of musical instruments. Henry and Martha Berry believed in strong Christian principles and a sound education. Young Chuck Berry, as a result of his parents' values, was exposed to good music, a quality education, and a strongly moralistic value system. These elements eventually coalesced into personality traits which made Chuck Berry the first poet laureate of rock-and-roll music.

It was this solid middle-class family background which made Chuck so unlike many blues singers, who were either the product of a poverty cycle or a split family. He was also not like many early rock-and-roll performers, who were either young country boys or poor city kids who looked to rock music for fame and fortune. His familiarity with many types and styles of music served to combine in Berry the elements of a black blues singer with the influences of young, white rock artists. In fact, Chuck might have grown up to be a latter-day Muddy Waters or John Lee Hooker had the blues been the main inspiration in his musical development. But Chuck Berry's early life in St. Louis revolved around the malt shop, the record store, the problems of school, the pressures of parents, and the need

1

Young Chuck as pictured on Chess's fold-out Bio album.

for an automobile, and it was these factors which helped to make Berry one of the Founding Fathers of rock-and-roll music instead. Eventually, he was to nurture these influences into major rock-and-roll records, and it was natural that what emerged was a type of mainstream rock music that celebrated the American way of life.

It is not easy to analyze the many musical styles which helped to mold Chuck Berry's music. The initial influences began as World War II raged. Chuck attended Sumner High School, where he developed his earliest performing talents in Mrs. Julia Davis' music classes. She worked extensively with Chuck, and eventually persuaded him to join the bass section of the school Glee Club. During his high school year, Chuck favored a smooth, ballad singing style characteristic of the early 1940s. He loved to tell his classmates that English, music, and math were his favorite school subjects. These classroom influences combined to create an early interest in songwriting, and at Sumner High Chuck began to show some tendency to pursue a career as a professional musician.

It was also during his years at Sumner High School that Chuck developed a unique and highly personalized performing style. His first guitar was a six-string Spanish guitar, and Chuck surprised almost everyone by playing a number of country-western songs. He was also a fan of big band music, and he would often play instrumental segments of Benny Goodman songs that he'd heard on the radio. Tom Stevens, a close high school friend, encouraged Chuck to continue his guitar playing, and it was Stevens who played guitar behind Chuck at the year-end school assembly, common to high schools in the 1940s. Chuck performed a show-stopping version of *Confessin' the Blues*. As popular music changed from swing to bebop in the early 1940s, Chuck purchased a number of records on the Esoteric label featuring guitarist Charlie Christian's music. Long before he listened intently to other guitarists, Chuck was playing Christian's version of *Confessin' the Blues*, and it proved to be an important influence during his formative years.

As a youngster, Chuck was a model student at Sumner High School, and had a strong curiosity about and interest in the local music scene. In the 1940s, St. Louis was a veritable training ground for some of the best American musical talent. During World War II, the Tune Town Ballroom on Grand and Olive near the Fox Theater featured Harry James, Benny Goodman, Glenn Miller and Tommy Dorsey. The big band era was responsible for producing swing music and the jitterbug, both important components in the rock-and-roll musical revolution.

In the late 1940s, the musical renaissance prompted a large number of small clubs to open after larger ballrooms like the Tune Town closed down. Suddenly, the Club Imperial and a sophisticated cocktail lounge in the Chase Hotel dominated the St. Louis music scene. The radio was filled with nationally syndicated musical shows, as well as local music broadcast from a number of well-known St. Louis clubs. In order to appeal to large numbers of people, certain nights were devoted to specific types of music. Tuesday nights generally featured jitterbug and dance contests. There were numerous Latin American bands playing on Wednesdays, while Thursday was big band night. The St. Louis clubs featured rhythm and blues music on Fridays to attract the college crowd, and on Saturday night there was every type of music available in the city. It was in the midst of this musical smorgasbord that Chuck Berry began formulating his songs about sweet little rock-and-rollers and school days, but it was to be a long time before Chuck's little poems, sketched on the backs of paper bags and written on yellow-lined paper, would mature into his own inventive brand of rock-and-roll music.

While he attended Sumner High School from 1940 to 1944, Chuck frequented the local clubs and studied music intensely. At Sumner High, for example, Chuck learned to play the guitar, the piano, the saxophone, and he was often in the music room trying to play the drums. This created a musical breadth which allowed Chuck to employ aspects of country-western, blues, rhythm and blues, pop music, and big band tunes in his musical repertoire. The clubs were important, because they exposed Chuck to instrumental riffs, vocal stylings, and stage mannerisms which were important in shaping his own act. Most studies of Chuck Berry's life indicate that he began his professional musical career in the early 1950s. There is some evidence, however, that Chuck was dabbling in the musical field in the 1940s. A number of Chuck's close friends have remarked that he was a sideman with the Ray Band Orchestra when it played in St. Louis. George Edick, the owner of the popular Club Imperial, remembers seeing Chuck performing in small lounges in the late 1940s. Although legend has it that Johnny Johnson hired Chuck for his first professional job, there are many people around St. Louis who remember seeing Chuck play in the late 1940s. In any event, Chuck emerged from Sumner High and the St. Louis club scene an experimental musician who blended a number of styles into a form very much his own.

There were a number of professional musicians who recognized Chuck Berry's early talents. Joe Sherman, a local rhythm and blues performer, gave Chuck his old Kay guitar to practice on after hearing Chuck play in a pickup jam session. This gift was enormously significant, because it not only inspired Chuck to practice daily but encouraged him to dream about his future musical career. It was also an indication that Chuck sought out the advice of professional musicians at an early age. He was intrigued with the sounds of the electric guitar.

When the Jay McShann Band appeared in St. Louis, Walter Brown, the band's lead vocalist, had an extraordinary impact upon Chuck Berry. Brown, a smooth blues singer, performed a version of *Confessin' the Blues* which Chuck used during his senior year performance in the Sumner High School Variety Show. Brown's lyrical realism in developing themes relating to alcoholism, poverty, and degradation in the black ghetto were fascinating to young Chuck Berry. He saw this story approach as a key ingredient in his own songwriting. The images, ideas, and lyrical approach were much different in Chuck's music, but the general approach to the "story song" remained intact. So, as Chuck watched blues singers weave stories of black tragedies, hypnotizing audiences with their lyrics and vocal delivery, he began to write his own versions dealing with teenage problems. In a decade, these early efforts would be translated into the first serious pieces of rock poetry. But in the 1940s, Chuck Berry was simply an obscure young kid waiting for his chance in the music world. It was the music which kept Chuck alive with enthusiasm in the chaotic post-World War II adjustment to the atomic bomb, the Cold War, and new politicians like Richard M. Nixon.

Shortly after he graduated from high school, Chuck Berry was involved in some problems with the law. He spent some time in a local reform school. After his release, Chuck went to work in a St. Louis General Motors plant. He married in the late 1940s and began to raise a family. Like any young man, he bought a car. In 1943, Chuck paid $34 for a 1933 Ford, and he later cited this automobile as the inspiration for some of the lyrics in *Maybellene*. The boy who could then only dream of a Cadillac began instead to write lyrics about a Cadillac and a Ford V-8. Ironically, these lyrics would later provide enough money for a half dozen Cadillacs.

As Chuck listened to the musicians of the 1940s, he was most influenced by a number of guitar players who were revolutionizing American popular music. As noted previously, the most significant guitarist in Chuck Berry's early life was Charlie Christian. Although he was a major recording and performing artist for only twenty-three months, Christian changed forever the evolution of the jazz guitar. Until Charlie Christian emerged, most big band guitarists were hidden in the rhythm section playing barely audible acoustic guitars. In 1939, when Christian mastered the electric guitar, still a very new instrument, he began to use this unique amplified sound to accompany a trumpet or saxophone. It was Christian's amazing instrumental prowess which inspired widespread acceptance of the electric guitar.

In the summer of 1939, Charlie Christian was accidentally

Chuck Berry "elevated" the electric guitar into *the* instrument of rock music.

discovered by Columbia Records executive John Hammond, who heard Christian playing in a small Oklahoma City cafe. The next day, Christian was hurriedly flown to Los Angeles where Hammond led him onstage to play with Benny Goodman. For twenty minutes, Goodman's musicians fed lines to Christian and he followed them in one of the most extraordinary jam sessions in American musical history. Christian was hired immediately and, by Christmas, 1939, he had recorded at Carnegie Hall with both Benny Goodman and the Kansas City Six. Christian's guitar solos on *Flying Home, Honeysuckle Rose*, and *Seven Come Eleven* permanently established the power and popularity of the electric guitar. During 1940 and 1941, Charlie Christian recorded and toured with the Benny Goodman Sextet. His instrumental skills were also featured on records by a number of other artists. Christian's music was ultimately much too sophisticated for Benny Goodman's swing and jazz style, however. As a result, Christian fled into the night clubs of Harlem to expand his musical opportunities. Christian loved the uptempo bebop of New York's black musical clubs, one of the most innovative sounds in American music, and one which eventually laid the foundation for rock-and-roll music.

It was the Gibson electric guitar, model ES-150, which was responsible for Charlie Christian's advanced sound. It is interesting to note that Chuck Berry uses a Gibson ES-355 with a number of extras: two humbucking pickups with separate pole pieces for each string, stereo wiring, and a solid maple center running through a semi-hollow body. There is little doubt that Christian's instrumental stylings, guitar techniques, and revolutionary approach to music influenced Chuck Berry. Charlie Christian gave the electric guitar its jazz voice, and Chuck Berry gave the electric guitar its rock voice. Perhaps Chuck's most important tribute to Charlie Christian was his February 1958 recording of *Rockin' at the Philharmonic*, which Chuck wrote as a celebration of Christian's deft guitar stylings.

There were a number of other significant guitarists who were important influences upon young Chuck Berry, too, such as T-Bone Walker and Carl Hoagan. It was the charismatic personality and stage presence of T-Bone Walker which first attracted Chuck Berry to this legendary bluesman. As a result of listening carefully to Walker's guitar work, Chuck began to practice new techniques on his electric guitar. T-Bone Walker's instrumental guitar stressed a lean, almost biting style with strong rhythm and blues overtones. This slow, drifting blues style of Walker's surfaced on a number of sides of Chuck Berry's Chess recordings. If Leonard Chess had effectively promoted these blues tunes, Berry would have sold well in the blues market. In *Wee Wee Hours*, for example, Walker's influence is pervasive. In fact, Walker's 1950 hit record, *Strollin' with Bones*, included an instrumental riff which is very similar to the guitar work on *Johnny B. Goode*. What Chuck adopted from Walker's records was an uncluttered solo guitar style. This helped Chuck to accentuate his clear, crisp vocals, which were patterned after Nat "King" Cole. Yet, in his St. Louis performances in the early 1950s, Chuck sometimes employed a biting, shouting blues tone in his music as well.

The least well-known guitarists influencing Chuck Berry were Carl Hoagan and Bill Jennings. For a brief period of time, Hoagan was the lead guitarist in the Louis Jordan band. When Louis Jordan appeared in St. Louis, Chuck Berry was intriguted by Hoagan's free-flowing performances. As a result, Berry practiced Hoagan-type guitar riffs and, in songs like *Carol* and *Reelin' and Rockin'*, there are musical characteristics with origins in Hoagan's inventive genius. Another guitarist in the Louis Jordan band, Bill Jennings, was also an important source of inspiration. In a number of extraordinary musical pieces, Jennings played his guitar in collaboration with Bill Doggett's piano, and the result was a sound much like the early rock guitar-piano duos of the mid-1950s. Bill Doggett's piano highlighted Jennings' guitar solos, and appreciative audiences clapped vigorously after these duets. In the 1950s, Chuck Berry's guitar pieces were similarly enhanced by Johnny Johnson's piano. When Chuck recorded for Chess Records, such keyboard giants as Otis Spann and Lafayette Leake were session musicians on many of Chuck's early hit records. It was Jennings and Doggett who convinced Chuck of the viability of the guitar-piano marriage.

Another significant influence upon Chuck Berry's music was Louis Jordan's own jump blues. Jordan, a singer and saxophonist, was at the peak of his career in the 1940s. In 1935, Jordan formed his famous Tympany Five and became one of the first black band leaders to attract a large white audience. The key to Jordan's musical success was a smoothly coordinated stage show featuring a number of talented musicians who practiced a creative form of musical diversity. Jordan's Tympany Five was in reality a seven or eight-piece band with horns, a boogie-woogie style piano, and a jazzy rhythm section. The band's instrumental offerings, however, centered around Jordan's gritty vocals and alto saxophone breaks, musical skills which he combined with an unprecedented sense of showmanship. His stage personality was so dominant that the Louis Jordan band appeared in a number of Hollywood films and musical shorts intended for local movie theaters. In 1944, Jordan's *Jumpin' at the Jubilee* demonstrated that black music could cross over into the gigantic and highly profitable white marketplace. In later years, Chuck paid Jordan the ultimate artistic compliment when he reflected: "I identify with him [Jordan] more than an other artist."

There were many things about the Jordan band that Chuck admired, but the single most significant ingredient was the professional manner which the group employed in concert. It was a lesson that Chuck perfected during this early years in St. Louis nightclubs. As Chuck worked on developing his level of music communication with the audience, he blended Louis Jordan's stage act into his own early performances.

As Arnold Shaw has suggested, Louis Jordan was one of the seminal figures in the development of rock-and-roll music. Not only did Jordan influence Chuck Berry, but Jordan's vocals and superbly crafted revue attracted numerous white concert audiences and record buyers. In addition, Jordan's records and movies made him a superstar, but his principal importance was as an inspiration to young artists like Chuck Berry. As a result of Louis Jordan's success, they sought a wider audience for their own music. Jordan also influenced white country singers like Bill Haley. In the late 1940s, Haley developed his initial musical ideas as a disc jockey, programming Louis Jordan and other rhythm and blues records on his WPWA radio program in Chester, Pennsylvania. In 1951, Bill Haley cut Jackie Brenston's *Rocket 88* for Philadelphia's Essex label, and this song helped Haley to launch his own career as one of America's rock-and-roll music pioneers.

When Bill Haley left Essex, Milt Gabler became Bill Haley's producer. To make Haley's sounds as commercially successfull as possible, Gabler brought the group to New York City to use a location which had been effective in recording Louis Jordan and the Tympany Five. This location was the Pythian Temple, an ex-dance hall on 80th Street in New York. When Gabler recorded Bill Haley and the Comets, he used arrangements and techniques similar to Louis Jordan's. Since none of the Comets, except piano player Johnny Grande, could read music, the idea was to equip them with a repertoire of arrangements in the style of the Louis Jordan band. In 1954, Haley's *Shake, Rattle and Roll* employed elements from Jordan's musical style to introduce a rock-and-roll version of Big Joe Turner's classic blues song. Bill Haley and the Comet's recordings became commercially successful only after Jordan's influence was ingrained in this fledgling country western dance band aggregation.

Not only did Louis Jordan influence rock-and-roll music generally, but he also brought comedic elements into the mainstream of rock music. In later years, the Coasters would become the clown princes of rock-and-roll music, and they publicly acknowledged the influence of the Louis Jordan band. When Chuck Berry reflected on Jordan's style, he commented: "I have a lot of flighty things like Louis had, comical things and natural things. . . ." In 1945, for example, Jordan's novelty song *Caldonia* contained humorous lyrics

9

The great showman clowns with his guitar in a '70s New York concert.

which became very popular with predominantly white audiences. The emphatic cry in Jordan's song, "Caldonia, what make your big head so hard," intrigued Chuck, leading him to experiment with his own humorous lyrics. Thus began the use of ingredients which were an important part of many Chuck Berry hit records. In songs like *Brown-Eyed Handsome Man, Almost Grown*, and *Around and Around*, Chuck composed tunes which were similar to Louis Jordan's.

Although Jordan had an important impact upon Berry's showmanship, there were a number of vocalists who were instrumental in Chuck's career. The key vocalists in the development of Chuck Berry's music were Frank Sinatra, Billy Eckstine, and Nat "King" Cole. The singer that Chuck Berry admired the most among these was Nat "King" Cole, because Cole's diction and phrasing allowed his music to cross over into the white record market. In 1972, Chuck reminisced to a *Rolling Stone* reporter that: " . . . when I started out I was singing everything blues, jazz, love ballads, and, well, I still try to sing as much smooth ballads as I can." Then Chuck confessed that the Nat "King" Cole songs were his favorite. A decade later, in the summer of 1982, Gene Nelson, San Francisco's premier oldies DJ on KYA radio, interviewed Chuck in a Lake Tahoe casino. When Nelson informed Berry that he was surprised to hear Chuck singing *Ramblin' Rose*, Berry smiled and again acknowledged his debt to Nat "King" Cole's music. Although Chuck Berry performed in a musical idiom different from Nat "King" Cole's, nonetheless, the communicative genius of Cole was an important influence upon Chuck Berry's own superb concert skills. As a tribute to Cole's influence, Chuck recorded *Ramblin' Rose* for Mercury Records in 1967 on the LP **In Memphis** (SR-61123).

There were also many blues musicians who added vocal touches to Chuck Berry's music. It is ironic that Chuck's precise diction and ability to use imagery prompted many blues enthusiasts to ignore his skills as a blues performer. Although the blues has not been a commercially important part of Chuck Berry's music, nevertheless, he has continued to record and perform successfully in a blues idiom. His Mercury Record albums from 1966 to 1969 contain some of the finest blues guitar work of Chuck's career. In the late 1960s, Chuck also tried to vary his performances with long, intricate blues riffs like those attempted in concerts at San Francisco's Fillmore Auditorium. The Fillmore crowds, however, continually hollered for old hits like *Johnny B. Goode*. This forced Chuck into performing in an "oldies-but-goodies" forum, which he often detested. In the 1970s, Chuck's ability to convey the old magic returned periodically but, at other concerts, he would appear listless and bored by performing the same

11

A reflection on the blues twenty years later.

material over and over. It was this failure to expand his musical appeal in the late 1960s which hurt his continued commercial success in the 1970s.

The demands of the audience have created problems for many blues performers. One of Chuck's favorite artists, Charles Brown, was unable to break away from his categorization as a slow blues singer. In 1945, Brown recorded *Drifting Blues* for Alladin Records, and this established the California rhythm and blues tradition as one of the foundation stones of rock-and-roll music. As a member of Johnny Moore's Three Blazers, Charles Brown became one of the giants of rhythm and blues music. It was Brown's almost frustrating way of phrasing his vocals which appealed to Chuck Berry. There was a passive sense of rejection in Brown's romantic musical style, and Chuck used this technique in songs like *Wee Wee Hours*. Chuck Berry listened intently to the majority of Brown's seventy *Billboard*-charted records from 1945 to 1950, and Berry eventually paid tribute to Brown's music in 1958 when he recorded *Merry Christmas Baby*. In 1960, Chuck also cut Brown's classic, *Drifting Blues*. The majority of the B sides on Chuck Berry's Chess Records are slow blues tunes reminiscent of Charles Brown, and this attests to Brown's enormous impact upon Berry's rock music.

It was Charles Brown's ability to mesmerize an audience with his blues ballads which intrigued Chuck Berry, and he spent an unusual amount of time working blues tunes into his early performances. There was another quality about Charles Brown that Chuck admired, and that was his broad interest in diverse types of music. Like many performers, Brown continually searched for new songs beyond traditional blues and rhythm and blues music. As a result, Chuck emulated Brown and often browsed in record stores looking for new material.

Country music was also one of the sounds which most influenced Berry's music. He listened to Tex Ritter, Gene Autry, and Hank Williams. One of the most interesting songs Chuck covered in his early years was *Cow Cow Boogie*, by Texas singer Ella Mae Morse. The song was included on an album entitled **Rockin' Brew**. When Chuck heard this country jazz-oriented song, he became intrigued with its sound. Berry also searched out other tunes by the writer of *Cow Cow Boogie*. Soon, he was performing Don Raye's *House of Blue Lights* and *Down the Road Apiece*. The importance of Don Raye's songwriting is evident in such Berry songs as *Too Much Monkey Business* and *Around and Around*. In these songs, Chuck translates Raye's highly sophisticated adult themes involving drinking, honky tonk conflict, and fighting into similar teenage musical themes. Part of Chuck's fascination with country music was the ability of key country songs to cross over into the pop market. This phenomenon occurred in 1946, when an uptempo, jazzy version of *The House of Blue Lights*, again by Ella Mae Morse, crossed over country western boundaries into pop music. When Chuck recorded *The House of Blue Lights* in 1958, his guitar work demonstrated an uncanny ability to blend country licks with rock music. The sound of the country pedal steel guitar was transformed into rock-and-roll on Chuck Berry's electric guitar. In 1957, few critics noted that the B side of *School Days* was a steel guitar-inspired instrumental song: *Deep Feeling*. The following year, Chuck's *Blues for Hawaiians* continued his eclectic use of country music in a blues-rock idiom. Chuck Berry has never discussed the importance of country western influences upon his music. When journalists broach the subject, Chuck usually changes the direction of the interview. But there is little doubt that Chuck was an avid country western musical aficionado.

Perhaps the most difficult influence to analyze in Chuck's career is that of Hank Williams. When Chuck wrote *30 Days* to pay tribute to Hank Williams' country music, he unwittingly acknowledged his debt to country music's most tragic legend. In fact, a number of blues artists have recognized Chuck Berry's pervasive country tone. Jimmy Witherspoon, when asked to describe Chuck Berry's music, replied, "Chuck Berry is a country singer. People put everybody in categories, black, white, if Chuck Berry was white . . . he would be the top country star in the world." Roy Brown, another blues legend, remarked: "Chuck Berry uses country music better than any contemporary performer, and his music is a perfect reflection of blending the blues and country music."

In sum, Chuck Berry's lyrical and musical heritage was a fusion of big band, jazz, pop, country/western, and blues music. It was an eclectic creation which defied description in the 1950s. But the anchor point to Chuck's music has always been a combination of revolutionary guitar playing and poetic lyrics. He was rock-and-roll music's first song-poet. In later years, song-poets like Van Morrison, Joni Mitchell, and Bob Dylan would follow Chuck Berry's lead with new themes and a new direction. Indeed, all the song-poets of the 1960s and 1970s owed much in the way of expanded musical horizons to the ground breaking efforts made by Chuck Berry in the 1950s.

In order to fully understand the development of Chuck Berry's art, it is necessary to next examine his career as a professional musician. Although he had played semiprofessionally, Chuck did not become a full-fledged professional until the early 1950s. For a number of years, Chuck had considered turning to music for a living, but he was also a responsible, middle-class family man who knew it could be a less than viable occupation. Although Chuck played in a number of St. Louis clubs, he was also an eager spectator at shows by the likes of Muddy Waters, Ike Turner, and Albert King. Despite their apparent success, Chuck considered a professional musical career a gamble. It was almost by accident, then, that he began to play professionally. In September, 1951, Chuck Berry got a phone call from Johnny Johnson, who headed a trio which played in local St. Louis clubs. The Johnny Johnson Trio was scheduled to play a December 31, 1951, New Year's Eve Concert, but the band's saxophone player had become ill. Chuck Berry was hired to fill in, an event which began his professional career.

The musical collaboration between Johnny Johnson and Chuck Berry was an immediate success. For years, rhythm and blues songs had used guitar-piano duos, and Chuck Berry's running guitar riffs were a perfect complement to Johnson's deft piano runs. "He had this trio," Chuck Berry recalled, "and we made a foursome. We had a tenor player and Eddie Harding on drums and . . . he just looked me up." Soon, the group was renamed the Chuck Berry Trio, and they played with Little Milton, Albert King, and Ike Turner in local clubs. Although Chuck remembers Ike Turner's Kings of Rhythm as being the most popular group in St. Louis, it was soon evident that the Chuck Berry Trio was equally as popular.

When Chuck joined the Johnny Johnson Trio, they were strictly an instrumental group covering other artists' songs. Soon, Chuck introduced country music and urban blues into their act. He also began to experiment with his own songwriting and onstage performances. At this point in his career, Chuck's strongest influences were Nat "King" Cole, Frank Sinatra, Muddy Waters, Elmore James, and Louis Jordan. "Actually, it was something new for a black man to be singing this type of song at that particular time," Johnny Johnson remarked. Another facet of young Chuck Berry's complicated personality was his penchant for country and western music. Carl Perkins remembers Chuck riding in the back of his brand new Cadillac writing the words and music to *Brown-Eyed Handsome Man.* There was little doubt in Perkins' mind that Chuck had a intimate understanding of country western music, and Perkins remarked that Chuck's songs developed themes similar to western music. During 1954--1955, the Chuck Berry Trio continued to work in clubs around St. Louis, but soon Chuck began to expand his musical horizons.

In 1954, a St. Louis radio station, KATZ, began broadcasting live concerts from local clubs. Such performers as Ike and Tina Turner were featured in concerts from small venues like Lindy's Hall in St. Louis. The concerts were increasingly attended by young whites, as the bands were perfecting a crossover sound, and Chuck Berry

Chuck Berry in 1955.

became one of the most popular performers because his music had a universal quality to it.

There were a number of local record labels interested in Chuck Berry's music, but they were small, unknown ones. Oscar Washington formed one such small company, known as the Ballad label. In 1952, after Washington released a record by The Swans, the label languished for a number of years. Constantly searching for new talent, Washington heard Chuck Berry in a local lounge. As a result, on August 13, 1954, Chuck was invited to the Premier Studios in St. Louis and, from one to three o'clock in the afternoon, he recorded *Oh Maria* and *I Hope These Words Will Find You Well*. Berry and the group recorded the songs under the name The Cubans; the musicians included Berry on rhythm guitar, Oscar Washington on guitar, Freddy Golden on bongos, and Joe Alexander doing vocals. Chuck's early recordings for Chess Records often had a Latin flavor, and *Oh Maria* was a good example of how different types of St. Louis music helped to form Chuck's musical makeup. The B side of the record, *I Hope These Words Will Find You Well*, featured the entire group and had a decidedly lighter Latin touch. Perhaps the most interesting aspect of this record was the guitar work of Berry and Washington. They, like Berry and Johnson, complemented each other, and such interaction was an integral part of Chuck's early musical training. Oscar Washington had a brief period of commercial success when he wrote the lyrics to *Night Train*. The bongo player, Freddy Golden, became a member of the Quartette Tres Bien, and went on to commercial success in Paris, France.

The Chuck Berry Trio used all these influences to become one of the most popular bands in St. Louis, but in 1954 Chuck, who was still uncertain about a musical career, enrolled at Annie Austin's Poro Beauty School. While he was training as a cosmetologist, Ms. Austin went to see Chuck perform in a number of clubs. She remembers that in 1954 he had a knack for exciting the audience with his original tunes. "He was a wonderful person," Ms. Austin said, "who was serious about his cosmetology studies and dedicated to his music."

By 1954, Chuck Berry was a twenty-eight-year-old cosmetologist who rented a $400 a month studio and was making some extra money as a part-time musician. One Saturday night, while staying at the Street Hotel in East St. Louis, Chuck wrote *School Day*. He also started to think about the lyrics to *Johnny B. Goode*. In addition, he took a number of unsuccessful trips to Chicago to search out a recording contract. When Chuck walked into the Vee Jay Studios and was rejected, he was crushed. Vee Jay had just released the Spaniels' 1954 hit *Goodnight Sweetheart*, which happened to be one of Chuck Berry's favorite songs. Another Vee Jay artist that Chuck

Berry listened to intently was Jimmy Reed. Reed was working in a Gary, Indiana, steel mill in 1955, and he was unable to make a living as a professional musician, a frustration which Chuck, uncertain about his own future, fully shared. As Arnold Shaw suggested in *Honkers and Shouters: The Golden Years of Rhythm and Blues*, "Young Chuck Berry is said to have a kindred voice in Reed's easy, humorous infectious style."

At any rate, while in Chicago, Chuck visited a number of Chicago blues clubs looking for new influences, and eventually his path crossed that of Elmore James. In April, 1952, James' *Dust My Broom* entered the Top 10 rhythm and blues charts, and he moved to Chicago to play in local clubs. Living in a local boarding house where Howlin' Wolf also resided, James soon became on of Chicago's most popular blues performers. It was common for Elmore James to open for Muddy Waters or Howlin' Wolf in a local club. By 1954, James was a legenday blues figure. One of James' backup musicians was Odie Payne, who was to become a session musician at Chess and play on a number of Chuck Berry Records. Matt Murphy, who played guitar in Howlin' Wolf's original band, was another musician who backed up Chuck Berry in the Chess studios. Also, Fred Below of the Aces played with Elmore James and was a session musician on a number of Chuck Berry records. So, Elmore James had both a direct and indirect musical influence upon Chuck Berry.

Elmore James' songstyling abilities also influenced Chuck Berry's music. After seeing Elmore perform in a number of clubs, Chuck used James' *It Hurts Me Too* as the model for *Our Little Rendezvous*. In January, 1964, shortly after James' death, Chuck Berry recorded James' *Dust My Broom*, with Odie Payne as backup. Chess Records did not release the song but, even though he rarely mentions Elmore James' influence, the rock side of Chuck's music is as much a tribute to this legendary Chicago bluesman as *Dust My Broom* was intended to be.

Ike Turner's Kings of Rhythm band traveled to St. Louis in the summer of 1954 to begin a new phase in their career. They brought a big band approach to rock music which also influenced Chuck Berry. Ike Turner had produced a number of Elmore James' most impressive songs in a Canton, Mississippi, nightclub and served as a talent scout for the Bihari brothers and Sam Phillips. As a result, when Ike Turner and the Kings of Rhythm began playing in East St. Louis nightclubs, they were a polished act which immediately became St. Louis' most popular black dance band. Jackie Brenston, whose hit, *Rocket 88*, had made Ike Turner's Kings of Rhythm a nationally known band, rejoined the group. While Ike Turner still feuded with Brenston, the band nevertheless recorded a number of songs for the Federal label in 1956 which remain collector's items.

Perhaps the most significant influence of the Ike Turner band on Chuck Berry was Jackie Brenston's lead vocals on *Rocket 88*, which gave Chuck ideas for songs with automobile lyrics. Chuck was intrigued by the use of automobile imagery, and he soon drafted songs using car themes.

Although a number of groups and individuals influenced Chuck Berry, it is nevertheless obvious that he was still a highly individualistic talent. A number of musicians in the East St. Louis clubs often remarked about Chuck's expertise in crafting his own songs and creating his own musical identity. Gabriel Hearns, a St. Louis musician, described Chuck Berry's music as having "a zing to it nobody else had." Chuck was a perfectionist who spent an inordinate amount of time working on his songs. The problems of Chuck's youth were soon transformed into song. There is no doubt that Chuck's musical ideas and lyrical creativity owe a great deal to his roots.

Apart from the musical influences upon Chuck, there were other important aspects of his early life which helped shape his future. Particularly significant was Chuck's musically talented family. Few recording artists have had the sophisticated musical training that the Berry family provided. Chuck's father and mother sang in the Antioch Baptist Church choir. His three sisters were highly accomplished musicians: Lucy Ann was a pianist and contralto, and she toured with a local gospel group; Thelma was an extraordinary piano player; and Martha was the best singer in the family. There was always good music in the Berry household. Since Chuck's family generally favored gospel music in the 1930s and 1940s, one can fully understand how he was affected by this traditional music. Old gospel tunes like *Talkin' Bout You*, for example, inspired his music in later life. In fact, it was common for Chuck to use other songs as a direct inspiration for his own music. When Chuck wrote *Blues for Hawaiians*, it was a remake of Floyd Smith's 1939 song, *Floyd's Guitar Blues*. The country singer Jimmy Wakely recorded a song entitled *Too Late* and this tune has the same lyrics but different music in Chuck Berry's version of *Too Late*. While there is no obvious plagiarism in Chuck Berry's tunes, the fact remains that he was obviously influenced by a wide variety of musical sources. When Fred Stuckey of *Guitar Player* magazine interviewed Chuck and pointed out the myriad influences upon his music, Chuck remarked: "I heard a lot of country stuff and copied a lot. I guess I couldn't have said I was playing country. But I was stabbing at it." The combination of gospel and country music was indeed an important part of Chuck's musical training.

In sum, Chuck Berry's music evolved over a fifteen-year period, from 1940 through 1954, and there was constant growth in Chuck's

"Thank you," says Mr. Berry.

songwriting and performing. In New York, at radio station WINS, Alan Freed had begun playing black music, setting the stage for the rock-and-roll revolution. The following year, rock music began to take over the *Billboard* charts, and by that time Chuck Berry was already well equipped to become one of the Founding Fathers of this new musical form.

Photo by Howard DeWitt

Chuck Berry at the Dixon, California May Fair, 1981.

CHAPTER 2

CHESS
1955

In March, 1955, Chicago blues artist Muddy Waters played a series of club engagements in St. Louis and, on his nights off, Muddy visited a number of local clubs. He wandered into the Cosmopolitan Club to hear the Chuck Berry Trio. Although he was familiar with Berry's musical craftsmanship, he was extremely impressed with Chuck's show. For the last three years, a number of musicians had told him stories of Berry's guitar and blues prowess. Although he was strictly a part-time local St. Louis musician, Chuck Berry already had a singular reputation for musical creativity. Curiosity had prompted Muddy Waters to drop by the East St. Louis club, and Muddy was so impressed with Chuck Berry's music that he went backstage and invited him to Chicago. Although Chuck had been turned down by Vee Jay Records, he listened intently as Muddy Waters discussed Leonard Chess and the Chess Records operation. Waters believed that Chess had a special ability to record black blues artists, and pointed out that the Chess studios contained the most sophisticated recording equipment in the Chicago area.

It was Muddy Waters' description of the Chicago blues renaissance which intrigued Chuck Berry. As Waters detailed the musical activity in the clubs, the diversity of artists, and the appreciation of local audiences, Chuck decided to take a month-long vacation in Chicago figuring that, even if he was not successful in securing a recording contract, at least he would enjoy the music. Not only were there a number of small record labels in the Windy City, but South Side bluesmen like Little Walter, Elmore James, and Howlin' Wolf were sharing the stage with rhythm and blues acts like Bo Diddley, the Moonglows, and the Flamingos. It was a time of musical change and the rock revolution was on the horizon. The stage was set for a black musical performer to merge gospel, blues, country, and pop music into the rock mainstream. In 1954--1955, Elvis Presley's Sun Record sessions created a product which allowed white artists to cross over into black markets. Chuck Berry was in many respects a black Elvis Presley. He crossed over into the white market and

Chuck performing in a Chicago club, 1957.

became the most popular black rock artist of the 1950s.

In 1955, Alan Freed recognized Chuck Berry's unique talent and watched him with great interest. After a successful three years (from 1951 to 1954) as a disc jockey and concert promoter for WJW in Cleveland, Ohio, Freed became a disc jockey at WINS in New York. After a short stint in the 11:00 p.m. to 2:00 a.m. slot, Freed became WINS' prime-time DJ, with a new evening slot from 7:00 p.m. to 11:00 p.m. at a salary of $75,000 a year and considerable power in promotion and recording circles. Freed was considered the most important disc jockey in the rock music business. In exchange for extensive airplay, Freed received co-writer's credit when Harvey Fuqua of the Moonglows composed *Sincerely*, a song which became not only a rhythm and blues hit but a smash pop record for the McGuire Sisters. When the Moonglows' version of *Sincerely* was released in November, 1954, it marked the beginning of a close working relationship between Freed and Chess Records. It was Alan Freed who was responsible for breaking Chuck Berry's first record, *Maybellene*, as a result of a deal made between Leonard Chess and Freed. It was quite common in the 1950s to pay a disc jockey to promote a record, but Chess Records was not financially strong enough to engage in large-scale payola. As a result, Leonard Chess informed Freed that he could pick a song to plug and, in return, Fred's name would go on the record as a co-writer. After listening to hundreds of Chess Record releases, Freed eventually selected Chuck Berry's *Maybellene*. The rest is music history.

To fully understand the rise of Chuck Berry's career, it is necessary to analyze the history of Chess Records. Small labels like Chess which emerged in th 1950s to produce rhythm and blues and early rock-and-roll records were new, unique, and unproven business ventures. Since the major record companies ignored black music, this opened up opportunities for shrewd businessmen to make a quick dollar marketing rhythm and blues songs. Alan Freed described labels like Chess, Duke, Modern, RPM, Crown and others as turning out "a river of music." Freed contended that the only real American music resulted from the small record labels like Chess and, by implication, that few other disc jockeys and large record producers — who were rejecting rhythm and blues — were able to understand the rock-and-roll revolution.

The early history of Chess Records is a complex and interesting story. When Leonard and Philip Chess arrived in Chicago from Poland in 1928, they settled in the city's Jewish section in a building at 1425 S. Karlov. A decade later, the Chess brothers opened the Macamba Lounge, becoming the proprietors of a club which featured legendary after-hours musical jam sessions attracting Chicago's finest musicians. The Chess brothers understood black music much better than their white contemporaries, and Leonard Chess believed that the larger record companies were especially unaware of the subtle nuances of Chicago's black music. It followed, therefore, that when a Hollywood talent agent came to the Macamba to listen to singer Andrew Tibbs, Leonard Chess became determined to record this young artist rather than allow another company to do it. The result was a hit record, *Union Man Blues* (Aristrocrat 1425).* The B-side was a controversial song, *Bilbo's Dead*, which was banned in the South due to its unflattering references to Mississippi Governor Bilbo. Leonard Chess had a knack for bringing out the best in Chicago blues musicians, and this initial recording was an example of his finest work.

To many black musicians in the late 1940s and early 1950s, Leonard Chess was a strange sight as he carried his tape recorder around Chicago's South Side searching out new musical talent. The first label Leonard Chess formed in 1947 was called Aristocrat Records. The early releases on Aristocrat were generally not commercially successful, but they demonstrated an uncanny talent for uncovering unique blues tunes. The Chess brothers were able to find this special blues sound because they operated the Macamba Lounge, a fertile spawning ground for original blues music. In fact, when the Chess brothers established Aristocrat Records, they already owned a number of nightclubs on Chicago's South Side. For the next few years musicians like Sunnyland Slim played in the Chess clubs, and Chess became one of the earliest Windy City entrepreneurs to attempt to record local artists in his garage. One of the best Aristocrat sessions took place late one night when Sunnyland Slim went into Chess' small garage and recorded two songs, *Johnson Machine Gun* and *Fly Right, Little Girl*. When this record sold moderately in Chicago, Sunnyland Slim demanded a large sum of money and Chess refused his request. A very public argument ensued, and Sunnyland Slim left Aristocrat Records. He recorded for a number of other independent Chicago labels, but Sunnyland Slim never again achieved the unique sound that Chess brought to his early recordings. Black musicians who were aware of Sunnyland Slim's differences with Leonard Chess urged him to remain with Aristocrat. It was obvious to these blues veterans that the other small independent labels in Chicago did not have the same skills as Chess in the production and marketing of blues records.

Although the early discs by Aristocrat Records were not nationally known, nevertheless, the groundwork was developed for the later triumphs of Chess Records. The first regional hit for Aristocrat

---

*Leonard Chess selected Aristocrat 1425 as his first release in order to pay tribute to his home on S. Karlov.

was Muddy Waters' *I Can't Be Satisfied*, backed with *I Feel Like Going Home*. On a Saturday morning in April, 1948, Leonard Chess began delivering records from the trunk of his car to the barbershops, shoeshine stands, liquor stores, grocery stores, and small record shops that dotted Chicago's predominantly black South Side. Chess sold the initial pressing of Waters' record out in one day. The *Billboard* race charts did not officially list Waters' record, but noted that it was a regional hit. The success of Muddy Waters' first 45 release astonished Chess; he was not prepared for the number of people who wanted the record. When Muddy Waters himself attempted to purchase five copies of his own record, a local merchant, Bernard Abrams, informed him that he would sell only one copy to a customer. (Waters complained that Abrams was selling his record for $1.10 when the list price was only 79 cents.) When Leonard Chess evaluated the reasons for Waters' success, he recognized that his music combined the Delta blues with recent urban themes. Blacks who migrated from Alabama and Mississippi recognized the blend of rural blues with the new urban influences, and they were responsible for most of the 80,000 records sold. There was also a sensual sexuality in Waters' recording of *I Can't Be Satisfied*, which created continuous sales among black women.

A hit record was a problem for the Aristocrat label. The company was largely a two-man operation, with songs recorded in Leonard Chess' garage. The number of records pressed by Chess initially never exceeded the orders placed by local retailers. Leonard Chess was learning the rudiments of record distribution by day, and searching out new musical talent by night. From 1947 to 1950, Chess had 180 accounts who regularly purchased his records, and he realized that new talent was needed to expand his business. As a result, Chess nurtured the early careers of such diverse performers as Willie Mabon, Bo Diddley, Sunnyland Slim, Howlin' Wolf, Little Walter, and Muddy Waters. The church-like storefront of Aristocrat Records was an invitation to ambitious black musicians to come in and cut a demo tape. The larger record companies had elaborate and highly ritualistic auditioning policies. Often when a performer entered Aristocrat Records he was greeted personally by Leonard Chess.

In 1950, Leonard Chess changed the name of Aristocrat Records to Chess. He also spent that summer traveling some 5,000 miles throughout the South searching out new talent. Chess carried a small Magnechord wire recorder into the fields of Mississippi, Arkansas, and Louisiana to tape blues songs, and it was during this journey that Chess discovered Chester Burnett, the Howlin' Wolf, in West Memphis, Arkansas. Chess immediately recorded Wolf's *Saddle My Pony* and *Worried All the Time*, with Ike Turner on piano and James

Cotton on harp. The Howlin' Wolf session was a fine example of the music available in the South.

In 1951, Leonard Chess visited Memphis, and he purchased a demo tape of Jackie Brenston's *Rocket 88*. This classic tune immediately rose to number one on the *Billboard* rhythm and blues charts. In the period from 1951 to 1953, Chess Records became one of the most significant rhythm and blues labels, with Little Walter's *Juke* topping the charts in 1952, and Willie Mabon's *I Don't Know* reaching number one in the 1953 *Billboard* rhythm and blues charts.

During his first Southern trip, Chess also met young Sam Phillips in Memphis. Phillips, an obscure dance promoter, was making a name for himself staging dances at the Hotel Peabody. In 1950, Phillips had opened the Memphis Recording Service in a small studio at 706 Union Avenue. In June, 1950, Phillips' first recording was a demo tape of jazz musician Phineas Newborn, which he sold to Modern Records in Los Angeles. When Leonard Chess heard the tape and watched Phillips record Joe Hill Louis in July, 1950, it had a tremendous impact upon the future of Chess Records. At this point in his career, Phillips recorded tapes and sold them to the Bihari brothers. The Biharis' Los Angeles record label, Modern, then issued the songs. Chess reasoned that, since the demo tapes made and sold by Phillips to the Biharis were not exclusive properties, he, too, would buy copies of the tapes and release these songs on this own label.

For some time, Chess had observed the Bihari brothers' success on the Modern record label. When Modern was formed by the four Bihari brothers in April, 1945, in Los Angeles, they pioneered the earliest discoveries of blues music. After signing John Lee Hooker, Modern recorded numerous early B.B. King songs and eventually such artists as Bobby Blue Bland, Jimmy Witherspoon, Junior Parker, Etta James, the Cadets, Johnny Moore's Three Blazers, and many other blues and rhythm and blues acts. The most important discovery for Modern Records occurred when a Detroit record distributor, Bernie Bessman, cut a demo tape of John Lee Hooker's *Boogie Chillen*, and sold it to the Bihari brothers. When *Boogie Chillen* was released, it established John Lee Hooker as an important blues artist. However, it was not until *Hobo Blues* reached the *Billboard* ratings in May, 1949, that John Lee Hooker had his first national hit. By 1951, B.B. King, Walter Horton, and Rosco Gordon had hit records due to demo tapes Sam Phillips recorded in Memphis and sold to the Bihari brothers. Leonard Chess recognized that Phillips had a keen ear for blues music, and he persuaded Sam to sell his demo tapes to Chess Records. The result was that, often, many blues artists had records released on different labels simultaneously. The industry was a fledgling one, and almost no one was concerned over threatened legal action.

And so it was that, in order to survive in the competitive jungle of rhythm and blues record production, Leonard Chess toured the South in 1950–1951. He argued persuasively with such artists as Sonny Boy Williamson, Little Walter, and Howlin' Wolf that they would be more successful living and recording in Chicago. Eventually, many blues artists made Chicago their home and recorded for the Chess label. Many of these blues veterans wanted to record for Chess, because Leonard Chess was considered a hit-making producer in the studio. Johnny Shines aptly summed up the attitude of local bluesmen when he remarked that: "Leonard Chess had a knack for getting the best out of musicians." On the other hand, Etta James has been quoted repeatedly in blues magazines to the effect that Chess had only a minimal understanding of the blues. She has suggested to a number of journalists that if a performer so much as tapped his or her foot, Leonard Chess would release that record as a single. There is undoubtedly a great deal of malice in Etta James' feeling toward Chess Records, and this makes her observations less than reliable. There are a number of bootleg LPs in which Chess can be heard arguing with Howlin' Wolf or Little Walter about the quality of their music. In heated and often profane arguments, Chess demonstrated both an in-depth knowledge of blues music and exceptional candor in explaining the strengths and weaknesses of his artist's music. This made Chess one of the most significant pioneer producers in the early and mid-1950s.

In analyzing Chess' musical growth, it is obvious that he entered the recording industry as a jazz music fan. He saw an opportunity to make a lot of money, and he possessed a virtually encyclopedic knowledge of Chicago music. Chess haunted the local clubs to find new talent, and in the late 1940s and early 1950s this was considered a sign of eccentricity. But what Leonard Chess discovered was that Chicago was not only a mecca for jazz but also for blues, rhythm and blues, rockabilly, and rock-and-roll music.

In 1952, Chicago's eclectic musical smorgasbord prompted Chess to form Cadet, Argo, and Checker as subsidiary record labels. The business strategy behind this move was a sound one. Cadet and Argo were designed as jazz, rhythm and blues, and rockabilly labels. In particular, Argo released some interesting early recordings like Eddie Fontaine's *Nothin' Shakin'* (Argo 5309), the Students' *I'm So Young* (Argo 5386), and the Sensations' *Let Me In* (Argo 5405). Significant Checker releases were Elmore James' *She Just Won't Do Right* (Checker 777), Little Walter's *Don't Have to Hunt No More* (Checker 767), and Otis Spann's *It Must Have Been the Devil* (Checker 807). These labels were an outgrowth of the success of Aristocrat Records from 1947 to 1950. When Aristocrat Records changed its name to

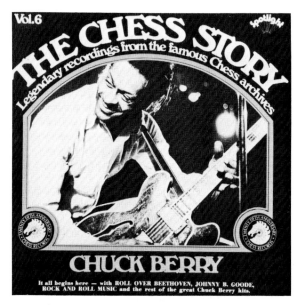

Chuck Berry repackaged by Chess for . . .

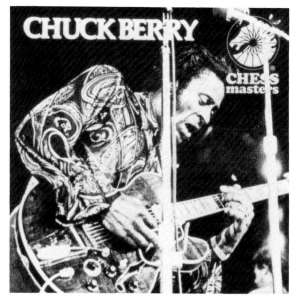

. . . Sweden (top) and the United Kingdom.

Chess in 1950, Leonard Chess began the process of forming what would become a million dollar recording empire. The subsidiary labels were the first indication of increasingly sophisticated production and distribution techniques by the Chess organization.

By the mid-1950s, the Chess label and its subsidiaries were well known to blues aficionados. Much of the early blues success of Chess Records was due to Muddy Waters. When Waters recorded *Rolling Stone* for Aristocrat Records, he established a strong regional market for Leonard Chess' label. Although *Rolling Stone* is Waters' best known song, it was not listed on the *Billboard* charts because it was sold in only three areas: Chicago, St. Louis, and Memphis. It was not until Waters recorded his first Chess side, *Louisiana Blues*, in 1951, that he had a *Billboard* hit. The success of Muddy Waters, John Lee Hooker, and Howlin' Wolf prompted Leonard Chess to concentrate his energies upon blues music. As a result of this blues resurgence, there was a steady stream of talent requesting auditions at the Chess offices at 71st and Phillips in Chicago.

Many people who bought blues music were intrigued by the echo or "reverb" which Chess was able to infuse into the records. This unique sound was the result of a primitive set up in the back of Chess' offices. By placing an open microphone in a tiny bathroom, an echo effect was added to the recordings. This constant experimentation by Leonard Chess led to some of the most innovative blues music of the 1950s. Marshall Chess, Leonard's son, believed that many of the sounds were accidential ones. There is no doubt an element of truth in this notion, but it should not obscure Chess' genius as a musical producer. In general, Chess Records developed into a magnificent blues and rhythm and blues label by 1955, and was on the verge of entering the mainstream rock-and-roll market.

Although bluesmen like Bo Diddley, Muddy Waters, and Howlin' Wolf were hitmakers, and rhythm and blues artists like the Moonglows also crossed over into the white record buying market, none of these artists or groups was a potential musical superstar. Of all these artists the closest to rock-and-roll music was Chester Burnett, the Howlin' Wolf. Leonard Chess' ability to produce excellent blues music was perhaps best evidenced in the career of Chester Burnett. Burnett was born in 1910 in eastern Mississippi, but he grew up in the Delta area where the blues originated. A Clarksdale, Mississippi bluesman, Charley Patton, taught him to play the guitar. Patton, who lived on Dockery's Plantation in Ruleville, Mississippi, began to show the young musician a number of guitar tricks. Burnett believed that Patton's music was old-fashioned, however, and began instead to pattern his style after a duo known as the Mississippi Sheiks. Memphis Slim was a member of the Mississippi Sheiks and Burnett was impressed by the vocal style and beat of this group. In the late 1920s, Burnett — Howlin' Wolf — began playing the guitar at local dances. In the 1930s, Wolf worked a party with legendary bluesman Robert Johnson. After meeting Johnson in Robinsville, Mississippi, he played some country parties near Greenwood, Ita Bena, and Moorehead. During these performances, Rice Miller (Sonny Boy Williamson No. 2) often joined Johnson and Howlin' Wolf on stage. After hearing Rice Miller play the harmonica, Wolf brought together a guitar-harmonica sound which blended perfectly with his infectious gravelly voice. The large, impressively built Howlin' Wolf did not become a professional musician, however, until 1948; he was thirty-eight years old. In West Memphis, Arkansas, Wolf had made a name for himself with a radio show on station KWEM. His band included Junior Parker on harmonica, Matt Murphy on guitar, and Willie Steele on drums. An obscure piano player known simply as "Destruction" often sat in on early gigs.

When Sam Phillips recorded Wolf's *Moaning at Midnight* and *How Many More Years* and sold it to Leonard Chess, a new dimension was added to Chess Records. Not only did Sam Phillips' acetate dub showcase Wolf's rasping vocals, but they were complemented by a heavy guitar background. When Chess and Modern threatened to take legal action against Wolf because he recorded for two labels, Wolf simply moved to Chicago in the fall of 1952 to record exclusively for the Chess label. During the next three years, Howlin' Wolf became a regional blues star. In 1954, *Cash Box* magazine voted Wolf the year's most promising new rhythm and blues performer. The forty-four-year-old Wolf had been playing music for a quarter of a century, and he chuckled over the belated recognition.

One of the obvious changes in Howlin' Wolf's musical career was the quality of his music. The recordings that he completed in Memphis were not distinguished ones, and it was not until he came under Leonard Chess' tutelage that Howlin' Wolf became a first-rate blues artist. It was a combination of excellent supporting musicians, first-class production techniques, and the careful selection of material which made Howlin' Wolf a legendary artist. By 1956, Wolf's versions of *Smokestack Lightnin'*, *Red Rooster*, *Back Door Man*, *Wang Dang Doodle*, and *Down in the Bottom* revealed a performer whose professional experience in the Chess studios and Chicago nightclubs had made him one of the most successful Delta bluesmen of his day.

There were also other important changes at Chess Records. Since 1947, Muddy Waters and Leonard Chess had worked together closely in the recording studio. Between 1947 and 1950, Waters recorded approximately eighteen songs for Aristocrat Records. Although Muddy Waters was not yet a nationally known bluesman, he was a very strong regional act. Many of the musicians who were important session players for Chess Records were a part of Muddy

Waters' band at one time or another. Such distinguished bluesmen as Otis Spann, Willie Dixon, and Jimmy Rogers played with Muddy Waters and subsequently played on Chuck Berry records. In 1954, Muddy Waters' *Hoochie Coochie Man* made inroads into white record-buying markets, but he never became the mainstream blues act that Leonard Chess envisioned.

In any event, due to the increase in business, the Chess brothers moved their offices to East 49th Street, and they intensified the production of rhythm and blues and rock-and-roll records. Much of the success of Chess Records' rhythm and blues sound was due to Harvey Fuqua. As one of two lead singers in the Moonglows, Fuqua was far ahead of his time in composing rock lyrics. He also had an intimate understanding of the trends and direction of early rhythm and blues rock music. When Fuqua wrote *Sincerely*, it was the beginning of a new era for Chess Records. *Billboard* magazine's survey of the musical year 1955 revealed that the Moonglows were the best-selling Chess group, with 250,000 copies of *Sincerely*. This seemingly insignificant statistic was the beginning of a mainstream record-buying cross over for rhythm and blues music.

So it was that Chess and rock-and-roll shared a coming of age. There was a performing energy and a songwriting skill in Howlin' Wolf's music which created one of the foundation stones necessary for the development of rock music. In addition, the successes of Muddy Waters and Harvey Fuqua and the Moonglows changed musical concepts and ideas. The release of *Sincerely* helped to establish attitudes and ideas about music which made it easier for performers like Chuck Berry, Bo Diddley, and Dale Hawkins to enter the recording business and rise to the forefront on Chess and Checker Records. An examination of the successes experienced by Chess artists in the mid-1950s provides a microcosmic analysis of the atmosphere necessary to bring about the rock revolution. The key to the rise of rock-and-roll was not only the talents of the Chess recording roster, but the talents and skills of Leonard Chess and his record company.

In 1955 and 1956, rhythm and blues records sold well enough to help place rock-and-roll music into the mainstream of the music business. Once rock music became commercially successful, the small record labels began to go bankrupt, since the major recording companies now started to compete with one another as well as with the small companies for new talent. The independent record companies were no longer able to sign the best-selling artists they needed in order to stay in business. There was also a trend toward more sophisticated production in the recording studio, and there were new marketing techniques to help place rock music at the center of the

The first Chess LP to feature Chuck (1957) . . .

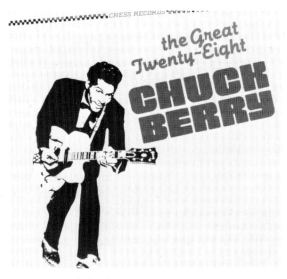

. . . and the latest repackaging (1982).

exploding popular culture of the 1950s.

The path which Chuck Berry took to a recording contract with Chess Records was a long and uncertain one. In 1954, Chuck had approached Vee Jay Records, but he was unable to convince anyone to listen to his tape. In fact, Chuck had prepared extensive demonstration tapes for Capitol, Mercury, and Vee Jay Records in 1954--1955. It was due to these tapes that he began to attract the attention of other artists. The key to Chuck Berry's popularity with other musicians was that they stopped by the clubs that he played in to listen to his music. Many recording executives who analyzed Chuck's music believed that his country-oriented guitar riffs were too sophisticated for any of the three established *Billboard* categories: pop, rhythm and blues, and country music. If Chuck's early demo tapes had been more blues directed, there is little doubt that he would have immediately been signed to a recording contract. His music, however, owed as much to Hank Williams and Nat "King" Cole as it did to Muddy Waters or Howlin' Wolf, and this confused talent scouts who sought out new material for record labels.

For a time, Chuck considered moving to Houston to record for Huey Meaux's Duke record label, or even to Memphis to approach Sam Phillips' Sun Record Company. However, Chuck Berry was a family man with a wife and children, and he believed that the strain would be too great upon his family. In addition, Berry was a successful cosmetologist, earning an extra fourteen dollars a night playing in East St. Louis nightclubs. It was not easy to uproot his family, and Chuck pondered the wisdom of a recording contract for some time. It was with these considerations in mind that Chuck Berry decided to take a four-week vacation to Chicago. In May, 1955, as he later recalled, "I visited a friend in Chicago and we went around to different places, listening to the blues artists." Chuck arrived in Chicago with his guitar, a small suitcase, and a little notebook filled with original songs, and he was not optimistic about his future in the record business. Before he left for Chicago, Berry's long-time piano player, Johnny Johnson, lectured Chuck about the country musical style which permeated Chuck's song, *Ida Red*, soon to be renamed *Maybellene*. He told Berry that it was too radical to appeal to a large scale commercial audience. What Johnson failed to realize was that Berry's mixture of country and blues music was very similar to Bill Haley's brand of rock-and-roll. There were already a number of Haley songs on the *Billboard* charts, largely due to his unique blend of country and blues music.

So it was that the route to a recording contract with Leonard Chess began in May, 1955, as Chuck Berry traveled from one blues club to another on Chicago's South Side. Berry was impressed and intrigued with the musical explosion in the Windy City, but he realized that while blues music was popular amongst blacks, it would not cross over to a white audience. Due to his education and extensive musical background, Chuck was more knowledgeable about popular songs than most novices in the record business. He performed in a number of small Chicago clubs, growing steadily more encouraged by the positive response to his music. Finally, at Chicago's Palladium Club on State Street, Muddy Waters asked Chuck to sit in with his band. After a particularly rousing set, Chuck and Muddy Waters talked backstage for a long time over drinks. As a result of this conversation, Chuck left the Palladium Club with a note written on the end of an envelope. On this tattered envelope were directions to see Leonard Chess at 2120 S. Michigan Avenue. Having already approached and been turned down by Vee Jay Records, just across the street from Chess, Chuck had no idea what to expect from the Chess label. As he entered the office, Chuck found Leonard Chess sitting out front, feet on a desk, smoking a cigar. After a brief conversation, Chuck realized that Chess was an astute judge of musical talent. The Chicago-based label was recording as many black artists as possible and, much like Sam Phillips, Chess had an ear for a unique new sound.

When young Chuck Berry walked through the front door of the Chess Record company he was understandably nervous. When Chess asked Chuck what his music sounded like, Chuck was so startled by the immediate attention from a recording executive that he could not think of an appropriate answer. Then Chess asked: "What kind of music do you play?" Berry replied: "Boogie." Chess suggested that Chuck make a demonstration tape. As a result, Chess lent Chuck a seventy-nine-dollar tape recorder, and he cut *Ida Red, Wee Wee Hours, Together We Will Always Be,* and *30 Days.* Chess listened intently to the tape and raved over *Ida Red.* Previously, when Chuck would play a tape of *Ida Red* for musicians, they were often perplexed by the tune. Leonard Chess, however, recognized that this song had the potential to be a hit record. The visionary Chess realized that *Billboard*'s country and western and pop charts would easily accommodate this cross over sound. In 1954, Chess recording artists the Moonglows had tremendous commercial success with *Sincerely,* which was covered by the McGuire Sisters. Leonard Chess had watched Pat Boone achieve enormous success with black music in the rock market, and he closely followed Sam Phillips' success with the career of young Elvis Presley. Chess saw Chuck Berry as a similar type of cross over musical artist, and made the decision to push Chuck's records solely in a white market. (As a result some of Chuck's early blues numbers were either relegated to the B sides of his records or not released.) For three years, Chuck had worked diligently to perfect a clear vocal delivery accentuated by country-type guitar licks during the instrumental breaks. Leonard Chess easily recognized the revolutionary commercial nature of Chuck Berry's music when most industry figures and a number of prominent musicians dismissed Chuck's music as "cream puff blues."

Chess made immediate plans for a recording session. A call was made to St. Louis, and Johnny Johnson rode the bus to Chicago to lend his piano skills to Chuck Berry's initial recording. In order to make Chuck Berry's sound as commercial as possible, Bo Diddley's maraca player, Jerome Green, was brought into Chuck's first session. Jasper Thomas played the drums, and Willie Dixon was the bass player on this session. On a warm Chicago evening on May 21, 1955, Chuck Berry cut thirty-six takes of *Maybellene* and nine takes of *Wee Wee Hours*. It was during the nine cuts necessary to get *Wee Wee Hours* in the can that Chuck demonstrated his uncanny ability to sing the blues. In his first session for Chess Records, Chuck remarked to Willie Dixon that his future was as a blues performer. He had recently witnessed the performance of most of Chicago's key bluesmen, and Chuck believed that his talents were superior to those of most other artists. When Leonard Chess began plugging *Maybellene*, Chuck Berry was surprised; he believed that his future was in the blues idiom. "We thought *Maybellene* was a joke," Chuck commented to a reporter. When *Maybellene* was played at the Cosmopolitan Club, it was a novelty number to commemorate Louis Jordan's influence. It was blues music that Chuck concentrated upon to please the St. Louis crowds. It was a music he loved and performed beautifully. But Leonard Chess saw another side to Chuck Berry's music. At Huff Gardens and the Cosomopolitan Club, Chuck had learned to excite a crowd and to work his original material into his stage show. By far the most requested Chuck Berry original had been *Ida Red*. When it was recorded in Chicago, with Leonard Chess' excellent sidemen and the title changed to *Maybellene*, it became one of the most significant early rock-and-roll songs.

The origin of the name "Maybellene" has intrigued rock historians for a long time. When Greil Marcus asked Chuck, during an interview before a number of students at the University of California, Berkeley, where the name "Maybellene" originated, Chuck responded: "the only Maybellene I knew was the name of a cow." This reinforced the legend that a story from a third grade reader at Simmons Grade School in St. Louis was the source of the name "Maybellene." Still other critics continue to point to the name of a popular hair creme in the mid-1950s to suggest the origins of "Maybellene." As to the song itself, there was a country song called *Ida Red*, which is often credited as the inspiration for Chuck's *Ida Red*, later *Maybellene*. The original *Ida Red* was recorded by Bob Wills and the Texas Playboys, and also by The Louvin Brothers, but it was

Chuck listens to the playback of an early Chess recording (1950s).

Wills' version which apparently influenced young Chuck Berry. In short, there is no agreement about the origin of a song which created a rock-and-roll revolution and changed the course of American popular culture.

One of the means of guaranteeing a hit record in the 1950s was to find a well-known disc jockey to plug it. When a disc jockey like Alan Freed shook the wrappers surrounding a 45 record, and a twenty dollar bill dropped out, he played the song. In later years, Leonard Chess would brag that payola was taken off the Chess Record payroll as a legitimate business deduction. Likewise, in the mid-1950s, if a popular disc jockey was given writing credit on a particular record, the DJ would push it. Leonard Chess also employed this tactic, and would invite important disc jockeys and record distributors to selected recording sessions. During Chuck Berry's *Maybellene* and *Wee Wee Hours* session, Russ Fratto, a Chicago record distributor and Chess' landlord, was invited to see Chuck's first recording session. Fratto was so impressed that he quickly called New York disc jockey Alan Freed, and they discussed Chuck's talents. Leonard Chess then flew to New York to confer with Freed, and the result was that Fratto and Freed were listed as *Maybellene*'s co-writers. Chuck has maintained for years that they contributed nothing to the song, but the Freed estate continues to receive royalties from *Maybellene*. It was virtually impossible to have a major hit record in the 1950s without payola, and so even a classic like *Maybellene* was forced to go begging for a sympathetic DJ.

When Leonard Chess met with Alan Freed, he pointed out that Berry's talent was a unique one. Not only was Chuck able to play a very lean and tight blues guitar, he could also vary his songs in the rock-and-roll idiom. He had much more range and depth than Bo Diddley, and his songwriting talents appealed to young *white* record buyers. When Chess later reflected on his initial feelings about *Maybellene*, he told Michael Lydon, "I liked it, thought it was something new." Chess also claimed that an acetate dub was taken to New York for Freed's approval. Chess's memory may not be accurate. A more plausible explanation is that Alan Freed simply agreed with Russ Fratto's assessment that Chuck Berry was an emerging rock-and-roll superstar.

So, when Freed played *Maybellene* for two hours on his popular WINS New York rock show, he promoted not only Chuck Berry's sound but his own financial empire. Alan Freed also staged rock-and-roll concerts, and Chuck Berry became his favorite performer and strongest gate attraction. Chuck has never allowed interviewers to gain any insights into his real feelings about Alan Freed, but the general consensus is that these two early rock giants respected each

Chuck, Sandy Stewart, Alan Freed and Jimmy Clanton in the 1958 movie "Go Johnny Go."

Photo by Howard DeWitt

San Jose blues artist Guitar Mac with Bo Diddley.

other and got along very well.

Bill Haley and the Comets were another strong influence in the success of Chuck Berry's music. Charlie Gillet, in his groundbreaking book *Sound of the City*, argues that Leonard Chess purposely arranged Chuck's music so that it resembled Haley's. In fact, Chess copied Bill Haley's arrangements and backup musical sounds to create Chuck's hit records. There is no mention of Bill Haley in any interviews by Leonard Chess or Chuck Berry, but it is safe to assume, in light of Haley's commercial success, that his influence on Chuck Berry's early recordings was not insignificant.

Once *Maybellene* was released, Chuck Berry began to tour extensively to support his Chess Record releases. By 1956, he was a legitimate rock-and-roll superstar. Leonard Chess's contribution to Berry's music was essentially in providing an atmosphere necessary to his art. The Chess studios not only boasted the finest equipment and the best session musicians, but Chess Records also allowed time for studio experimentation. It was a time of great creativity in the rock recording industry, and it would have been impossible without the astute guidance of Leonard Chess.

During this period, one of Chuck Berry's closest friends was Bo Diddley, and they influenced each other a great deal. It was difficult for Leonard Chess to market Bo Diddley's material extensively among white audiences, but there was a hard-core Bo Diddley faction who were also strong Chuck Berry fans. In 1955, though, the major record labels failed to take artists like Chuck Berry and Bo Diddley seriously. Mitch Miller voiced the prevailing attitude when he suggested that artists such as Perry Como, Joni James, Frank Sinatra, and Dean Martin would continue to dominate popular music. Almost every executive in the music industry believed that rock-and-roll was simply a passing fad. The corporate leadership at RCA did not seek out another serious rock act after signing Elvis Presley in 1955. Privately, RCA executives swore that they would never sign another rock artist. Presley's records sold in such large quantities that RCA was forced to contract with rival companies to press his records, but this still did not change the opinion of RCA executives about rock music. Although the RCA accounting department announced that Presley's sales totaled twenty-five percent of the company's overall business, RCA continued to ignore the figures. It was not until the mid-1960s that RCA talent scout Joe Di Imperial signed another rock act. After watching concerts at San Francisco's Fillmore and Avalon ballrooms, Di Imperial stood outside the Matrix nightclub in San Francisco and counted the number of patrons who paid to see each act. After two weeks, Di Imperial signed the group that had drawn the largest crowds. Luckily for RCA, this newly discovered talent was the Jefferson Airplane.

There was little doubt that the rock music business was a new departure for the major record companies. In 1955, Chuck Berry's *Maybellene* spent fourteen weeks on the *Billboard* Hot 100, and rose to number five on the charts. It heralded the arrival of rock music. But, to knowledgeable recording exeuctives, *Maybellene* was simply not a particularly successful release. What they failed to realize was that the lyrics, the musical direction, and the energy in Chuck Berry's music was a portent of the impending revolution in American popular culture.

Many early rock-and-roll artists were intrigued with Chuck Berry's music. In 1955, Elvis Presley sang *Maybellene* on the "Louisiana Hayride,"and he also featured the song in performances throughout the South. Marty Robbins was the first important artist to cover *Maybellene*, and the Gadabouts recorded Chuck Berry's *Too Much Monkey Business* in 1956. By the 1980s, more than 800 cover versions of Chuck Berry songs were available worldwide (see the Appendix in this book). In the 1980s, Chuck remarked to San Francisco disk jockey, Gene Nelson, that he had written 208 songs, and he was tickled each time he heard a cover version of one of his tunes.

Although *Maybellene* reached number one on the *Billboard* rhythm and blues charts, giving Chuck Berry the satisfaction of replacing Bill Haley's *Rock Around the Clock*, he was discouraged by the fact that it did not sell as well as Haley's song on the *Billboard* Hot 100. On white AM radio stations, *Maybellene* received only limited airplay. Across the country, black disc jockeys like "Jumpin' " George Oxford at KSAN, then an AM station in San Francisco, recognized the commercial potential of the new rock musical acts. Soon, caravans of nine or ten predominantly black rock acts toured local movie theaters and small auditoriums doing three to five shows a day. Jimmy Beasley, a recording artist with Crown Records, recalled: "I remember playing seven shows a day for Alan Freed at fifty bucks a show. I thought that I was making a lot of money." Beasley's reference was to the Paramount Theater Shows in New York. In California, there were fewer shows but the musicians still worked long and hard for a few dollars.

As a result of *Maybellene*'s success, Chuck Berry began to work in small clubs, concert halls, and at teen dances. His first concert as a Chess rock-and-roll recording star was in June, 1955, in an Ohio movie theater. Soon, Chuck was on the road more than 300 days a year. It was the beginning of the rock-and-roll revolution, and the early tours were filled with backbreaking days of travel blended with raucous nights performing under makeshift conditions. Although travel was difficult, accommodations were poor, and the pay often disappeared into the pockets of dishonest promoters, Chuck Berry loved the rock-and-roll lifestyle. He had waited a long time to play his music professionally, and he began to press Leonard Chess for better bookings. It was difficult to obtain television exposure, and the major clubs were not yet ready for rock music. So, Chuck Berry's early odyssey was one of travel and frustration.

In summary, 1955 was the beginning of Chuck Berry's professional career in rock-and-roll music. He found a suitable record label in Chess, and his music gained national exposure on the *Billboard* charts. Although Chuck appeared to some to be an overnight sensation in the music business, nothing was further from the truth. He had already spent almost a decade practicing his craft in one form or another. By the time Chuck traveled to Chicago, he was a seasoned performer, and an accomplished songwriter. Still, there were few people in the recording industry who either recognized Berry's enormous talent or his subtle influence upon popular culture. The significance of Chuck Berry's first few months at Chess Records lies in the fact that he had found an excellent record company, and he was one of the earliest important rock-and-roll artists to write both the lyrics and music to his songs. His themes were ones which were universally suited not only to rock music, but to the vibrant cultural changes transforming America. The stage was set for the musical explosion which became the first golden age of rock-and-roll music: 1956 and 1957.

Chuck performing in California, 1978.

CHAPTER 3

THE FIRST GOLDEN AGE
OF ROCK MUSIC: 1956-1957

In 1956–1957, rock-and-roll music entered its first golden age, and five performers dominated the mainstream of the rock music business. The most exciting performer was Elvis Presley, whose appearances on the "Tommy and Jimmy Dorsey Stage Show," the "Steve Allen Show," the "Milton Berle Show," and the "Ed Sullivan Show" helped to popularize rock music amongst adult listeners. Elvis brought rock-and-roll into the living rooms of American homes, and demonstrated the strong commercial potential of this new music. Bill Haley and his Comets caught the imagination of the American public with what became the national anthem of rock music, *Rock Around the Clock.* When this song was featured in the movie "The Blackboard Jungle," rock-and-roll became a movie as well as a television phenomenon. Little Richard was another important performer in the germinal stages of rock music, as he introduced a wild piano style and exaggerated vocal delivery which helped set the stage for a highly theatrical approach to rock music. Fats Domino lacked the personal charisma of Little Richard, the mainstream appeal of Bill Haley, and the raw energy of Elvis Presley, but Domino's New Orleans musical heritage and his pronounced rhythm and blues styling made his contribution equally as important. The music of Elvis Presley, Bill Haley, Little Richard, and Fats Domino was written in collaboration with other songwriters, arrangers, and musical handymen. The fifth Founding Father of Rock and Roll Music was Chuck Berry, who was the only rock pioneer to write the lyrics and music for his songs. Elvis did not write songs, but simply put his name on tunes written by artists like Otis Blackwell. Little Richard, Fats Domino, and Bill Haley wrote some of their own music, but they needed musical and lyrical assistance to complete their songs. Chuck Berry sat up late at night in small hotel rooms, penning the words to his own songs, weaving the lyrical poems which transformed rock-and-roll music. Chuck was the poet laureate of a new music at a time when few people understood anything about the rising crescendo of rock. It was Chuck Berry who provided the first realistic images of teen-age life in his music and lyrics. As Lillian Roxon suggested, "Chuck Berry may be the single most important name in the history of rock . . . . "

When Chuck Berry's music began to receive extensive radio play, it quickly changed the direction of rock-and-roll music. Elvis Presley's *Heartbreak Hotel* was the pop music approach to rock-and-roll. Fats Domino's *Blueberry Hill* had a nostalgic aura, because it brought back older music in a new form. Little Richard's *Ready Teddy* and *Rip It Up* had a raucous feel, but it was not as popular as Chuck Berry's musical and lyrical approach to rock music. Chuck realized that rock-and-roll meant more to young people than just music. He saw his lyrics as a means of attacking conformity, racism, and the everyday problems of life in the 1950s. But in his first year with Chess Records, Chuck recorded only fourteen new songs because he was so busy touring to support his previous hit records.

In 1956, only five Chuck Berry songs were recorded for Chess Records. In the February sessions, Chuck was backed by Johnny Johnson on piano, Willie Dixon on bass, Fred Below on drums, and L.C. Davis on tenor sax. These sessions produced important Chuck Berry songs, such as *Drifting Heart, Brown-Eyed Handsome Man, Roll Over Beethoven*, and *Too Much Monkey Business*. The only song from this session to reach the *Billboard* Hot 100 was *Roll Over Beethoven*, entering the charts on June 20, and peaking at number twenty-nine during its five week residence on the charts. In October, 1956, Jimmy Roger's guitar and Willie Dixon's bass were brought in for a brief session, and *Havana Moon* was cut for future release. This song had a calypso-reggae direction, a sound far ahead of its time. It was released as the B side of *You Can't Catch Me*, and went virtually unnoticed by the general public. The fact that Chuck was almost continuously on tour precluded any type of intensive recording sessions, and helps to explain why he had only one hit record on *Billboard*'s Hot 100 in 1956.

It was on the rhythm and blues charts that Chuck Berry made his greatest impact in 1956. *Billboard*'s rhythm and blues charts listed three Top 10 Berry tunes: *Roll Over Beethoven, Too Much Monkey Business*, and *Brown Eyed Handsome Man*. Another song, *No Money Down*, reached number eleven on the rhythm and blues charts, and there was constant demand for Chuck's records by rhythm and blues record buyers. It was often difficult to buy Chuck Berry records in many towns. In Seattle, Washington, for example, Chuck's discs were sold at a shoe shine stand near the Birdland Club on Capitol Hill. The major record stores did not carry Chess releases, and this relegated Chuck to small stores on Seattle's Jackson Street. It was this way all over America, as Chess was not able to match the distribution of Elvis Presley's RCA label.

Chuck Berry circa 1956.

As Chuck Berry traveled from one city to another, however, he brought his revolutionary lyrics and energetic performing style into the mainstream of American popular culture. The good-looking, well-dressed Berry was the picture of the *Brown Eyed Handsome Man* as he cavorted about the stage in the movie theaters and small ballrooms which served as the backdrop for the early rock-and-roll revolution. Once he appeared before an audience, they never forgot the image of the tall, wavy-haired performer with the slouching duck walk and pleasing personality.

The demands of Chuck's early performing career were impossible ones, but local promoters could always count upon him to give a quality show. He was a cordial, pleasing stage personality who seemed unaffected by the pressures of constant touring. After years of obscurity in East St. Louis nightclubs, Chuck certainly was prepared for stardom. He was unprepared, however, for the unequal treatment he encountered in the South, the racial slurs by promoters, and the success of artists whose talents were inferior to his own skills. It was a frustrating time for Chuck Berry, as even constant touring did not produce the financial rewards that white rock stars like Elvis Presley and Bill Haley enjoyed. Yet, much to his credit, Chuck never complained about the racial, monetary, or artistic inequities of the rock music business. He was a survivor who made the best of an impossible situation.

In 1972, Chuck Berry reflected on his early years. While working one of Richard Nader's Rock N Roll Revival Shows at New York's Madison Square Garden, Chuck reminisced: "Elvis and I were bumping heads, that cat and me. I was more popular then he was. I was busting my ass to push him over, to bust him out of number 1. I did it, too. *Sweet Little Sixteen* bumped *All Shook Up*, but *Roll Over Beethoven* couldn't knock over *Heartbreak Hotel*." With characteristic honesty, Chuck acknowledged that his music did not reach the vast number of people, or have the financial success, that Elvis Presley's music did under RCA and Colonel Tom Parker's tutelage. Always a gentleman, Chuck never publicly complained about Chess Records' poor distribution, or their failure to advertise his record releases extensively. There is no doubt that *Sweet Little Sixteen, School Day*, and *Rock and Roll Music* deserved "gold" status, but it was not until the early 1970s that Chuck was finally presented with the official gold records for these hits. Much of the difficulty in collecting royalties and documenting gold records can be traced to management in the record business. Although Leonard Chess was honest and paid a fair royalty, he often found it difficult to control the distributor and the disc jockeys. Moreover, Chess Records' pressing statistics were often haphazardly kept, a reflection of the prevailing business procedures in the industry which unwittingly cheated both black and white artists alike.

The attitude of the executives in charge of the major recording companies was demonstrated when Ahmet Ertegun of Atlantic Records approached Columbia Records with a deal to distribute a number of Atlantic's popular acts. When Ertegun informed Columbia executives that he paid his artists a three percent royalty, a Columbia vice-president responded: "You're paying those people royalties? You must be out of your mind!" The interview ended with the Columbia representative calling the Atlantic singers a group of "Nigger artists." Clive Davis, the president of Columbia Records, exhibited a similar attitude in the 1970s, when his memoirs described Chuck Berry as not really being a mainstream rock-and-roll artist. These prejudices suggest that race, not music, was the reason that Chuck Berry never really experienced extraordinary financial success in the record industry. It is notable, as a result, that it was not until the 1970s that Columbia Records had a number one hit record with a rock group. Paul Revere and the Raiders were signed in the mid-1960s as Columbia's first rock artists. Paul Revere, however, had to first convince Mitch Miller that his music was "wholesome," and not a threat to American youth. There have been few musicians as shrewd as Paul Revere, and even he was amazed at the absolute power of Columbia's A and R chief.

In 1956--1957, Chuck Berry experienced a blend of rapid commercial success, and personal and racial slights. He toured incessantly and traveled to all parts of the United States. He encountered numerous bullies, hostile Sheriffs, and irate parents. The concert settings were often like the one at Seattle's Eagle's Auditorium. It was a long, upstairs concert hall with a small balcony. There were only a few seats, and most people simply stood around and watched eight to ten acts perform in a three-hour period. In the South, in towns like West Memphis, Arkansas, the racially mixed audience was separated by a chicken wire fence, with a grimacing sheriff stalking the room. After such shows, Chuck would disappear into the black section of town for a blues jam in a small club. It was ironic that Chuck Berry could sit in at jam sessions only in the black part of town to play the blues. This was a good indication of the role of race in the categorization of musical styles; young white audiences had not yet discovered the blues.

To combat the rigors of the road, Chuck Berry carried an elegant looking briefcase filled with a hot plate and cans of food. Many early observers of the rock music scene found Chuck's habits strange ones. Marshall Chess remembers: "Chuck would tell me he was never hungry . . . and then I'd catch him cooking a can on a hotplate." To survive in the midst of this lifestyle, Chuck drank very little and ate good food. "Twinkes and that kind of shit," Chuck reflected, "it'll rot out your stomach forever."

In January, 1956, Chess Records released *No Money Down* and *Down Bound Train* (Chess 1615), and *Billboard* described this record as an example of Berry's humorous approach to rock music. *Billboard* noted that the flip side, *Down Bound Train*, had an "almost country-style blues" tone to it. The May 19, 1956, issue of *Billboard* described *Roll Over Beethoven* as a humorous song with a driving beat. These descriptions were much like those that *Billboard* accorded Louis Jordan in the 1940s. What *Billboard* failed to recognize was that there was a great deal of lyrical significance to Berry's early music. In *No Money Down*, for example, the high pressure sales tactics employed by automobile dealers in the 1950s were parodied. In lyrics which were critical of the sharkskin-suited, suede-shoed salesman who sold an inferior product, Chuck was speaking out against the conformist mentality of the Eisenhower-Nixon years. Another example of Chuck's early use of humor occurred in 1958, when he included riffs from the Gillette razor commercial in the midst of *Jo Jo Gunne*. The Gillette razor theme was used to promote the Friday night television fights, and the use of this riff was typical of Chuck Berry's musical mirth.

There was also a great deal of diversity in Chuck Berry's music. This musical breadth was demonstrated in a February, 1956, recording session. To make Chuck as comfortable as possible, Leonard Chess brought in Johnny Johnson from St. Louis to play the piano. Once they practiced together, Chuck began to work very smoothly with Johnson, drummer Fred Below, tenor saxophonist L.C. Davis, and bass player Willie Dixon. During the recording of *Roll Over Beethoven*, Chuck mentioned *Blue Suede Shoes*, which was recorded by Carl Perkins on December 26, 1955. This reference not only indicates that Chuck listened to current Sun Records rockabilly releases, but was his own personal way of letting people know that he had eclectic musical interests.

There was also a serious side to the February, 1956, Chess Record session. In an effort to make Chuck Berry's music commercially more appealing, Leonard Chess switched Willie Dixon to an electric bass guitar. One of the mysteries of this session is an unidentified trumpet player who added some brilliant musical touches. Although such Chuck Berry classics as *Brown-Eyed Handsome Man, Too Much Monkey Business*, and *Roll Over Beethoven* emerged from this session, none of the songs were particularly successful on the radio or *Billboard* pop charts.

Barber shops, liquor stores, small mom and pop grocery stores, and records shops served at first as the principal dispensing points for Chuck Berry's music. As a result, Chuck did not receive adequate or timely post-sale royalties from his recordings, and got into the

Chuck recording in the Chess studios (late 1950s).

habit of demanding cash payments *before* performing live in concert. This helped to develop his reputation as a no-nonsense, uncompromising performer with a mercurial temperament. Because it was common for promoters to short-change rock acts in the 1950s, Chuck refused to sign contracts or receipts. He simply put the cash he received in a briefcase before going on stage. In this way, he was able to control malevolent and parasitic rock promoters. The concern which Chuck demonstrated with the business side of the industry was the main reason that he was cool toward rock entrepreneurs such as Alan Freed. In a number of interviews, Chuck Berry very slyly pointed out that Freed neither wrote any of Berry's songs, nor was as influential in their success, as rock historians have suggested. Chuck remarked to Dan Fries of *Goldmine* magazine that he was "ripped off" in his early days in the music business.

Chuck' recollections differ considerably with Marshall Chess's assessment of Chuck Berry's early years. In an interview with *Blues Unlimited* magazine, Chess stated that Chuck agreed to allow Alan Freed's name to be added to *Maybellene* because it would guarantee a hit record. "It wasn't anything behind Chuck Berry's back," Chess remarked, "he was definitely a party to it." Over the years, Chuck has coyly suggested that he was naive about the business side of the industry. "I was basically unknowledgeable about the business," Chuck told one reporter, "and when the time came to sign papers . . . well I signed!" As Berry lamented to *Goldmine* magazine, he was still learning the business end of the recording industry in the late 1970s. If Chuck found the financial aspects of the record industry perplexing, it was not a deterrent to his songwriting and performing skills, however.

In the summer of 1956, Chuck Berry was an integral part of the rock-and-roll musical explosion. Even with *Roll Over Beethoven* on the *Billboard* Hot 100 for only five weeks, it guaranteed Chuck a good number of concert dates. His second hit was also rock music's first serious protest song, and *Roll Over Beethoven* influenced a generation of fledgling songwriters. In Hibbing, Minnesota, Bob Dylan started out pounding away at the piano, emulating Little Richard. By the 1960s, Dylan carried Chuck Berry's protest lyrics to an entire generation. Another important attribute of *Roll Over Beethoven* is that it influenced a considerable number of musicians who were still learning their craft. When the Beatles and Rolling Stones brought the first wave of English rock-and-roll music into America in 1964, Chuck Berry tunes were standard numbers in their concert repertoire.

Due to the innovative lyrical nature of Chuck Berry's music, his pioneering of the use of word pictures in his songs, other composers of the generation of the 1960s were presented with models and forms which they could employ to speak out against war, nuclear weapons, racism, and poverty. The prototype of the protest record appeared in October, 1956, when Chess Records released *Too Much Monkey Business*, backed with *Brown-Eyed Handsome Man*. Both of these records were similar to themes Bob Dylan developed in *Subterranean Homesick Blues*. In effect, Berry criticized middle-class values which kept the blue-collar worker, in his words, "hard workin at the mill." The demands for revolt against conformity in Chuck Berry's music were apparent in *Too Much Monkey Business*, when he intoned: "Want to marry, get a home, settle down and write a book. Ah, too much monkey business for me to be involved in." By rejecting the conformity of the mid-1950s, Chuck Berry sounded the national anthem of teen-age rebellion.

It was Chuck Berry's lyrics which molded the thoughts and ideas of young Bob Dylan. As Michael Gray's excellent book, *The Art of Bob Dylan: Song and Dance Man*, suggests, "Berry offered an urban-slang sophistication slicker than any city blues man before him." It was Chuck's ability to write songs with simple themes about automobiles, highways, refrigerators, and modern buildings which intrigued young Bob Dylan. For example, *Too Much Monkey Business* and *Memphis, Tennessee*, are songs in which a pay phone is a significant image. There were few rock songwriters who could carry off a popular tune with these lightweight lyrical props; Chuck Berry was the only one able to use the phone as a symbol of teen-age rebellion effectively in music.

When Bob Dylan wrote *Talkin' World War III Blues*, he employed similar telephone symbolism: "So I called up the operator . . . just to hear a voice of some kind. 'When you hear the beep it will be three o'clock.' She said that for over an hour." This is perfect Chuck Berry imagery in a Bob Dylan song, and it attests to the enormous influence that rock-and-roll's first poet laureate had upon the folk poets of the 1960s. In 1965, Bob Dylan released the **Bringing It All Back Home** and **Highway 61 Revisited** albums, and there was a distinct Chuck Berry influence in these folk-rock recordings. Although Dylan's images are more obscure than Chuck Berry's, nevertheless, Dylan uses many of Chuck's themes in his music.

Equally provocative in Chuck Berry's music was the message underlying the lyrics to *Brown-Eyed Handsome Man*. While Bob Dylan wrote deliberately about black civil rights activists like James Meredith, Chuck's writing had to be very subtle due to the pressures for commercial material in the entertainment business. Few people realized that *Brown-Eyed Handsome Man* was, in reality, the story of an interracial love affair. Implicit in the lyrics was a strong criticism of the double standard that society developed to separate the races.

The brown-eyed handsome man in concert.

As the civil rights movement of the 1950s made some minor gains, rock music reflected the changing social climate. To Chuck Berry, this song was simply an artistic rendering of the changes epitomized by the mixed audiences that applauded his music in St. Louis' Cosmopolitan Club. There, it was as common to see mixed couples as it was in Seattle, San Francisco, Los Angeles, Chicago, New York, and Detroit. The media and general public ignored this social revolution, but Berry's lyrics were a clear reflection of the fundamental level of social change occurring in American culture.

The movie industry was another important force in the changing direction of American society. In December, 1956, the movie "Rock, Rock, Rock" was released in theaters around the nation. Tuesday Weld played a teen-ager who lost her boyfriend, Teddy Randazzo, to the new girl in town. In counterpoint to a dull and dreary plot, there were twenty rock-and-roll songs featuring such artists as Chuck Berry, LaVern Baker, Frankie Lymon and the Teenagers, the Johnny Burnette Trio, the Moonglows, and the Flamingos. Chuck's version of *You Can't Catch Me* was one of the many musical highpoints of the film. In an attempt to capitalize on the movie's music, Chess Records issued the first rock-and-roll soundtrack album, **Rock, Rock, Rock**, which featured such Chuck Berry songs as *30 Days, Maybellene, Roll Over Beethoven*, and *You Can't Catch Me*. Rock-and-roll movies became an important factor in altering attitudes concerning rock music, race, and entertainment in the 1950s, and Chess Records' LP proved to be just such a catalyst to changing racial views.

As the nation modified its attitude on race and desegregation, rock-and-roll music became an important force in advancing social change. A number of white rock artists were booked by promoters to play black clubs, for example, because they had the "negro sound." When Buddy Holly and the Crickets had their first hit, they were booked into New York's famous Apollo Theater. A quiet, predominantly black audience at first greeted Holly's band with an uncomfortable silence when they appeared on stage. After two nights of lukewarm audience acceptance, Holly wandered into a Harlem Club, which featured Bo Diddley in concert. After listening to Bo's raucous music, Buddy Holly and the Crickets hastily put together a set of Bo Diddley and Chuck Berry songs. Once Holly launched into *Brown-Eyed Handsome Man* and *Bo Diddley*, the Apollo audience danced in the aisles. It was a refreshing sight to see four country boys change the social taboos against white performers singing black music.

In 1956, Buddy Holly recorded *Brown-Eyed Handsome Man* because he believed that it bespoke the reality of the new musical and cultural ideas coming of age in America. But Buddy Holly and

Chuck Berry were more than just professional musicians who admired each other's work. In 1957, both Berry and Holly were touring together as members of "The Biggest Show of Stars." As they rode the old bus each night to the next concert, they developed a strong friendship. In the back of the bus, Holly and Berry played cards, shot craps, and talked music. This led to in-depth discussions on how to phrase lyrics, compose music, and set the mood for a song. It was a time of growth and education for both of these rock-and-roll giants. Unfortunately, Holly's untimely death in 1959, and Berry's reluctance to discuss their friendship, makes it impossible to assess the full impact of the conversations.

During the first Golden Age of Rock-and-Roll music, Chuck Berry began to employ his famous duck walk to establish himself as one of America's most exciting rock performers. None of his stage tricks was as popular as the duck walk. In January, 1956, while performing in one of Alan Freed's shows in New York's Paramount Theater, Chuck introduced his showman's trademark. The audience responded with shrieks and applause, and the low-crouched walk became a permanent fixture in Berry's act. There are many legends surrounding the origins of the duck walk. One critic has speculated that it was devised to hide the wrinkles in a twenty-two dollar suit. The story maintains that Chuck bought himself and his band members twenty-two dollar seersucker suits to wear on stage at the Paramount Theater. The oppressive New York summer heat wrinkled the suits, and Chuck simply went into his duck walk to hide the wrinkles. This is a good story, but an inaccurate one. Many years before, Chuck had developed his duck walk at home, when he would scoot under the kitchen table of the amusement of visiting relatives and his family. In the East St. Louis nightclubs, Chuck frequently duck-walked around the stage. In 1956, therefore, this showstopper came naturally to Chuck Berry because he had used it for years. In an interview with *Goldmine* magazine, Chuck recalled, "The duck walk got laughs and later, well I just sort of went into it on stage one time, and it went over big. So I've been doing it on certain numbers ever since."

Perhaps the duck walk was also one means of injecting some humor into Chuck's rigorous tours. In June, 1956, for example, when Chuck was a member of "The Biggest Show of Stars," he was the most popular act even though the first tour featured Fats Domino. The traveling conditions were terrible ones, and Chuck's piano player, Johnny Johnson, remembers long, all-night bus rides and second-rate hotels as the tour's highlights. One of the most interesting aspects of these 1956 concerts was that after Chuck performed *Maybellene* and *Roll Over Beethoven*, the audience immediately

Chuck's trademark: the show-stopping 'duck walk' in Europe (1970s) . . .

. . . and again in Oslo, Norway, in May 1977.

called out for *30 Days* and *No Money Down*. Even though these songs were neither played on the radio nor listed on the *Billboard* Hot 100, they were still favorites of young record buyers. (There was an avid group of record aficionados who purchased anything that Chess Records produced, and artists like Chuck and Bo Diddley also benefited from this insatiable desire for Chess's brand of rock-and-roll music. If Chess Records had had the facilities and connections to distribute and publicize their product, there would have been far greater sales and recognition for its artists.)

In 1956, the rigors of touring took a toll on Chuck Berry's writing and recording activities. The lengthy tours, the constant travel, and the need to promote his existing records via interviews left Chuck no time to write and record new material. In fact, when he cut *Havana Moon* in October, 1956, at what was originally to be a lengthy recording session, what resulted was only the one song. This was because Leonard Chess had hundreds of requests for Chuck Berry concerts. So, Chuck was quickly sent back on the road to reap the profits from his new-found commercial success. There was also some strain between Chess and Chuck over the direction of his music. Chess did not feel that *Havana Moon* had a strong enough rock focus, and he urged Chuck to write songs with a stronger rock beat. There was a calypso-reggae touch to *Havana Moon* that Chess believed was too far from rock music's mainstream. Chess was unaware that Chuck had played *Havana Moon* with the Jimmy Rogers group at the 708 Club in Chicago as early as 1955; when Rogers was brought into the studio with Chuck Berry, he supplied a fascinating new guitar sound to which Chess was apparently oblivious.

After a year and a half at Chess Records, Chuck Berry had recorded only fifteen tracks. His reputation rested on the chart success of only two songs, *Maybellene* and *Roll Over Beethoven*. Yet, a rival company, Mercury Records, thought enough of Chuck's music to produce a cover version of *Too Much Monkey Business*. The Gadabouts 1956 version of Chuck's song was a humorous one, however, and it indicated that many record companies still looked upon Chuck Berry's music as nothing more than fun rock-and-roll. The spectre of Louis Jordan's stageshow continued to haunt Chuck's career, and *Billboard* continued to describe releases like *Roll Over Beethoven* as "humorous songs."

Nevertheless, despite a temporary hiatus from recording and song writing, Chuck Berry's popularity continued to grow among young record buyers. *Roll Over Beethoven* became the Marseillaise of a generation who were throwing off the shackles of Patty Page, Perry Como, Frankie Laine, and Kay Starr. The pop musical performer was no longer the most popular, and the emerging rock singer was suddenly a commercial success.

In 1957, Chuck Berry's career took a number of very positive turns. He recorded fifteen more songs for the Chess Record label, and he placed three releases on the *Billboard* Hot 100. Two of these songs, *School Day* and *Rock and Roll Music*, were Top Ten hits. In addition, *School Day* (on Columbia Records) was Chuck's first English release, and it reached number twenty-four during its two-week stay on the British Top 50. By 1957, Chuck Berry was established as one of the key figures in the rock-and-roll musical revolution.

"The Biggest Show of Stars" for 1957, produced by Irwin Field, was the first successful, large rock-and-roll touring show. For an average ticket price of two to three dollars, the eighty-day cross-country tour brought rock fans face-to-face with Fats Domino, Buddy Holly and the Crickets, the Drifters, Frankie Lymon and the Teenagers, LaVern Baker, Jimmie Bowen, Buddy Knox, Clyde McPhatter, Paul Anka, and Chuck Berry. Each act performed two or three numbers and quickly exited. This tour helped to popularize rock music in all parts of America, and the rock concert business became an important part of the music industry.

Other important developments in the popularization of rock music were the concerts and television shows produced in New York by Alan Freed. From July 12 through August 2, 1957, Freed presented four rock-and-roll shows, and the two most exciting performers were Chuck Berry and Jerry Lee Lewis. There was a potpourri of musical talent, featuring such diverse acts as Connie Francis, the Everly Brothers, Ferlin Huskey, Andy Williams, Bobby Darin, Fats Domino, and Frankie Lymon and the Teenagers. The strategy behind the Big Beat Shows was to present as diverse a musical aggregation as possible, in hopes this would help to draw a broad-based audience.

In December, 1957, Alan Freed booked a twelve-day musical extravaganza known as the "Holiday of Stars" at New York's Paramount Theater. The sellout shows featured fourteen acts in a two-hour time slot, allowing Freed to present seven shows a day. Jerry Lee Lewis complained to Freed that Fats Domino should not have top billing. When Freed reminded Lewis that Domino had six number one hits compared to two Top 10 songs for Lewis, the Killer replied that he was the hottest entertainer in rock music. When Buddy Holly also complained to Freed that his name was too far down the list, there was a tension in the air which made most performers uncomfortable. Although Chuck Berry was not a part of this show, nonetheless, he was aware of the increased difficulties in bringing together so many ego-oriented rock performers. Much to his credit, Chuck was an easy artist to work with at this stage of his career. He realized that the rock revolution was a growing phenomenon, and he was more intent upon maintaining his place as a sought-after concert artist than in topping the bill.

The cross-pollination of musical styles was another important outgrowth of the 1957 rock-and-roll tours. As the tour buses and concert dressing rooms crowded with different types of artists, there was an interaction of musical ideas and concepts which helped to broaden the scope of rock music as a whole. The fruits of a fertile exchange of musical ideas was apparent in Chuck Berry's 1957 recording sessions for Chess Records. In January, Leonard Chess brought Johnny Johnson on piano, an unidentified session musician on guitar, Fred Below on drums, and Willie Dixon on bass into the Chess studios to cut seven songs. These sessions were not particularly successful ones. Chuck demonstrated some difficulty in the studio, and his version of *Rock and Roll Music* was too slow for commercial release. In fact, this unreleased take of *Rock and Roll Music* had such a listless guitar sound that Leonard Chess wondered if it could possibly be recut into a hit record. Yet, there were two excellent guitar instrumentals, *Deep Feeling* and *Blue Feeling*, completed during these sessions, both revealing new facets of Chuck's talents and the benefits of touring with musicians of so many different stripes. It was in the song *Deep Feeling* that Chuck demonstrated guitar techniques which revealed him to be one of the foremost blues artists of his day. The January, 1957, recording session also produced a Latin song, *La Juanda*, and an unreleased version of *Wee Wee Hours*. The highlight of this session was an excellent version of *School Day*. Later in 1957, *School Day*, after entering the charts in March, rose to number 3 on the *Billboard* Hot 100. *School Day* remained on the charts for twenty-six weeks and proved a milestone in Chuck Berry's commercial success.

After a number of single concert dates and a couple of brief Alan Freed tours, Chuck was brought back to the Chess studios to record another batch of songs. In May, 1957, Leonard Chess brought in Lafayette Leake on piano, Willie Dixon on bass, and Fred Below on drums to accompany Chuck. This session resulted in eight songs, but only four were considered suitable for release. The session was a tension-filled one for Chuck. He was experimenting with his music in an attempt to fuse a number of blues elements with the principal attributes of rock. This caused a great deal of disagreement with Leonard Chess, who believed that Chuck had never appealed to the narrow blues audience, and that he would lose his rock audience if he diluted his style with blues.

One of the more interesting songs from the May, 1957 session was *21*, which was a song much like *Johnny B. Goode, Roll Over Beethoven* and *Rock and Roll Music*. It told the story of a young

60

man who wanted to marry his girlfriend, but who was forced to wait until she turned twenty-one. The song lacked the power and emotion of many of Chuck's hits, but it contained many of the same lyrical themes. A sequel to this song was *21 Blues*, which extended the theme behind the song *21*. The young man was now able to date the girl and discuss their future life. The guitar work on *21 Blues* is outstanding, and it demonstrates Chuck's willingness to pursue a good idea.

The experimental nature of Chuck Berry's music was further evidenced in the song *13 Question Method*, from the same session. In this song, a sequence of questions is used to chart the progress of a romantic date, and when it comes time for question number thirteen, the record fades off into romantic bliss. This song was an excellent example of Chuck Berry's wry humor and his ability to carry out an intricate story far beyond the sophistication of *School Day*.

The May, 1957, Chess sessions demonstrated the unusually broad songwriting and musical talent at Chuck Berry's command. Although only *Rock and Roll Music* and *Oh Baby Doll* were chart songs, nevertheless, the sessions provided a clean sound and some highly experimental music. There is no doubt that a strong rhythm and blues tone permeated these sessions, and that Chuck had obviously been influenced by the burgeoning Chicago rhythm and blues scene.

School Day was a number one rhythm and blues hit, Chuck's second *Billboard* chart topper. It had been two years since *Maybellene* peaked on the r and b charts, and this hiatus was the reason that Chuck's earlier records continued to sell well to r and b aficionados. *Rock and Roll Music* was also a Top 10 r and b chart record. Both songs had strong messages, but one rock critic, Richard Goldstein, believes that *School Day* was the first message rock sound. In April 1957, *Billboard* made *School Day* its spotlight pick, and this helped the chart progress of the record.

During the summer of 1957, Berry toured incessantly. *Oh Baby Doll* was released in July, but it appeared only briefly on the *Billboard* Hot 100 at number 57. Despite its lack of sales, *Oh Baby Doll* remained on the charts for seven weeks, while *School Day* was listed for twenty-six weeks and *Rock and Roll Music* for nineteen weeks. The obvious conclusion was that Chuck Berry was an enormously popular artist, and that the appeal of his songs was translated into a lengthy stay on the *Billboard* charts.

In 1957, there were a number of important changes in the rock music business. Perhaps the most significant was the changing attitude of the media toward rock-and-roll. On February 23, 1957, the *New York Times* ran an in-depth story on Alan Freed's rock-and-roll show at the Paramount Theater. The *Times'* front-page headline

Chuck on stage at New York's Paramount Theater.

read: "Rock N Roll Teenagers Tie Up Times Square Area." There were also four separate stories on the rock music explosion, and, predictably, the *New York Times* ran a follow-up article on the monetary success of the rock-and-roll revolution. The Paramount Theater reinforced the commercial aspect of Freed's successful shows by announcing that 15,200 customers had paid $29,000 for the six performances. The movie shown at this Paramount show was fittingly entitled: "Don't Knock the Rock." It was a 1956 feature, starring Alan Freed and Billy Haley and His Comets. A cameo appearance by Little Richard singing *Tutti Frutti* and *Rip It Up* was the best part of the movie. "Don't Knock the Rock" was quite different from other rock-and-roll movies, in that it had something of a plot. The movie involved a rock singer accused of corrupting the local kids. In the end, the movie's theme developed the notion that rock-and-roll music was no worse than big band tunes. An added bonus in this movie were four songs by Bill Haley and the Comets. The Paramount shows proved so popular than teen-agers began lining up at 4:00 a.m. in the morning to see the concerts. There was no doubt that rock music had crossed over into the mainstream of popular entertainment.

Chuck Berry came of age as a performer during this first "golden era" of rock-and-roll music. It was a time of experimentation and change, and it was also a very important period of growth. Perhaps the most interesting phenomenon of the period, late 1957, was the emergence of the white "teen idol." Paul Anka entered the charts on July 15, 1957, with *Diana*, and Dick Clark's "American Bandstand" spotlighted Frankie Avalon, among others. But it was the publicity over the influence of rock music which made it grow. At Columbia University, Dr. Joost A. Meerlo completed a study of rock dancing which compared it to St. Vitus's Dance, a nervous disorder. In Jersey City, New Jersey Commissioner of Public Safety, Lawrence Whipple, made national headlines when he denounced rock music over national television. At the same time, Southern ministers warned of the dangers of rock music. The end result of this hysteria was the ever-increasing popularization of rock-and-roll among American teenagers; it became a matter of teen-age integrity to defend their music against adult critics. The conflict certainly did not hurt music sales; Elvis Presley's records were responsible for twenty-five percent of the singles and albums sold by RCA Victor records. The frenzy over rock music's expansion finally prompted the moguls of the record industry to begin to analyze this new phenomenon. The result was not only that singles and albums were more attractively packaged, but that there were large sums of money spent on advertising these products.

Chuck Berry occupied a prominent place in the rock revolution. Although his record sales were not as impressive as those of Bill

Haley, or Elvis Presley, nevertheless, he was the model for many young artists aspiring to success in the rock music world. In 1957, a Philadelphia high school student, Danny Rapp, introduced a song on Dick Clark's "American Bandstand" entitled *At the Hop*. It was followed in a few months by *Rock and Roll Is Here to Stay*. Young Rapp, like many teenagers, was first awakened to rock music by Chuck Berry's *Maybellene*. In April, 1983, Rapp committed suicide in an Arizona motel, an obvious casualty of the "oldies-but-goodies" mold that many of the early artists were forced into as rock music matured, but in 1957 Danny and the Juniors were one of many young show business acts who owed their success to Chuck Berry's pioneering influence upon rock-and-roll music.

In 1956–1957, the First Golden Age of Rock and Roll Music established Chuck Berry as one of the Founding Fathers of a new generation of musical enthusiasts who were altering the framework and structure of American society. Once the rock revolution had taken hold, there occurred a number of important changes in the entertainment business which paralleled those occurring in this intense period of social and cultural change.

CHAPTER 4

ROCK MUSIC'S
YEAR OF TRANSITION: 1958

In 1958, Chuck Berry experienced his most commercially successful year in the rock music business. Eight of his songs appeared on the *Billboard* Hot 100, and he had his second English hit when *Sweet Little Sixteen* rose to number sixteen on the U.K. Top 50. The fact that more white record-buyers were purchasing his music than blacks was demonstrated when only four Chuck Berry songs appeared on the predominantly black *Billboard* rhythm and blues charts. In an almost backhanded compliment, however, *Billboard* named Chuck Berry its outstanding *rhythm and blues* performer for 1958. It is difficult to understand how an artist who had twice as many chart songs on the *Billboard* Hot 100 could only be named the outstanding rhythm and blues artist of the year, unless the role of racial prejudice in the selection process is fully appreciated. The racial side of the record industry was still a deterrent to full stardom for black performers in the Hot 100.

There were a number of other controversial events in rock-and-roll history which changed rock music's direction during 1958. In January, after completing an Australian tour, Little Richard denounced rock music, and enrolled in Oakwood College, a Seventh Day Adventist school in Huntsville, Alabama. Little Richard's desire for a religious education, a reflection of the identity crisis which he was experiencing at this point, caused him to retreat to this fundamentalist school. Art Rupe, the President of Specialty Records, has pointed out that Little Richard thought that a signal from Sputnik was the instrument of a divine inspiration directing him to the ministry. Whatever the reasons, the publicity over Little Richard's announcement that he would study for the ministry kept the argument over rock music's intrinsic values alive.

The outcry surrounding Jerry Lee Lewis' marriage to his young cousin, Myra, was symptomatic of the moralistic crusade against rock musicians. Although Lewis was married in the United States with little publicity, he made the mistake of talking to English

An ad for "Go Johnny Go," the 1958 movie in which Chuck sang three songs.

reporters. In jest, Jerry Lee stated that his new bride was nine years old, and the British press ripped the marriage apart. It made sensational headlines, and suddenly record companies and major distributors were not interested in Jerry Lee Lewis' records. Dick Clark refused to book Jerry Lee on his shows, Sun Records was unable to merchandise his 45s due to radio blacklisting, and the concert audiences who had once enjoyed his music were no longer interested. Before the scandal broke, Jerry Lee Lewis and Chuck Berry were part of Alan Freed's "Big Beat Show." From March 28 to May 10, 1958, the "Big Beat Show" toured the eastern and midwestern sections of America, as well as a portion of Canada. This rigorous tour began with five shows at New York's Paramount Theater, and then continued with sixty-eight shows in thirty-seven cities.

During the "Big Beat Show" of 1958, Chuck Berry was listed as the headliner, and Jerry Lee Lewis, Buddy Holly, Danny and the Juniors, Larry Williams and twelve other acts completed the revue. There was less than an enthusiastic reponse to Alan Freed's "Big Beat Show" in New York City, however. One New York newspaper headlined: "Alan Freed's Big Beat Loaded with Amateurs." Then, the newspaper went on to give Chuck Berry a rave review, and suggested that his hit songs made him the most worthwhile performer in the show. When Alan Freed's "Big Beat Show" stopped in Boston, on Saturday, May 3, 1958, the Mayor cancelled the performance due to pressure from Rev. J. Joseph Delaney, who was the local CYO (Catholic Youth Organization) director. The subsequent dates in Troy, New York, were cancelled, but a show in Lewiston, Maine, went on without a hitch. The press, in their zeal to uncover controversy, reported that a fourteen-year-old boy was arrested for climbing on the stage.

Part of the controversy over the "Big Beat Show" of 1958 resulted from the confrontations between Chuck Berry and Jerry Lee Lewis. In order to upstage Chuck, Jerry Lee closed his show by dousing his piano with lighter fluid, and then playing the last strains of *Great Balls of Fire* on the burning piano. Dave Garroway's "Today Show" featured a performance by Jerry Lee Lewis playing *Down the Line*, but no appearance by Freed's black headliner. The competition between Chuck and Jerry Lee did draw thousands of extra fans to Alan Freed's shows, however.

Another important forum for Chuck Berry's music in 1958, and one more liberal in its attention to black artists, was the "Dick Clark Show." Chuck frequently visited Clark's daytime show in Philadelphia, where he would lip-synch his latest hit record. On Saturday nights, Chuck Berry was often featured on the "Dick Clark Show," broadcast from New York City. Beechnut Gum, the sponsors, used buttons and sloganeering to make the "Dick Clark Show" America's first popular prime time rock-and-roll series. When Chuck Berry introduced *Sweet Little Sixteen* on Clark's afternoon show from Philadelphia, the response was so strong that the telephone switchboard was blown out from incoming calls.

In 1958, Chess Records brought Chuck Berry into the recording studio for five separate sessions. Leonard Chess personally supervised the recording of twenty-seven songs, and only six languished as unreleased cuts. Chuck Berry classics such as *Sweet Little Sixteen, Reelin' and Rockin', Johnny B. Goode, Around and Around, Carol, Sweet Little Rock and Roller*, and *Memphis, Tennessee* were cut during these sessions in the Chess studio. The longest and most productive Chuck Berry recording session took place in February, with Lafayette Leake on piano, Willie Dixon on bass, and Fred Below on drums. Of the ten songs cut at this session, *Sweet Little Sixteen* and *Johnny B. Goode* were Top Ten *Billboard* hits. During the session, there were two excellent instrumentals cut. One was *Guitar Boogie*, which was an attempt to pay tribute to a number of musical influences, and the other was *Rockin' at the Philharmonic*, which was an affectionate tribute to Charlie Christian. Another important influence reflected in these tunes was the music of Pee Wee Crayton. One of Chuck's favorite records was Crayton's *Central Avenue Blues*, backed with *Texas Hop*, songs which Chuck used to practice his guitar riffs.

A number of problems developed at the February, 1958, Chess recording session, however. One of the controversies was Chuck's demand that Leonard Chess use backup vocalists to enhance the commercial appeal of his recordings. (In February, 1959, when Chuck recorded *Do You Love Me*, the production finally employed a haunting backup vocal accompaniment.) It is difficult to assess Leonard Chess's role in the February, 1958, sessions; as his son, Marshall, has stated, these were recordings completed prior to the emergence of the so-called "producer." In essence, Leonard Chess viewed his role as that of a supervisor. Marshall Chess, speaking to *Blues Unlimited* magazine: "These were the days before record producers, before all this bullshit of record producers and what my father and my uncle, and what I was taught to do was 'supervise' recording sessions." This meant that the artist, his musical sidemen, and the producer all contributed to the sound. Willie Dixon actually produced and arranged the music for these sessions in the modern sense, but Leonard Chess certainly assisted in the production area.

Leonard Chess's historical significance to rock-and-roll music is that he allowed talented musicians and songwriters, like Chuck Berry, the freedom to produce their own material. This technique permitted black producers, such as Willie Dixon, to become important

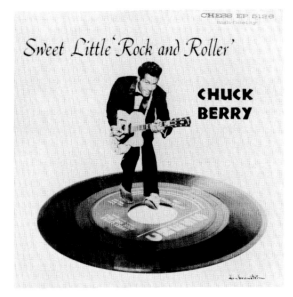

Sweet Little Rock And Roller   Chess 5126 (EP)

After School Session   Chess 1426 (LP)

figures within both the business and the production sides of the recording industry. It would be erroneous to suggest that black producers had made any headway with the major labels, but the quality of the music on small labels like Chess, Checker, Specialty, RPM, Modern, Duke, and Peacock rested on the freedom given to the black artists in the recording studio. The real historical importance of the Chess Records--Chuck Berry collaboration, therefore, was in the recording studio, a partnership which laid the foundation for some of the most innovative rock music of the 1950s.

This studio freedom prompted Chuck to add some interesting personal touches to his music. For example, when Chuck recorded the instrumental song, *In-Go*, it was a clever tribute to his nine-year-old daughter, Ingrid Gibson Berry. In the song *Reelin' and Rockin'*, Chuck applied a humorous mathematical formula involving eleven minutes time-breaks. He used the times 9:21, 9:32, 9:43, and 9:54, so that the song would progress in steady rhythmic increments. Another important Chuck Berry musical device was evident in *Carol*. In this song, he used a contradiction to make a more serious point. "You can't dance I know you wish you could, I've got my eyes on you cause you dance so good." This seemingly incongruous lyrical juxtaposition of ideas was common in Chuck Berry's music. He believed that the lyrics simply highlighted the contradictions of American life.

During the April, 1958, recording session *Around and Around* was quickly recorded, so that it could become the B side to *Johnny B. Goode*. The songs, *It Don't Take But a Few Minutes, Blues for Hawaiians* (which Chuck rewrote from Floyd Smith's 1939 song, *Floyd's Guitar Blues*), *In-Go*, as well as *Around and Around*, completed this session. After this recording series, Chuck Berry went back on the road and continued his extensive touring. The *Billboard* Hot 100 reported *Johnny B. Goode* on the charts in April, *Beautiful Delilah* in July, and *Carol* in August. These hit records created quite a demand for Chuck Berry concerts in the summer of 1958.

A brief tour through the South in July, 1958, gave Chuck a chance to try out a rewrite of an old song, *21* or *21 Blues*, which Chuck simply retitled *Vacation Time*. This light tune was an attempt to commercialize the summer vacation routine of American teenagers and, in August, Chuck recorded it in the Chess studios. It is ironic that *Vacation Time* received so little airplay and did not become a hit, dealing, as it does so well, with so many of the staple themes soon to be employed in countless other "summer fun" songs and movies.

While performing in Tulsa, Oklahoma, a young man named Jerry Keller heard one of Chuck's earliest renditions of *Vacation Time*.

The following year Keller moved to New York City and wrote *Here Comes Summer* as a result of Chuck Berry's influence. During a brief tour of New England, a group of young musicians soon to be called the Jamies also heard Chuck's *Vacation Time*; when Tom Jameson and his sister Serene subsequently formed the Jamies and cut a dub of Jameson's original tune, *Summertime, Summertime*, they sent the acetate dub to Sherm Feller at WEZE in Boston, and he arranged a recording contract with Epic Records. The irony was compounded by the fact that Feller had attended the very concert at which Chuck Berry performed *Vacation Time* in front of the Jamies. There were many others inspired by Chuck Berry. In 1963, in Southern California, three brothers, Dennis, Brian, and Carl Wilson (known as the Beach Boys) released the Berry-inspired *Surfin' USA*. In Seattle, Washington, the Ventures, the Frantics, and the Wailers played Chuck Berry tunes in local clubs. In 1964, the Ventures recorded the song *Go*, featuring easily recognizable Berry guitar riffs. These groups all developed a unique instrumental sound based largely on Chuck Berry riffs, practiced reverently in their garages in the mid-1950s. The level of Chuck's influence was unparalleled. There was never any similar attempt made by serious musicians to emulate Elvis Presley, Little Richard, Bill Haley, or Fats Domino to such a degree. In the formation of the rock music revolution, Chuck was overwhelmingly the model of young, popular musicians in America.

In England, Chuck Berry's influence was an equally pervasive one. There was a difference in the approach of young English musicians, however, because they were often influenced by more obscure Chuck Berry songs. A good example of this phenomenon was *Beautiful Delilah*, which rose to only number eighty-one on the *Billboard* Hot 100. Yet, in Britain, Ray Davies of the Kinks was captivated by the song, one of the earliest rock-and-roll records motivating his attempt to form his own band. When the Kinks later recorded *Beautiful Delilah*, they added their own personal touch to it. Although an enormous number of British musicians embraced Chuck Berry's music in the summer of 1958, no group was as significant as the young men who listened to Chuck in Liverpool.

In July, 1958, John Lennon left the Quarry Bank School. He was a poor student who had recently failed the 0 level examinations. Art was Lennon's only strong subject. To relieve his sense of frustration over school, Lennon played with a rock band known as the Quarrymen. A factor in the development of English rock music was Liverpool's prominence as a seaport city. John Lennon and Paul McCartney soon learned that the sailors who docked in town often brought records by American artists into port, and they pursued them eagerly. There were only two Chuck Berry songs available to John Lennon, *School Day* and *Sweet Little Sixteen*, and he listened to these

Chuck and John Lennon on the "Mike Douglas Show" in 1972 (see page 145).

tunes over and over again. Although young Lennon loved the skiffle music of Lonnie Donegan, his primary interest was in American rock-and-roll. In 1957, Buddy Holly and the Crickets toured England, and this further excited the imagination of young British musical enthusiasts. It was the inspiration of Buddy Holly and Chuck Berry which prompted young John Lennon to begin writing his own songs. *I Lost My Little Girl* was an example of an early Lennon song which owed its inspiration to American rock music. The Quarrymen soon changed their name to Johnny and the Moondogs as a tribute to Chuck Berry's inspirational rock-and-roll music.

In May, 1958, Leonard Chess brought Chuck Berry back into Chess studios to record seven songs. Despite his heavy touring schedule and the necessity to continue promoting his Chess Record releases, Chuck needed fresh material to satisfy his rapidly expanding army of fans. From this session, *Beautiful Delilah* was released immediately, and *Carol* came out the next month. There were three unreleased cuts: *Oh Yeah, Time Was*, and the *House of Blue Lights. Hey Pedro* was an interesting novelty tune in which Chuck continued to use Spanish musical influences, and unwittingly demonstrated a Tex-Mex rock-and-roll sound. During early 1958, Chuck had toured Texas and was influenced by the diverse musical sounds in the southern part of the state.

The continued consumer demand for Chuck Berry records brought Chuck back into the recording studio in October, 1958. This session was one of the best in Chuck's fledgling career. He recorded *Sweet Little Rock and Roller*, which rose to number forty-seven on the *Billboard* charts, as well as *Jo Jo Gunne*, which hit number eighty-three in 1958, and *Anthony Boy*, which peaked at number sixty on the Hot 100. Although *Memphis, Tennessee* was not an American chart song, it rose to number six on the British Top 50 in 1963. In this session, Johnny Johnson's piano work and Willie Dixon's bass were outstanding; Fred Below's drums were added after the session to round out the sound. It was the presence of Bo Diddley's infectious guitar, however, which made the sessions so successful. Since Bo and Chuck were close friends, this helped to make these recordings some of the most notable ones in Chuck's musical life.

For the first time in his recording career, Chuck Berry was credited with producing a song. Leonard Chess listed Chuck Berry as the producer of *Memphis, Tennessee*. In reality, Chuck had been producing his own records for three years, but this was an appropriate new means of giving recognition to Chuck's talent. When *Memphis, Tennessee* was finally released, Leonard Chess added a new drum background and remastered the tape. Although it did not receive a great deal of airplay, *Memphis, Tennessee* was eventually covered by more than a hundred different artists. Almost every major modern rock performer has either recorded *Memphis*, or used it in live concerts. It is ironic that a song which never made the American charts could have been so influential in the evolution of rock-and-roll music.

As the pressure of being a rock-and-roll performer mounted, Chuck Berry became more difficult for concert promoters, disc jockeys, and radio and television personalities to understand. He was expected to perform virtually every day, and to use his free time to help promote his latest Chess Record release. As a result of his hectic schedule, Chuck often became rebellious. Dick Clark recalls the first time Chuck appeared on his afternoon "American Bandstand" show. After an all-night automobile ride, Chuck came into Philadelphia tired and cranky. When Clark informed him that he was to lip-synch his song and do his duck walk to the left of the stage, Chuck flatly refused. He told Clark that he didn't want to perform his duck walk. In fact, he might not even feel like going on. A frantic Dick Clark placed a quick telephone call to Leonard Chess and, after a lengthy conversation with Berry, Chuck performed. "He's never gotten any easier to get along with," Clark remarked, "he's still an ornery son of a bitch, but I love him dearly." Clark has also pointedly remarked that without Chuck Berry, rock-and-roll music would not have evolved into its present form.

The signs of rebellion evidenced in Chuck's stage performances were similar to those embodied in his lyrics. As fame, wealth, and public recognition were bestowed upon Chuck, he experienced all the usual tensions that accompany rock-and-roll stardom. No longer was he able to move freely about without someone asking for an autograph, an interview, or an opinion. After three years, the rock-and-roll life began to wear on Chuck Berry. He was no longer the friendly, gregarious soul who performed out of love for rock-and-roll music. After being left penniless by unscrupulous promoters, insulted by Southern sheriffs, and badgered by loyal but intense fans, Chuck was beginning to feel the need for privacy. These pressures resulted in massive personality changes. It was also evident that Chuck's musical artistry suffered slightly from the grind of steady touring, quick radio and television appearances, and the demand for instant hit records in the Chess studios.

Dick Clark was one of the few people that Chuck Berry could trust in the 1950s. Clark never asked for a penny of payola to play Berry's records. When *Sweet Little Sixteen* was debuted on "American Bandstand," Clark recognized that it was a blockbuster rock-and-roll song. As a result of Clark's regularly featuring this song, Chuck made numerous appearances on the "American Bandstand" show.

Throughout the years, they have maintained a close working relationship without ever really becoming friends, a good example of Chuck's somewhat aloof personal manner. There is another dimension to this relationship, however. It is the blend of Clark's pop personality with Berry's lyrical musical sophistication which makes the interaction of these two rock music giants so interesting. In 1977, when Dick Clark hosted *Rolling Stone* magazine's Tenth Anniversary Special, Clark selected Chuck Berry to close the show. Despite some personal differences over the years, both men feel at ease with each other, and Chuck Berry and Dick Clark have long remained professionally appreciative of each other's talents.

During 1958, Chuck Berry was one of the highest paid rock acts in America. As a result of his new affluence, he made plans to open the Club Bandstand in St. Louis. He also established his own publicity organization, and a recording company was set up to produce new Chuck Berry records. Chuck also searched for new musical talent, and briefly considered founding his own record label. It was uncommon for a recording artist to pay such careful attention to business details. Financial planning and the strains of touring were not Chuck's only pressures; he also considered offers to tour abroad. Despite all the new demands on his time and attention, Chuck continued to be instrumental in the many changes taking place in the entertainment business. B.B. King has pointed out that Chuck Berry's concerts helped to open up new performing venues for blues artists. In 1956 and 1957, King noticed that his concerts were attracting many more whites, and he suggested that this was largely due to Berry's songwriting and performing genius. As B.B. King observed, forces from both black and white musical styles had merged into a new art form: rock-and-roll music.

In early December, 1958, Chuck was brought into the Chess studios to record two Christmas songs. Charles Brown's *Merry Christmas Baby*, and Johnny Marks and Marvin Brodie's *Run Rudolph Run* were quickly pressed for the Christmas season. On December 12, 1958, *Run Rudolph Run* was released and rose quickly to number sixty-nine on the *Billboard* Hot 100, and *Merry Christmas Baby* ascended to number seventy-one during its three weeks on the charts. Dave Edmunds and Keith Richards have both recorded excellent versions of *Run Rudolph Run*, and it remains one of rock music's premier Christmas classics. As 1958 drew to a close, Chuck had eight songs appear on the *Billboard* Hot 100, two of which became Top Ten hits. There was no doubt that rock-and-roll music was no longer a suspect commercial art form.

In a March, 1958, issue of the *New York Times*, Dick Clark was promoted as the symbol of rock music success. The *Times* placed great emphasis upon Clark's clean cut appearance and polite personality. Rock-and-roll music was so popular in 1958 that Clark was on television six days a week. After he finished his five-afternoon-a-week show from Philadelphia, "American Bandstand," Clark journeyed to New York City to present his Saturday night show, sponsored by Beechnut Gum. The earliest personalities in the rise of rock-and-roll music suddenly found themselves upstaged by Dick Clark. There were also strong concerns over the use of payola to promote hit records. Since the early 1950s, Alan Freed had been the symbol of rock music in New York, but he came under federal investigation for income tax evasion and payola. It was a time in which politicians, clergymen, and self-prolcimaed protectors of public morality were looking for a scapegoat. They found one in Alan Freed. In 1959, both Alan Freed and Chuck Berry experienced problems with the law. While there was no connection between their problems, nevertheless their identification with rock-and-roll music prompted local law enforcement authorities to engage in virtual vendettas against Freed and Berry. In was an omen of the general trouble that rock music would face in the late 1950s.

Chuck Berry in concert in the 1960s.

Chuck at the Olympia in Paris, France, February 24, 1975.

CHAPTER 5

THE VACUUM ROCK YEARS: 1959-1962

By 1959, Chuck Berry had become one of rock music's most popular performers. From 1955 through 1958, thirteen of Chuck's songs appeared on the *Billboard* Hot 100. He was a financially and artistically successful performer who owned a nightclub in St. Louis, a management company, and a number of real estate investments. This success was short-lived, however; his songs increasingly had difficulty reaching local radio hit charts. In 1959 and 1960, Berry did have six songs appear on the *Billboard* Hot 100, but only two, *Almost Grown* and *Back in the USA*, entered the Top 40. During the 1960s, only one of Chuck's songs was a Top 10 entry on the *Billboard* charts, but his songwriting influence and performing genius continued to permeate all parts of the rock music world. The years from 1959 to 1962 were frenetic ones for Chuck Berry. Not only did his record sales decline precipitously, but he was involved in a number of business and legal problems which drove him to the brink of bankruptcy. He was sentenced to jail for violating the Mann Act, which forbade transporting women across state lines for immoral purposes, and he lost his nightclub while he served his jail sentence.

During the same period, there were a number of sweeping changes in the rock music business. Elvis Presley was in the army. Bobby Darin no longer sang rock-and-roll songs, and concentrated upon entertaining adult audiences at New York's Copacabana Club. Bill Haley and His Comets ceased to be a popular touring act, and Haley's problems with alcohol made it impossible for him to perform a complete set. It was not uncommon for Haley to sing only two or three songs in a hour show. Fats Domino's seemingly inexhaustible string of hits also ended and, although he continued to tour more than 300 days a year, the old excitement over Fats Domino's performances vanished. Little Richard was retired, studying to be a minister. Jerry Lee Lewis had married his cousin, and found it virtually impossible to secure concert bookings. On February 3, 1959, Buddy Holly, the Big Bopper, and Ritchie Valens died in a tragic plane crash. Finally, the following year, on April 17, 1960, Eddie Cochran was killed in England while on tour with Gene Vincent and Tony Sheridan. The Fleetwoods, the Coasters, Dion and the Belmonts, Paul Anka, Connie Francis, Fabian, and Frankie Avalon could not fill the void left by the death and decline of these original 1950s rock artists. The rise of folk musicians, coupled with the fluidic decline of rock as a whole, also hurt Chuck Berry's career.

It was not just the music which changed dramatically in the late 1950s and early 1960s, but the record business as well. During the years from 1955 to 1959, record buying was very strong in the United States, with retail sales jumping as much as thirty-six percent a year. In 1960, however, rock-and-roll record sales declined for the first time. From 1960 to 1963, it was common for rock record sales to increase by as little as two percent a year. In essence, rock music was experiencing its first significant recession. The excitement generated in the First Golden Age of Rock Music had subsided, and, with the exception of the "girl groups," there was little that was new in American rock-and-roll music. It was not until the emergence of the Beatles and the California "surf" sound, popularized by the Beach Boys, that the rock music slump abated, and it was not until 1963--1964 that the musical decline ended. Being one of the country's most significant rock artists in the middle of the worst commercial period in rock-and-roll musical history did not help Chuck Berry's record sales at all. Dave Marsh and Kevin Stein's study, *The Book of Rock Lists* (1981) identifies, as one of the "discredited rock theories," the notion that rock-and-roll music died from 1959 to 1964. To support the idea that rock-and-roll was alive and well in the United States, Marsh and Stein listed records by such giants as Lloyd Price, Wilbert Harrison, the Drifters, Del Shannon, Ernie K-Doe, Roy Orbison, Gary "U.S." Bonds, Little Eva, the Four Seasons, the Crystals, the Chiffons, and Stevie Wonder as irrefutable evidence that rock-and-roll music weathered the storm. What is wrong with the Marsh and Stein notion is that not one of the artists listed had a strong cult following among rock-and-roll record aficionados, or, with the exception of Stevie Wonder, can be said to have persisted through the years to the heights of superstardom. They were simply individuals and groups with hit records, some of whom continued on to ever greater achievement, and some of whom faded into oblivion. Others, like Gary "U.S." Bonds, Del Shannon and Mitch Ryder, were brought back in the early 1980s by artists like Bruce Springsteen, Tom Petty, and John Cougar. Not one of these artists had the mass appeal of the early Founding Fathers of rock-and-roll music, however. There is little doubt that if rock music was not dead from 1959 to 1962, it was at least in critical condition.

By examining Chuck Berry's career during this vacuum period in rock's history, it is possible to learn a great deal about the industry's adjustment to the recession, and Chuck's reaction to the first failures in his hitherto distinguished musical career. In January, 1959, Chuck Berry toured Hawaii and Australia as part of a very important rock-and-roll show. The General Artist Corporation package, featuring Bobby Darin, George Hamilton IV, JoAnn Campbell, and Chuck Berry, performed for four days at the Civic Auditorium in Honolulu in order to work out all the problems before a week-long tour of Australia. The reaction to Chuck's music in Honolulu was overwhelming, and he was captivated by the relaxed, racially mixed Hawaiian Island setting. It became one of his favorite performing places. When the General Artists Corporation package played in Sydney and Melbourne, it was only Australia's second important rock-and-roll show. In January--February, 1958, Buddy Holly, Jerry Lee Lewis, Paul Anka, and Jody Sands toured Australia. The next year, Chuck Berry's tour proved to be a commercial and artistic success, and created an Australian market for Chuck's record releases. When he returned to Chicago after the Australian tour, Chuck immediately wrote *Back in the USA* to express his strong feelings over the hamburgers, freeways, and rock music he had briefly left behind in the United States. It was an interesting song, because its lyrics demonstrated Chuck Berry's ability to use typical American images in his own inimitable fashion. Chuck made other attempts to reach into new lyrical areas. In February, 1959, for example, his song *Anthony Boy* heralded a number of new themes in Berry's songs by chronicling an intricate tale of an Italian wedding which Chuck had attended in Boston. *Anthony Boy* was one of the best story-songs of 1959, but it rose to only number sixty on the *Billboard* Hot 100. America's lukewarm response stood in contrast to Britain's, where, for example, *Anthony Boy* was performed, shortly after its release, in a Liverpool club by the Mersey group Rory Storm and the Hurricanes. The song was not released in England, but the Cunard Line sailors brought in a number of copies from New York record stores and avid British Berry-ites snapped it up immediately. At the same time, Alan Synter's Cavern Club in Liverpool was taken over by Ray McFall, who booked John Lennon and the Quarrymen. After the Quarrymen energetically performed six Chuck Berry songs, they were informed by McFall that they would not be rehired at the Cavern. McFall believed that Berry's tunes attracted an unsuitable audience, and he told John Lennon that this type of music was merely a passing fad.

Ray McFall was influenced in his conclusion that rock music was a transitory phenomenon after seeing the movie "Jazz on a Summer's Day," which played in Liverpool in the early 1960s. This brief, eighty-six-minute movie was filmed at the 1958 Newport Jazz

Festival, and included Chuck Berry singing *Sweet Little Sixteen* and performing his famous duck walk. It was an extraordinary moment in Chuck's career, with Jack Teagarden's band backing Chuck's performance. A number of knowledgeable music professionals like Ray McFall believed that rock, folk, and jazz music were merging into a new sound, and would not persist as distinct forms. It was obvious that rock music was evolving in a number of exciting directions, but it was the advent of the folk era, and of Congressional investigations into payola, which made the rock-and-roll music industry a focus of public attention in the early 1960s, and not the music itself.

The Congressional investigation of rock music was largely due to the prevalent practice of bribery in the industry. Breaking into the Top 40 hit list was one of the most demanding aspects of recording rock-and-roll music. The pressure on record companies to produce hit records prompted regional industry promotional men and local disc jockeys to engage in the exchange of payola. In 1959--1960, the results of a Congressional investigation led to the firing of Alan Freed from New York's WABC radio station. Freed had previously been fired at New York's WINS for payola violations. Then, after going back to work for KDAY in Los Angeles, Freed was indicted and convicted of accepting $30,000 in payola bribery, and given a suspended sentence. There was little doubt when Freed died in 1965, it was in part due to his harassment by federal authorities. A heavy drinker, Freed was forced to endure the unrelenting prospect of being indicted for rather minor crimes on a number of occasions. Like Chuck Berry, Freed was finally convicted of evading payment of income tax.

The most revealing aspect of the 1960 House of Representatives investigations, conducted by Representative Owen Harris, an Arkansas Democrat, was that Dick Clark held the copyright to more than 150 songs played on his "American Bandstand." Representative Harris' Committee listed a number of interesting statistics: from 1958 to 1960, for example, eleven Duane Eddy records were played more than 240 times on "American Bandstand." This not only helped to promote the records, but also profited Clark, who owned the publishing rights and also stock in Eddy's recording company, Jamie Records.

Dick Clark's business practices were common ones in the recording industry, and the use of payola was a widespread phenomenon. There was a great deal of public pressure to reform things, but payola continued to exist into the 1960s and 1970s. Most radio stations today hire consultants, maintain strict playlists and constantly conduct airchecks on the disc jockeys. While payola is virtually dead, some of the raw energy and excitement has also gone out of rock-

and-roll radio because of the stultifying oversight procedures involved.

Radio remained, in the late 1950s and early 1960s, the most significant influence upon fledgling young musicians, however. The pirate radio stations which began broadcasting off the English coast in the spring and summer of 1959 brought a number of new converts to the rock music revolution. In Liverpool, a sixteen-year-old musician, George Harrison, listened to Radio Luxembourg, and practiced Chuck Berry riffs on his guitar. Back in America, in June, 1959, as radio stations blared out Ronnie Hawkins' *40 Days*, a remake of Chuck Berry's *30 Days*, Levon Helm, a drummer with Ronnie Hawkins, jotted down notes for more songs. He dreamed of a superstar band in which every member contributed equally to the music. When The Band became one of the hottest rock acts of the late 1960s, Helm pointed out that his earliest songs were written to Chuck Berry's music. Helm more pointedly acknowledged his debt to Berry when The Band recorded *The Promised Land*.

Although the future of rock-and-roll music appeared bright in 1959–1960, there were cataclysmic changes awaiting stars like Chuck Berry; Chuck himself had no way to foresee the impending crisis in his personal and professional life. In St. Louis, Berry's life was idyllic. His wife, Thelmetta, and their four children lived comfortably with him in one of the best sections of the city. He was a sensible, hard-working businessman, an energetic performer, and a creative songwriter who hoped to eventually score musical soundtracks and act in the movies.

In 1959, Chuck Berry, businessman, began the practice of demanding half his concert fee in advance. This was the result of a contract to perform in Fayetteville, North Carolina. A promoter sent Chuck a contract for $750 to perform in a local concert. After driving all night, Chuck arrived in Fayetteville to find that the concert site was a small ice cream parlor, with about twenty paying customers. After Chuck played this abortive concert, the promoter handed Chuck his share of the night's proceeds: $1.75. After his experience in Fayetteville, Chuck began to demand half his fee in advance. During the 1959 to 1962 era, when Chuck often did not receive the other half of his fee, he began collecting his entire concert fee in advance. When Chuck would play Bill Graham's Fillmore Auditorium in the late 1960s, Graham always had a check ready for Chuck. Once Chuck endorsed the check, Graham provided a little bag of money. Although there was never any question that Graham would pay Chuck Berry, they both enjoyed this ritual, an excellent example of how far the rock music business had progressed in a decade. Performer Chuck Berry, because of the increasingly sophisti-

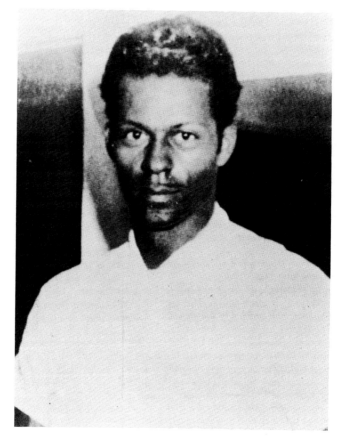

Chuck Berry in 1959.

cated pressures of the music business, was forced to become inordinately concerned with business details. In the early 1960s, Chuck shrewdly managed every aspect of his career. Berry's careful attention to fiscal detail was reasserted in 1972, when he remarked to a *Rolling Stone* reporter: " . . . any man who can't take care of his own money deserves what he gets."

The rise of folk music in 1959 was a serious challenge to the continued growth of rock-and-roll music. In July, the first Newport Folk Festival drew almost 15,000 people, with Joan Baez and the Kingston Trio sharing the media spotlight, and receiving much of the audience's applause. The crowd was younger, and there was a noticeable rock-and-roll feeling among many of the tunes played by many of the more obscure performers. The Newport Folk Festival began the slow fusion of folk music into the rock mainstream and, by the mid-1960s, the term folk-rock was a fitting designation to the marriage of two popular musical styles.

There were two significant personalities to emerge from the Newport Folk Festival — Joan Baez and Albert Grossman. Baez was the most important performer, and she was instrumental in popularizing the influence of folk music among rock aficionados. It was a time in which artists like Bob Dylan, Roger McGuinn, Barry McGuire, and Gram Parsons were developing their musical talents. By the mid-1960s, the folk-rock revolution owed much of its popularity to Joan Baez's music. Albert Grossman was the talent agent who managed many of the most successful rock acts of the 1960s, among them Bob Dylan and Janis Joplin. Grossman began to make his earliest management connections in the midst of the folk music revolution. He was the owner of the Gate of Horn Club, in Chicago, and also the co-producer of the Newport Folk Festival. It was Grossman's vision which resulted in the formation of Peter, Paul and Mary, whom he guided to superstar status. Grossman also had an incredibly keen ear for commercially appealing music, and he counseled record companies and key concert promoters, scrambling for new talent, to simply pay close attention to unsigned or obscure groups which appealed most to the rock audiences casting their votes at the box office.

In the midst of these musical changes, Chuck Berry, performer, committed a serious error in judgment while touring Texas and New Mexico in 1959. A young Spanish-speaking Apache girl persuaded him to bring her back to St. Louis to work at his Club Bandstand as a hatcheck girl. This innocent gesture of kindness almost ended Berry's career. When Chuck met this young girl, he had no idea that she was fourteen years old, and had worked as a prostitute. Upon her arrival in St. Louis, she worked nights in Berry's club, allegedly plying her trade in other parts of the city on her own time. Eventually

Chuck performing in the late 1950s.

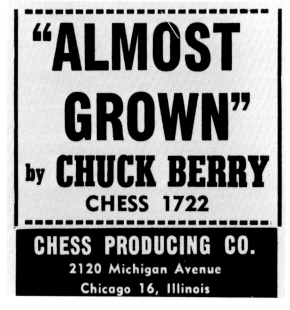

A Chess publicity release, 1959.

the St. Louis police investigated and, despite weak evidence, spent an inordinate amount of time developing a case. Chuck was prosecuted for violating the Mann Act. This legislation made it illegal to transport women across state lines for immoral purposes. The St. Louis police were particularly persistent about the investigation, and more than one of Berry's close friends believed that it was due to the fact that the Club Bandstand had opened in a predominantly white section of St. Louis. This began a legal odyssey which almost destroyed Chuck Berry's career.

Although he continued to record and perform in concert, Chuck spent almost two years engaged in two lengthy court trials to clear his name. The first trial resulted in a guilty verdict, but was overturned on an appeal. The judge demonstrated considerable bias, and continually referred to Chuck as "that Negro." The second trial was also lengthy and intense, with St. Louis authorities apparently determined to prove that a rock-and-roll singer was the cause of St. Louis's racial tension. In 1961, a St. Louis court convicted Berry for violating the Mann Act; he was sentenced to three years in prison, and fined $5,000. St. Louis newspapers had a field day with Berry's case. A typical headline read: "Rock N Roll Singer Lured Me to St. Louis, Says 14 Year Old." On February 15, 1962, as the *Peppermint Twist*, by Joey Dee and the Starlighters, topped the charts, Chuck Berry surrendered to federal officials at the Springfield, Missouri prison. When Chuck was released on October 18, 1963, his career was on the verge of extinction.

Prior to the final adjudication of his legal problems, Chuck had continued to record and perform, but the strain of his personal and professional life adversely influenced his recordings. During four separate recording sessions in 1959, Chuck cut sixteen songs, but only ten were suitable for release to the general public. The Moonglows and the Equadors supplied excellent vocal backups at these sessions, and Johnny Johnson's piano, Willie Dixon's bass, and Fred Below's drums provided the musical accompaniment. Such Chuck Berry classics as *Almost Grown*, which rose to number thirty-two on the charts, and *Back in the USA*, which occupied the number thirty-seven position on the *Billboard* Hot 100, were recorded in these sessions. *Let It Rock* and *Too Pooped to Pop*, which peaked at sixty-four and forty-two respectively on the *Billboard* charts, were also cut during the 1959 sessions.

It is understandable that Leonard Chess did not release some of the songs from the 1959 sessions, but not because of any particular lack of quality in them. *County Line* and *Blue On Blue*, for example, were two Chuck Berry songs that were not released because Chess felt that they were too blues oriented. In 1974, when Chess released **Chuck Berry Golden Decade Volume 3**, these previously unreleased songs were included on the album. Two other then unreleased songs, *Do You Love Me* and *One O'Clock Jump* are available now on the U.K. issue of **Golden Decade Volume 3** and **Chess Masters** respectively. There is also an excellent bootleg LP featuring these recordings. In these songs, Chuck displayed his amazing musical range, as well as a singular mastery of the blues sound. In not releasing the songs earlier, Chess Records hoped to maintain Chuck's appeal in the rock-and-roll market. Leonard Chess's strategy was a smart business move, because blues records sold very poorly in the late 1950s and early 1960s.

One of Chuck Berry's obscure 1959 hits, *Little Queenie*, had a humorous impact upon Jerry Lee Lewis's life. For three years, Jerry Lee and Chuck were mortal rivals in a number of concert tours. Each artist demanded that he close the show while on tour, and when Chuck and Jerry Lee were booked on the same tour there were numerous arguments, and often fistfights. There are a number of stories concerning Chuck and Jerry Lee's infamous differences. One story alleged that Jerry Lee's father, Elmo, held a shotgun to Chuck's head during a concert in Baltimore. Another story alleges that Chuck held a knife to Jerry Lee's throat during a subsequent concert. Still another story has Chuck and Jerry Lee engaging in a fistfight. These tales are impossible to substantiate, but they have crept into a number of books. While there is little doubt that Chuck Berry and Jerry Lee Lewis were less than friendly, no credence can be given to many of the mythical stories concerning their lives without more support from others. One tale, however, is true, and it is a hilarious one.

In 1959, Jerry Lee Lewis' mother, Mamie, asked Myra Gail Lewis to write Jerry Lee for a copy of Chuck Berry's *Little Queenie*. Myra recalled: "I suppose that next to Jerry, Chuck Berry is her very favorite." Jerry Lee Lewis reacted in a rage, and he immediately called Sam Phillips to set up a recording session. "I want to get into the Sun studios as soon as possible, Sam," Jerry intoned. "I have a debt that I am going to settle." Sam Phillips was astonished when Jerry Lee demanded an immediate recording session, and once he learned the reason, he roared with laughter. Jerry Lee Lewis wanted to record his own version of *Little Queenie*. Phillips could not accommodate Jerry Lee on such short notice, however. Jerry Lee then went home to Ferriday, Louisiana, only to find himself awakened each morning by his mother's stereo blasting out Chuck Berry records. After hearing Chuck's version of *Little Queenie* for two or three hours at his parents' home, Jerry Lee almost went through the roof. Finally, on May 28, 1959, Jerry Lee called a session at the Sun studios solely for the purpose of recording *Little Queenie*. After recording the song, Jerry Lee traveled back to Ferriday with a sample record, and promptly broke the Chuck Berry version into a number of little pieces. Jerry Lee Lewis was infuriated that his mother preferred Chuck Berry's music to his own. He believed that the devil was working on his family. In 1962, when Jerry Lee recorded *Sweet Little Sixteen*, he confided to his session guitarist, Scotty Moore, that he was finally getting even with Chuck Berry.

There were other 1959 Chuck Berry songs which influenced musicians in other ways. In Liverpool, John Lennon and Paul McCartney listened to *Back in the USA* on a portable stereo. After repeatedly listening to *Back in the USA*, a number of ideas germinated in Lennon and McCartney's minds. In later years, Chuck Berry's song was McCartney's inspiration for the White Album Beatle song, *Back in the USSR*.

As 1959 ended, rock-and-roll music reached a crisis period. With artists like Johnny and the Hurricanes, Bobby Rydell, Fabian, and Sandy Nelson rising on the charts, mediocrity seemed to have taken over the rock music art form. When Mark Dining's *Teen Angel* hit the *Billboard* charts in December, 1959, many teen-agers wondered what had happened to the old wave of rock-and-roll music.

Despite the depressing changes in American music, there was still a strong market for Chuck Berry records. Although he continually toured, he was able to record sporadically in the Chess studios. The rock LP was still in its infancy, but Leonard Chess realized that Chuck Berry's successful singles meant that another album would also be successful. The first two Chess LPs had been issued in late 1958, more than three years after Chuck began recording for Chess Records. His chart success in 1959 was consistent, and, as a result, another LP was planned. In September, 1959, Chess Records released Chuck's third LP. It was entitled **Chuck Berry Is on Top** (Chess 1435). The album was an excellent one, and contained such songs as *Almost Grown, Carol, Maybellene, Johnny B. Goode, Little Queenie, Anthony Boy, Sweet Little Rock and Roller, Jo Jo Gunne, Around and Around, Roll Over Beethoven, Hey Pedro*, and *Blues for Hawaiians*. This was an album in which Chuck was happy with every song; he did not consider any of the tunes "fillers." The album sold very well, and Chuck began preparations for yet another album. In fact, the success of **Chuck Berry Is on Top** was strong enough to persuade Leonard Chess to spend a couple of months in the studio recording Chuck's new material. In addition, Chuck also believed that he could now diverge into other musical areas. As a result, he planned a blues-oriented recording session. It was time to finally develop a commercially-based blues sound. Chuck was tired of recording an entire album of rock-and-roll songs. He was eager to demonstrate his prolific blues talents, and to expand his songwriting in new directions.

Chuck ...Berry Is On Top   Chess 1435 (LP)

During early April, 1960, Leonard Chess arranged a recording session in the Chess studios. There were some new musicians brought into this session. Among them was Matt Murphy, a legendary Chicago guitar player, who worked with Howlin' Wolf. The seven cuts from this session also feature L.C. Davis on tenor sax, and Johnny Johnson on the piano. An Elmore James-inspired version of *It Hurts Me Too* had been a Chuck Berry favorite for some time, and during this session he recorded his own version of the Elmore James classic. Another important song Chuck wrote and recorded during 1960 was a blues-oriented classic, *Our Little Rendezvous*. It was a remake of Johnny Lee "Sonny Boy" Williamson's *Good Morning Little Schoolgirl*, and Chuck had frequently heard the song performed by a number of Chicago bluesmen. This served as an inspiration to Chuck to do a version. Matt Murphy's guitar work was a potent musical force during the session for this song; Murphy had played with all the early Chicago blues giants, and he added a unique interpretive touch to Chuck's recordings. Another song from this session, *Bye Bye Johnny*, was a clever commentary on Elvis Presley's decision to concentrate upon studio recording and acting in Hollywood movies, and to forego live concert performances. There was a historical significance to *Bye Bye Johnny*; in effect, Elvis abandoned traditional rock-and-roll music to concentrate upon a career in the mainstream of the entertainment business. A humorous side of the song describes Elvis taking a Greyhound bus to Hollywood to find a new career, but there was also a serious side to *Bye Bye Johnny*, as Chuck never forgot that Elvis had more number one rhythm and blues *Billboard* hits than he did. It didn't upset Chuck that Elvis was such a popular artist on the *Billboard* Hot 100, but the fact that a white artist could outsell the black artists on the rhythm and blues charts bothered him.

As an indication of his strong desire to write and record rhythm and blues songs, Chuck often did renditions of favorite tunes by others, adapting the existing music and lyrics to his own style. An example of this tendency was Chuck's arrangement of Fats Domino's *Don't You Lie to Me*. This song was recorded during the same sessions that Chuck did versions of Elmore James and Sonny Boy Williamson tunes. During the lengthy April 1960 sessions, three of the seven songs were old blues tunes, either rerecorded or substantially rewritten by Chuck Berry. In the summer of 1960, Chuck cut thirteen songs for Chess Records, but none of these tunes were important *Billboard* chart songs. Two of these recordings carried with them a sense of deja vu. *Confessin' the Blues* and *Down the Road Apiece*, were old favorites of Chuck's that he had performed in small clubs around St. Louis for years. It was on these tunes that Chuck displayed his remarkable ability to render sensitive reinterpretations of classic Chicago and Memphis blues music. However, the general quality of such songs as *Diploma for Two, Sweet Sixteen,* and *The Way It Was Before* were not up to Chuck Berry's usual high level. A combination of exhaustive touring, personal problems, and extensive changes in the music business had taken a toll on his songwriting talents; he was no longer a one-man show, capable of turning out a half dozen hit songs each year. In fact, in 1960, only *Too Pooped to Pop* and *Let It Rock* entered the *Billboard* Hot 100, and neither song was a Top 40 hit.

In 1960, Chuck Berry began to perform Maceo Merriweather's classic blues tune, *Worried Life Blues.* This song was an accurate reflection of Chuck's own feelings about the direction of his career. He realized that important changes were taking place in the recording industry, but was determined to continue developing his songwriting and recording skills. During the 1960 Chess sessions, such songs as *Stop and Listen* and *13 Question Method* emerged as examples of innovative new musical directions in Chuck Berry's music. The presence of a number of talented new session musicians added musical diversity. Matt Murphy's guitar was given more freedom than in previous Berry recording sessions. In addition, L.C. Davis' tenor saxophone brought a new degree of flexibility to Chuck's music. These musical changes were not conducive to producing *Billboard* Hot 100 chart songs, however.

Despite the decline of his ability to record hit records, Chuck was in demand for television appearances. He was a regular on the various Dick Clark shows, and he continued to appear on other local television bandstand shows. In 1960, Chuck's concert appearances also declined, part of an industry-wide problem which *Newsweek* magazine pointed out in a piece dealing with the rock-and-roll music field. In June, 1960, a *Newsweek* article, entitled "It's Folksy, It's Delightful, It's a Craze," detailed the changing patterns in music during an analysis of the folk music renaissance. When the second Newport Folk Festival was held, during the last week of June, more than 10,000 attended, and half that many were turned away at the gates. Although folk music was still essentially nonpolitical, John F. Kennedy's 1960 presidential campaign helped change its course. The Massachusetts Democrat fired the imagination of young people, and soon folk artists like Tom Paxton were turning out topical songs. For many years the Weavers had been highly political, but they failed to excite the commercial imagination of young record buyers. When Tom Paxton wrote his apochryphal song, *A Rumblin' in the Land*, it sparked a new genre of folk-protest songs.

There were also other changes in rock-and-roll music. Elvis Presley no longer offered the same exciting music he had in the 1950s. Such Elvis hits as *Now or Never, Stuck On You,* and *Are You Lone-*

some Tonight? seemed to be tired rehashings of old themes. New, sophisticated production techniques threatened the raw, emotional power of 1950s' style rock-and-roll music. By the early 1960s, the Drifters, in songs like *This Magic Moment*, employed a large string section, and this spelled doom for the First Golden Age of Rock and Roll Music. Pop duets by artists like Brook Benton and Dinah Washington further eroded the definitions of rock music in the early 1960s. The *Billboard* charts underwent dramatic changes, with country songs like Johnny Horton's *The Battle of New Orleans* entering the rock music listings. Although Horton's hit was in the summer of 1959, nevertheless, it was a harbinger of the identity crisis facing rock music in the 1960s. The old rock-and-roll artists like Fats Domino, Little Richard, Larry Williams, and Chuck Berry were giving way to pop musicians. Occasionally, one of many 1950s rock groups would temporarily return to the charts, like Hank Ballard and the Midnighters. In August, 1960, Ballard's *Finger Poppin' Time* revived his dormant career, and the song spent twenty-six weeks on the *Billboard* charts. No one realized that the periodic comeback of artists like Hank Ballard was simply a reflection of the developing "oldies-but-goodies" syndrome, which would soon dominate the format of a number of radio stations.

Another major musical divergence, surf music, came to the fore in the early 1960s. In Seattle, Washington, the Ventures were playing surf music at the Spanish Castle and Dick Parker ballrooms. In Los Angeles, Jan and Dean were already national rock stars using a surf genre. When surf music was fused with the rock music revolution in the early 1960s, Chuck Berry was an important influence upon a number of groups. Carl Wilson of the Beach Boys told Dick Clark that he listened primarily to Chuck's music, adapting it as the basis of the Beach Boys' music. Dean Torrance of Jan and Dean also credits Chuck's music as the most important influence in the evolution of the surf sound. Brian Wilson defined surf music as a "Chuck Berry guitar with Four Freshman harmonizing." The rise of surf music had the salutary effect of temporarily reviving record sales of early rock-and-roll artists like Chuck Berry.

In an attempt to continue promoting Chuck Berry records, the Chess label recycled old songs on albums with new names. In June, 1962, the **Twist with Chuck Berry** (Chess 1465) album was released; it included 1950s hits like *Maybellene, Roll Over Beethoven,* and *Johnny B. Goode.* This ploy alienated large numbers of potential Chuck Berry record buyers, as most people had purchased these songs in the 1950s. The strangest repackaged album in the early 1960s was entitled **Bo Diddley and Chuck Berry: Two Great Guitars** (Checker 2991). The album was an accident in time, and an exercise in greed. In March, 1964, Bo Diddley was in the Tel Mar Recording

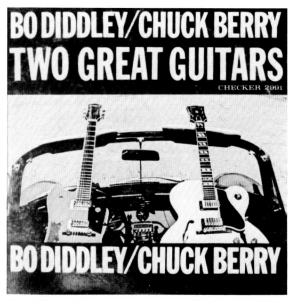

Two Great Guitars   Checker 2991 (LP)

End of concert!

Studio in Chicago, and he had a half-an-hour of studio time left. As a result, Bo and Chuck began to play together. The result was the song *Bo's Beat*, and another appropriately entitled *Chuck's Beat*. Neither Bo Diddley nor Chuck Berry believed that these songs would ever be released. Chuck's *Liverpool Drive* and Bo's *When the Saints Go Marching In* were added to make a four-song "album." The liner notes for the LP proclaimed: "The musicians, the engineer, people in the control room; people who produce hundreds of records every year, did applaud every take, every song in this album." The liner notes then stated that the album contained "the most exciting, spirited instrumental session ever put on record." The reality was that Chess Records badly needed new Chuck Berry records, and this album was released in an attempt to fill the void. It was a disaster which did not help Chuck's recording career, and a further indictment of the early 1960s as a period in which vacuum rock dominated the musical scene in America. Money-grabbing repackagings of earlier rockers, and groups of white, boring, minimally-talented performers playing pseudo rock-and-roll and dreaming of playing in New York's Copacabana nightclub were the norm. It was a grim time for rock-and-roll music.

In August, 1960, as Chuck Berry's musical influence waned in the United States, it was on the rise in Europe. Few people at the time recognized how important Chuck's music was in the development of the new age of rock which was coming. The Beatles were playing at Bruno Koschmider's Hamburg, Germany, club, the Indra. When they opened in this dank, second-rate little club that August, the Beatles featured Chuck Berry's *Too Much Monkey Business* each night in their set. A number of British rock stars, notably Cliff Richard, Wee Willie Harris, Billy Fury, Tommy Steele, and Johnny Kidd and the Pirates were influenced by Chuck Berry's songs. Virtually every singer and group who became part of the so-called first British Invasion in 1963--1964 was weaned on Chuck Berry music.

In America, European rock-and-roll appeared as novel and exciting as that same music had once been in the U.S., and was no more. Those elements which were alien and different in foreign recordings overshadowed the fact that what really gave them the energy and bite of bygone days were an underlying reliance on the music of Chuck Berry, whose current music, sadly, was on the decline in the United States even as that of his "children" was on the rise. In June, 1960, a Chess album entitled **Rockin' at the Hops** (Chess 1448) was released, and went virtually unnoticed by the rock press. This LP contained seven excellent original Chuck Berry songs, as well as five songs by other artists. The songs on this album included: *Bye Bye Johnny, Worried Life Blues, Down the Road Apiece, Confessin' the*

Blues, Too Pooped to Pop, Mad Lad, I Got to Find My Baby, Betty Jean, Childhood Sweetheart, Broken Arrow, Driftin' the Blues and *Let It Rock*. To advertise the single for *Bye Bye Johnny*, Chess Records distributed a simulated playing card featuring the song title in the middle of an Ace of Clubs. Although this was Chuck's fourth album for Chess Records, it was not as strong as his previous efforts. The long tours and the increased attention to personal business had taken its toll.

The frequency of Chuck's recording sessions declined in 1961. The changes in rock music, another temporary recession in sales, and the emergence of other Chess artists combined to reduce his time in the studio. In January, 1961, Chuck went into the Chess studios with Johnny Johnson on piano, Eddie Hardy on drums, and an unknown club player. The result was three songs: *Route 66, I'm Talkin' About You*, and a cover version of Little Richard's *Rip It Up*. The remake of the Little Richard song is undoubtedly the worst recording of Chuck's distinguished career, but it points up his willingness to take a chance on a song and musical style that is alien to his nature.

There were a number of problems between Chuck Berry and Chess Records in the early 1960s, but he continued to record and Chess Records produced two more Chuck Berry LPs during 1961--1962. In June, 1961, the album **Juke Box Hits** (Chess 1456) was released, with *I'm Talking' About You, Diploma for Two, Rip It Up, Thirteen Question Method, The Way It Was Before, Don't You Lie to Me, Little Star, Route 66, Sweet Sixteen, Stop and Listen, Away from You*, and *Run Around* included on this album. It was obvious that this album was conceived and recorded in the midst of Chuck's legal problems, as the original songs were poorly crafted and lacked spontaneity. *Don't You Lie to Me* and *I'm Talkin' About You* were the only two excellent songs in an otherwise dull album. The main reason that this album was so substandard was that Chuck's legal problems forced him to tour constantly to pay his lawyers' fees. During this time of controversy, Leonard Chess stood firmly by Chuck Berry, and was one of his staunchest defenders; it was a losing battle, however, and Chuck could not escape the eagerness of the St. Louis authorities to prosecute him for a crime that they would have ignored had he been a white man.

In August, 1961, Chuck entered the Chess studios for the last time before serving his prison term. On this session Chuck's sister, Martha, supplied the back-up vocals for Chuck on *Come On, Go, Go, Go, Trick or Treat*, and *The Man and the Donkey*. It was a short session, and only one of the five songs was a hit record. *Go, Go, Go* reached number thirty-six on the U.K. charts in July, 1963, but was not an American hit. Another song, *Come On*, was an important tune, and had a strong influence on England's Rolling Stones.

While Chuck Berry was in prison, a number of important changes occurred in rock music. Suddenly, rock-and-roll music was overwhelmed by the white teen idol, and names like Fabian, Frankie Avalon, Bobby Rydell, Paul Anka, and Bobby Vee came to the fore. There were also a plethora of minor league white rock idols like Jimmy Clanton, Vic Dana, and Joey Dee with *Billboard* chart hits. As 1962 ended, there was another decline in rock record sales. Not only were the songs stale and talentless recyclings of old themes, but there were few new rock acts that excited the imagination of record buyers. On the eve of the emergence of the Beatles and the Rolling Stones, American rock music was in the midst of a crisis. For Chuck Berry, the 1959--1962 era was a time of lows and highs, and his career seems nearly to exactly parallel the roller coaster fortunes of rock music.

Chuck in the early 1980s.

CHAPTER 6

FROM OBSCURITY BACK TO THE BILLBOARD HOT 100: 1963-1964

During 1963--1964, Chuck Berry's career was at its lowest point, and his personal life was also in disarray. Chuck had served time in jail, he had lost his Club Bandstand, and he was no longer certain that his records would continue to sell. The constant changes in rock music made it difficult for Chuck to foresee a future as a successful recording artist. He had not had a single on the *Billboard* Hot 100 since 1960, when *Let It Rock* peaked at the number sixty-four position, and the *Billboard* rhythm and blues charts no longer listed Chuck Berry records. In July, 1963, Chess released **Chuck Berry On Stage** (Chess 1480), the first in a strange procession of Chuck Berry albums put out in 1963--1964. The album contained *Memphis, Sweet Little Sixteen (Surfin' USA), Rockin' on the Railroad (Let It Rock), Maybellene, Surfing Steel (Blues for Hawaiians* with the second guitar track omitted), *Go, Go, Go, Brown-Eyed Handsome Man, Still Got the Blues, Jaguar and the Thunderbird, I Just Want to Make Love to You, All Aboard, The Man and the Donkey, Trick or Treat*, and *How High the Moon*. Musical tastes had changed dramatically since the late 1950s, and the album was not a best-seller because much of the material consisted of old hits or second-rate studio cuts. Another problem was that the album dubbed-in applause from an "audience." However, *Go, Go, Go* and *Jaguar and the Thunderbird* were important songs despite the dubbed applause.

The advent of surfing music was the main reason that Chuck Berry's music returned to the charts. In 1963, the Beach Boys released a record entitled *Surfin' USA*, with Brian Wilson of the Beach Boys listed as the songwriter. Dean Torrance, of Jan and Dean, recalled that when he heard *Surfin' USA*, he recognized immediately that it was a remake of Chuck Berry's *Sweet Little Sixteen*. After Arc Music sued the Beach Boys, Chuck Berry's name was placed on the song as composer. Inadvertently, the legal problems over *Surfin' USA* helped to revive Berry's musical career in Europe.

Although rock-and-roll music in the United States was in serious

Chuck Berry in London, England, February 19, 1975.

trouble, Chuck's records sold very well in England and throughout Europe. Like many 1950s rock-and-roll stars, Chuck was able to survive artistically due to foreign record sales. At home, the *Billboard* Hot 100 was increasingly filled with songs by artists like Peter, Paul and Mary, the Rooftop Singers, and the New Christy Minstrels. Bob Dylan's album **The Freewheelin' Bob Dylan**, was released in May, 1963, and the folk music revolution increasingly turned to protest lyrics. In May, 1963, Joan Baez and Bob Dylan appeared at the Monterey Folk Festival, and the overwhelming public response brought folk music to the forefront of the record industry. The California audience greeted Dylan and Baez with thunderous applause. During the summer of 1963, the continued success of folk music was demonstrated when 200,000 civil rights advocates descended upon Washington, D.C. to hear Martin Luther King's historic "I Have a Dream" speech. Much in evidence as a political and moral force at such gatherings, the voices of folk musicians began to fill the radio airwaves.

As the folk musical revival engulfed America, Chuck Berry was quietly released from jail in the summer of 1963. The other Founding Fathers of rock-and-roll music were now either in Hollywood, or touring with oldies shows. Jerry Lee Lewis, Bill Haley and His Comets, and Little Richard were no longer significant recording acts. Fats Domino had a few hits, but his strength remained as a strong live concert draw. Elvis Presley was ensconced in Hollywood, no longer a part of the live concert milieu, and no longer recording elemental rock. Another change on the American music scene was the rise of the Motown sound. Mary Wells, Smokey Robinson and the Miracles, Martha and the Vandellas, and the Supremes made Berry Gordy, Jr.'s Motown conglomerate a new force in the recording industry. There was also a resurgence of female singers, as Little Peggy March, Leslie Gore, Deedee Sharp, Linda Scott, and Sue Thompson scored with hit records. The Ronettes, the Angels, the Chiffons, and the Jaynettes pioneered the "girl group" sound, bringing new diversity to rock-and-roll music.

The changes in audience tastes in the United States made it difficult for Chuck Berry to return to the charts. His music was no longer in style, and the energy of such producers as Phil Spector made it obvious that the old rock acts of the 1950s were no longer a part of the mainstream of rock-and-roll music. As a result, Chuck requested that Chess Records plan a European tour. As he served out the last two months of his jail sentence, Chess Records quietly negotiated with a number of English booking agents. As a result, the British rock bible, *Melody Maker*, headlined in June, 1963: "Chuck Berry to Tour in Autumn." English interest in Berry's music coincided with the appearance of a number of Berry tunes on the U.K.

Top 50. *Go, Go, Go, Let It Rock/Memphis, Tennessee*, and *Run Rudolph Run* were all chart hits. *Memphis, Tennessee* rose to number six, and spent thirteen weeks on the English charts. The fact that it was not an American chart song is hard to explain, but since Chuck was in jail and the *Billboard* charts were often apparently controlled by unfathomable forces, it is not surprising that one of Chuck's songs was the victim of the sometimes malevolent rating practices. As a result of the British success of *Memphis, Tennessee*, however, Chuck determined to continue his songwriting and recording career. The period that Chuck spent in jail had only reinforced his commitment to excellence. America was not alone in snubbing Chuck, however; the stuffy promoters who controlled the British concert halls believed that Chuck Berry was not a suitable family act. Consequently, Chuck's first English tour was temporarily postponed, but the bad publicity helped the sales of another record, *Brown-Eyed Handsome Man*. Although this song did not appear on the U.K. Top 50, nevertheless, it sold very well in record shops. The growing popularity of English rock groups such as the Animals, the Beatles, the Rolling Stones, and the Yardbirds, also helped to popularize Berry's music. He began receiving an unaccustomed amount of publicity as one of rock music's Founding Fathers. When the Beatles had their first, and unsuccessful, audition for Decca Records in 1962, they had included a rendition of Chuck's *Memphis, Tennessee*. The Rolling Stones recorded *Come On*, which became a hit for them in July, 1963, and the Yardbirds version of *Too Much Monkey Business* was a favorite of London pub fans.

On August 1, 1963, while on a temporary work furlough from prison, Chuck Berry entered the Chess recording studios for the first time in more than two years. It was not easy for Chuck to return to the studio and immediately record a hit record. Things did not go smoothly, and only three songs were cut during the lengthy recording session. *No Details* was released, but not on a 45 record. The remaining cuts, *Nashville*, and a remake of *Brown-Eyed Handsome Man*, were not considered suitable for commercial release. It was peculiar that Leonard Chess refused to release *Brown-Eyed Handsome Man*; it had an innovative reggae-calypso feel to it, and featured some exciting horn bursts.

While he was in prison, Chuck began to work on an autobiography which promised to discuss many of the more controversial aspects of his music career. (For the next twenty years he thought, wrote, and conceived this book. By 1983, it was finished, and Chuck Berry was negotiating with major publishing houses.) The cartharic experience of writing a book on his life inadvertently helped Chuck to revive images of his youth. As a result, he penned two new hit songs while in prison. These tunes, *Nadine* and *No Particular Place to Go*, evoked memories of Chuck's earlier hits, and were perfectly crafted choices for his return to the *Billboard* charts.

Shortly after he was released from prison, Chuck spoke with a British journalist, Chris Roberts, about his career. Surprisingly, Chuck did not appear bitter during the interview, and he was unusually cooperative with the *Melody Maker* reporter. There was no doubt that Chuck Berry realized his precarious position in the record industry, and he reverted to the image of a pleasant, amiable artist. His usually bellicose and uncooperative manner was temporarily abandoned, so that he could resume his career. The *Melody Maker* interview was an important one, because it revealed that Chuck was intent on developing an amusement facility known as Berry Park, in Wentzville, Missouri. He also indicated that an English tour would take place in 1964, and discussed a forthcoming recording session in the Chess studios.

In 1964, the *Billboard* Hot 100 charts were dominated by some of the worst rock acts in history. The Singing Nun's song, *Dominique*, was a Top Ten hit, and the Kingsmen's version of the Richard Berry classic, *Louie Louie*, topped the *Billboard* Hot 100 in January. Both these songs provided evidence of the sorry condition of rock music. In February, 1964, the American music scene was shaken to its foundations by the arrival of the Beatles, and *I Want to Hold Your Hand*'s seven-week number one stay on the *Billboard* charts. American rock music could muster only tunes like Leslie Gore's *You Don't Own Me*, the number two *Billboard* song. The subsequent English invasion, and the popularity accorded the Beatles, was devastating for home-grown rock-and-roll artists.

As these changes took place, Chuck was preparing for a recording session. In January, 1964, when Chuck Berry entered the recording studio, he had no real feel for all the revolutionary changes that had taken place in American music. The session was an interesting and productive one, however. Although nine songs were recorded, only four were released by Chess Records in America. In Europe, three songs were issued on different labels. Among the unreleased songs was an excellent version of Elmore James' *Dust My Broom*; Chuck had watched Elmore James perform a number of times at Silvio's Tavern at 2254 W. Lake Street in Chicago, and he was particularly impressed with James' presentation of *Dust My Broom*. Other songs recorded during this session included a version of *Ain't That Just Like a Woman*, heavily influenced by Fats Domino. Chuck also recorded an excellent rendition of the country song *Fraulein*, a Ray Charles tune, *I'm in the Danger Zone*, as well as one of his most original songs, *You Never Can Tell*. All of these tunes were enhanced by the session drummer, Odie Payne, who was well known for his

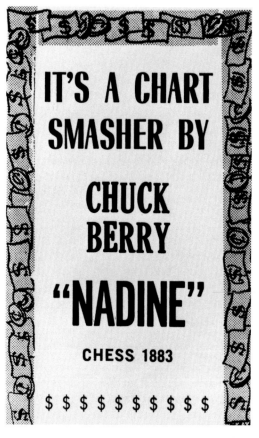

A promotional poster for *Nadine*, 1964.

work with most of Chicago's top blues performers. In the early 1950s, Payne's crisp drumming was an integral part of Elmore James's sound. While playing with James, Payne developed into one of the best blues drummers in the Chicago area. After more than a decade as a leading studio and club musician, Payne helped to propel Chuck Berry's music back into the mainstream of rock-and-roll.

The success of this session prompted Leonard Chess to schedule another. A February 25, 1964, recording date was set, with Lafayette Leake on piano, Payne on drums, and one other unknown club player. Of the four songs recorded during this session, *The Promised Land* and a novelty tune, *Brenda Lee*, were the best. In 1964, *The Promised Land* appeared on both the American *Billboard* charts and the Top 50 in England. It was also a song which virtually every obscure British band played during rehearsals and live concerts. (Eric Burden was particularly influenced by Chuck Berry's music in the early 1960s. When the Animals emerged as one of England's premier rock groups, such Berry classics as *Memphis* and *Let It Rock* became an integral part of the Animals' concert repertoire. Reportedly, during the early Animals' tours, Burden often looked into a mirror in his hotel room and suddenly began singing *The Promised Land*. In Hollywood, another famous rock star, Elvis Presley, sat quietly in his Bel Air home listening to *The Promised Land*. Eventually, Elvis returned to live performing, incorporating a number of Chuck Berry songs in his concert repertoire.) The quality of the songs from the February 25th sessions was apparently appreciated only by Leonard Chess at the time. On March 26, 1964, another Chess session resulted in three more excellent songs, *No Particular Place to Go*, *You Two*, and *Liverpool Drive*. There was little doubt in Chess's mind that Chuck Berry had been rejuvenated as a major songwriting talent, and that his keen eye for musical trends had returned. The song *Liverpool Drive*, for example, was an insightful, if humorous, comment on the rise of English rock-and-roll music.

After the Dave Clark Five became the first English group to tour America, and the Beatles appeared on the "Ed Sullivan Show," there was an influx of English recording groups. Soon, the Kinks, Gerry and the Pacemakers, Freddy and the Dreamers, Peter and Gordon, the Rolling Stones, Chad and Jeremy, and the Animals brought a revitalized avalanche of rock music from England. Ironically, Americans were rediscovering Chuck Berry through the British Invasion, which depended so heavily upon his music for inspiration.

In 1964, the *Billboard* Hot 100 was once again filled with Chuck Berry songs. In March, 1964, *Nadine* was released, rising to number twenty-three in its ten-week stint on the charts. In May, *No Particular Place to Go* reached the number ten spot. *You Never Can Tell* rose to number fourteen, and *Little Marie* went to number fifty-four.

105

With four chart records, Chuck Berry was solidly back on the *Bill-board* Hot 100. In England, *Nadine, No Particular Place to Go*, and *You Never Can Tell* were hits on the U.K. Top 50. In fact, *No Particular Place to Go* became Chuck Berry's best-selling English 45, rising to number three and remaining on the British charts for twelve weeks. The premiere British rock magazine, *New Musical Express*, named Chuck Berry its number seven personality in rock music, and its number eight world male singer, an indication of the English fascination with Chuck's music.

Although Leonard Chess felt he had been witness to Chuck's rejuvenation as a songwriter and musical master, there was some question in Chess's mind that Chuck Berry could resume his career as a major touring attraction. After a long absence from the charts, a great deal of negative publicity over the Mann Act conviction, and the increasingly moral tone trumpeted by disc jockeys and concert promoters in the aftermath of the payola scandals, there was reason for concern. In order to guarantee a reasonable profit from a diminished concert fee, the decision was made to employ pickup bands of local musicians in Chuck's personal appearances. This often made the performance ragged and imprecise, but it did increase the profits reaped by Chuck and Chess Records, and was an important step in reviving his career. Since many concert promoters were reluctant to spend big money on an over-the-hill oldies artist, garnering most of the $350 to $750 concert fee was an important aspect of Chuck's financial comeback. The new practice also attests to the shrewd management skills of Leonard Chess. Ultimately, however, it hurt Chuck's music and led to a number of later confrontations between Chuck and Chess Records.

The differences between Chuck Berry and Chess Records in 1964 became pronounced when, after his jail sentence, Chuck began touring. Marshall Chess, the twenty-two-year-old son of Chess Record founder Leonard Chess, had become Berry's road manager. Apparently, Berry and Chess fought a great deal, and Marshall Chess remarked to a writer for *Blues Unlimited*: "He was a real cheap bastard, Chuck Berry. He would tell me he was never hungry. I'd be starving, and then I'd catch him cooking a can on a hotplate . . . he'd carry a little electric hotplate in his suitcase . . . too cheap to buy a meal." It apparently never occurred to Chess that perhaps Chuck just didn't care to eat *with him*.

After a concert at San Francisco's Cow Palace, Chuck wandered down to Jimbo's Bop City on Fillmore Street and played a series of blues sets in that after-hours nightclub with a number of local musicians. The San Francisco blues scene was a small but impressive one, and Chuck was able to play a number of his favorite blues tunes, notably Elmore James' *It Hurts Me Too* and Louis Jordan's *Saturday Night Fish Fry*. Although *Nadine* and *No Particular Place*

Chuck's *No Particular Place To Go* and . . .

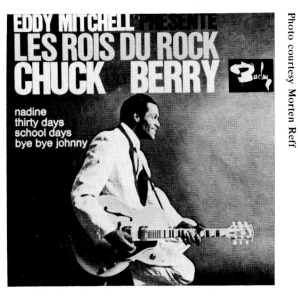

. . . *Nadine* were hits on both sides of the Atlantic.

to Go had once again brought Chuck Berry back to the *Billboard* Hot 100, he still had a fervent desire to play the blues. In 1964, Jimbo's Bop City was an excellent psychological escape for Chuck, who was determined not to let the cataclysmic changes in American music destroy his basic approach to rock-and-roll.

The temporary resurgence of Chuck Berry's recording career, as well as the release of new albums, resulted in a large number of bookings. Suddenly, his touring schedule was a hectic one. Although Chuck was still capable of performing excellent concerts, and actively participated as a guest on radio talk shows, there was a noticeable difference in his personality. If Chuck liked a newspaper or magazine reporter, the interview was very positive. More and more, however, Chuck's temperament and personality were given over to volatile high and low points. The roller coaster ride of "success" in the rock music business was a difficult one for most artists, and, after a decade in the business, Chuck yearned for a time of relief and isolation from the constant demands of touring and recording. And so it was that, after he left prison, Chuck moved to a small, German-dominated town of almost 3,000, Wentzville, Missouri. In the solace of a farm he dubbed Berry Park, Chuck rebuilt his life and began to make plans to continue his musical career; Berry Park was even equipped with a guitar-shaped swimming pool. After concert tours Chuck returned to his farm to rest amidst the quiet, rural Missouri countryside. It was the perfect retreat from the hectic, often overwhelming rock-and-roll life style. After five blissful years at Berry Park, Chuck reflected upon his career. In a question-and-answer session at the University of California, Berkeley, moderated by Greil Marcus and reprinted in the June 14, 1969 issue of *Rolling Stone*, Chuck explained his move to Berry Park as a mystical one: "How I ever drove stakes there, I don't really know," Chuck remarked. It was obvious from the interview that his need for solitude, time to write and think, and for a reprioritizing of personal values were major reasons for the move to Wentzville. Although Chuck presently lives much of the year in Los Angeles, he maintains Berry Park as a retreat from the pressures of show business.

A major factor in the resurgence of Berry's career in 1963--1964 was the newly emerging English superstars, the Beatles. In a February, 1963, issue of *Melody Maker*, for example, John Lennon stressed the importance of Berry's songs in his own development as a songwriter. As already noted, as part of the Beatles' audition for Decca Records, they played *Memphis, Tennessee* as one of their songs. In October, 1962, when the Beatles played at the Embassy Theater in Peterborough, *Memphis, Tennessee* was again performed (to a virtually silent family audience). In later years, Lennon's instrumentals in *Get Back* revealed very similar patterns to those in Chuck Berry's music.

There were also other significant Chuck Berry influences upon the Beatles' early career. Not only was Chuck Berry's *Roll Over Beethoven* featured by the Beatles, with George Harrison singing the lead, but there was an attempt to mimic Chuck's guitar wizardry. In the 1964 summer and winter American tours, *Roll Over Beethoven* was one of the strongest songs the Beatles performed in concert. The following year, Chuck's *Rock and Roll Music* was released by the Beatles, with John Lennon singing the lead, and George Martin supplying a strong piano accompaniment. The intensity of this song prompted the Beatles to continue using it in the live shows from 1964 to 1966. During the 1964 Christmas show, *Rock and Roll Music* brought the loudest and most sustained applause from Beatle fans. John continued to feature the song in the 1965 European tour, and in the final American tour in 1966. On August 29, 1966, 25,000 spectators partially filled San Francisco's Candlestick Park to hear the Beatles perform *Rock and Roll Music*, among other songs, in what was to be their last live concert appearance. It was entirely fitting that a Chuck Berry song stands as one of the most popular tunes performed during the Beatles' final live performance. Apart from live concert lists, Chuck Berry's songs were featured when the Beatles began performing on BBC radio programs. In 1963, a BBC series called "Pop Go the Beatles" included fifteen weeks of interviews and live performances. Berry's *I Got to Find My Baby* was one of the songs regularly performed on this program, although the Saturday radio show included a wide variety of Berry tunes in sporadic appearances from 1963 to 1965. John Lennon summed up the Beatles attitude in 1963: "Don't give me any sophisticated crap, give me Chuck Berry."

One of the main attractions of Chuck Berry's music for British teenagers was the fact that the BBC had banned some of Berry's tunes due to references to commercial products, such as a V-8 Ford and a Cadillac Coupe de Ville. The BBC had a regulation against playing songs which promoted a commercial product. This rule only served to make Chuck Berry's music even more popular. In the late 1970s, Paul Simon's *Kodachrome* had similar difficulties in securing BBC airplay. In 1975, Dion DiMucci's *Make the World Love Me* was banned on BBC, due to a reference to Levi jeans. While the BBC's regulations have hampered many artists, their policies did not hurt Chuck Berry's record sales, or dampen the enthusiasm of his English fans.

Amid the hoopla over banning some of his records on BBC radio, Chuck traveled to England and West Germany for a series of concerts. This brief 1964 tour included Carl Perkins, and Eric Burden

Chuck in Copenhagen, Denmark, January 25, 1973.

and the Animals. Carl Perkins noted that Chuck was no longer the gregarious, friendly performer he had toured with in the 1950s. Perkins made it a point to be as friendly as possible with Chuck, but Berry was no longer quite as open as in the past. The years of rock-and-roll performing, and a host of personal problems, had taken their toll on Chuck Berry's personality. The European tour was an important one, however, because most English rock and blues bands were heavily influenced by Chuck's music. The live performances throughout England revived his career, and refocused attention upon his pioneering status in rock music. The better known English bands, particularly the Beatles and Rolling Stones, have acknowledged their debt to Chuck Berry. However, there were hundreds of middle-level bands, and a few other internationally known British rock groups, who never fully acknowledged the debt they owed to Chuck Berry.

A good example of just such an influential English band, one viewed primarily as a blues band but in reality influenced more directly by Chuck Berry, was the Yardbirds. This band provides a fascinating case study of Berry's importance to English rock music. In 1962, when American and British music was dominated by artists like Frankie Avalon, Bobby Vee, Tommy Steele, and Cliff Richard, seventeen-year-old Keith Relf met a fellow art student, Paul Samwell-Smith, and they began to play blues and rock-and-roll music together. Keith and Paul listened to recordings by Elmore James, Howlin' Wolf, B.B. King, Bo Diddley, and Chuck Berry in their homes, small coffee houses, and record shops. Soon, while still attending the Kingston Art School, Relf, Samwell-Smith, and another young musician, Laurie Bain, began to play rhythm and blues and rock-and-roll in the rough English pubs. The origins of the Yardbirds can be traced to the Ealing Rhythm and Blues Club, founded in the spring of 1962 by Cyril Davies and Alexis Korner. This club booked bands which strictly adhered to traditional blues repertoires, but the club was often played by bands with a bent for Chuck Berry-Bo Diddley music. While the Yardbirds only listened to the music at the Ealing Rhythm and Blues Club, they made appearances at such nearby clubs as the Metropolis Blues Quarter. The Yardbirds officially formed as a group in early 1963, when Keith Relf persuaded bassist Paul Samwell-Smith to accept a stock exchange employee in the group as the drummer. When Jim McCarty became the drummer, the Yardbirds' main musical problem was solved because, like the Beatles, they had a very difficult time finding an acceptable drummer. Chris Dreja was brought in to handle the rhythm guitar chores, and fourteen-year-old Anthony "Top" Topham was the lead guitarist.

Once the Yardbirds launched their musical career, they were even more strongly influenced by traditional American blues music. Since the Yardbirds more often practiced to Chuck Berry records than to other blues artists, their sound was heavily influenced by his style. When Anthony Topham left the Yardbirds, Eric Clapton became the lead guitarist. At this stage in his career, Clapton was mesmerized by Chess artists. As a guitar player with such obscure English groups as the Roosters, and Casey Jones and the Engineers, Clapton displayed extraordinary talent in interpreting the guitar work of Jimmy Reed, Elmore James, and Chuck Berry. It was Clapton's guitar solos which eventually made the Yardbirds such an important rock-and-roll band.

When the Yardbirds replaced the Rolling Stones as the resident band at the Crawdaddy Club in the Station Hotel in Richmond, Surrey, they were shifting their musical direction toward Chuck Berry-oriented rock music. Although this was not the vehicle that brought them international stardom, nevertheless, it is an interesting reflection on Chuck Berry's pervasive musical influence in the mid-1960s. In March, 1964, the Yardbirds' most requested concert song was Chuck's *Too Much Monkey Business*. In 1965 and 1966, the Yardbirds performed this song a number of times on the BBC "Top of the Pops" program. "At first I played exactly like Chuck Berry for six or seven months," Eric Clapton recalled. "You couldn't have told the difference when I was with the Yardbirds."

What is ironic about the Yardbirds' use of Chuck Berry's material was that he was in jail, or at least out of touch with the music scene, while they were developing in 1960--1962 as a major concert act. When Chuck was released from the Missouri Federal Prison, he immediately became aware of the extent to which his and other early rock-and-roll songs were being used by songwriters responsible for mid-1960s rock-and-roll. In fact, Chuck believed that many songs were simply remakes of his old tunes. As previously recounted, the lyrics and music to the Beach Boys' *Surfin' USA* bore a none-too-coincidental similarity to *Sweet Little Sixteen*. It is unfortunate that Berry was not able to take a more active personal part in the controversy over *Surfin' USA*, which was handled by Arc Music. The suit left such a bitter feeling among the Beach Boys that even as late as 1966, when they released the revolutionary **Pet Sounds** album, they categorically stated that Chuck Berry was no longer an important influence upon their music.

Most rock historians have neglected to point out the continued importance of Chuck Berry's music in the early and mid-1960s. As a black artist who crossed over strongly into white markets, Chuck was a pioneer who strongly motivated a young man named Berry Gordy, Jr. When Gordy's Motown company emerged as a major recording label in the early 1960s, Chuck Berry's influences were apparent. Gordy appreciated the financial potential of crossover songs, and spent a great deal of time crafting Motown soul songs for maximum impact in the white market. In 1964, for example, the success of the

In Gothenburg, Sweden, August 1976.

A promo poster for *Dear Dad*, 1965.

Mark Naftalin, a frequent keyboardist for Chuck.

Four Tops' hit single, *Baby I Need Your Lovin'*, prompted Levi Stubbs, Jr., the Four Tops' lead singer, to state that he owed Chuck Berry an enormous musical debt. The relationship between Chuck Berry and Motown was so close that Chuck recorded a session with Motown's rhythm section in Flint, Michigan. Berry Gordy refused to sell the tapes to Chess Records, because he believed that they were worth more money than Leonard Chess was willing to pay.

In the mid-1960s, electric blues bands became an important part of the American music scene. The strong emphasis upon folk and blues music in the early and mid-1960s had led to a revived form of electric blues. Most of the practitioners of this new music were young, white, college-age musicians like Al Kooper, Steve Katz, Tommy Flanders, Danny Kalb, Andy Kulberg, and Ray Blumenfeld, who together formed the Blues Project in 1965. Among the early songs that this electric blues group used in concert was Chuck's *You Can't Catch Me*. At the Cafe A Go Go on Beeker Street in New York, the Blues Project became one of the first successful electric blues bands in the 1960s. Although both the blues and Chuck Berry's traditional rock-and-roll music were a part of the electric blues band renaissance, there was suddenly a demand for older, more traditional blues tunes. Groups like the Paul Butterfield Blues band formed in Chicago in 1965; it included names like Elvin Bishop, Mike Bloomfield, Mark Naftalin, Jerome Arnold, and Sam Lay. This blending of white and black blues musicians was a revolutionary mix of talent, and bands like Butterfield Blues helped to revive traditional blues music. John Mayall's Bluesbreakers, featuring Peter Green, was another group which was in the forefront of the English blues revival; Mayall's British band further popularized American blues songs.

The changes in musical interests made it difficult for Chuck Berry to continue to release hit records, since the market for songs like *Sweet Little 16*, *Rock and Roll Music*, and *School Day* no longer was a viable one. Perhaps Ahmet Ertegun, the founder of Atlantic Records, analyzed the problem most astutely when he stated: "The little white girl in school loved to dance to Chuck Berry, but somehow John Lennon looked more like her dream." (It is ironic that Lennon himself believed that Chuck Berry was the most influential rock musician of the twentieth century.) If American record buyers did not respond to Berry's songs in the 1960s as they had in the previous decade, the passage of time had no effect upon his European sales. In England and on the Continent, Chuck Berry's music flourished in countries starved for traditional rock-and-roll. In fact, when Berry played a week-long engagement at London's "Beat City" in 1964, the club was packed nightly to hear the man they credited with giving birth to rock-and-roll music.

Chuck in Oslo, Norway, 1980.

In America, there was still a strong demand for Berry's concerts, if not for his records. In 1964, he performed at the Newport Jazz Festival with such diverse acts at Phil Ochs, Judy Collins, and the Lovin' Spoonful. Rock historicans have labeled the Newport Festival of 1964 as the year of musical fallout. This was because traditional rock-and-roll music was replaced by a sophisticated, message-oriented type of music. The feeling at Newport was aptly summed up in Phil Ochs' *The Year of the Topical Song*. It was a strange time; no one seemed ready to acknowledge that Chuck Berry was the originator of the topical song. When Chuck wrote *Too Much Monkey Business*, he introduced most of the elements which characterized 1960s' political protest songs. Somehow, the pseudo-intellectual biases pervading the rock and folk music businesses allowed for the dismissal of any reference to the lyrical significance of *Sweet Little Sixteen, Johnny B. Goode*, and *Roll Over Beethoven*. There was one new performer who paid tribute to Chuck Berry's importance, however; this was Richie Havens. After making his Festival debut, Havens quietly acknowledged his strong feelings over Chuck's music, and he skillfully pointed to Berry's lyrical accomplishments. It was in Berry's lyrics, Havens noted, that topical folk artists initially found their inspiration.

There were many who did not follow folk music trends of the 1960s, of course. The rise of clubs like the Whiskey A Go Go in Los Angeles, and the Peppermint Lounge in San Francisco, brought large numbers of people back to the dance floors. The popularity of television rock-and-roll shows, such as "Shindig" and "Hullaballoo," created a renewed demand for vintage rock. In effect, the British Invasion and the rise of electric blues music had split the rock music field into two competing, and often hostile camps. A stellar gathering of one arm of rock's divided camp occurred in 1964 at the Civic Auditorium in Santa Monica, California. The "TAMI Show" was filmed at this concert location, during which Jan and Dean sped onstage aboard two skateboards as prelude to a feature-length movie featuring some of the best rock acts of the mid-1960s. Chuck Berry was included, along with James Brown, the Rolling Stones, and Gerry and the Pacemakers. The "TAMI Show" was released in Europe, where it was titled "Gather No Moss." It was produced by Steve Binder, who was responsible for the Elvis Presley comeback show in the late 1960s on American television. The eighty-five-minute movie was filmed using a strange new process called Electronovision. Chuck Berry performed *Sweet Little Sixteen, Johnny B. Goode*, and *Maybellene* in the show, which brought together such diverse acts as the Supremes, the Beach Boys, and the Barbarians on the same stage. It was a portent of things to come in the music business; the years from 1965 to 1970 witnessed some of the most revolutionary changes in rock music.

117

In concert at the Circle Star, San Carlos, California in the 1970s.

CHAPTER 7

THE FILLMORE
AND THE FESTIVALS: 1965-1970

From 1965 to 1970, rock-and-roll music continued to branch out in new directions. A number of new promoters entered the rock music business, and the older concert halls gave way to the rise of new venues like the Fillmore Auditorium and the Avalon Ballroom in San Francisco. There was a new freedom and a sense of experimentation in the rock world. A generation of young promoters, typified by Bill Graham and Chet Helms in San Francisco, helped to turn a rock concert into a special social and cultural event. The advent of light shows, free breakfasts after holiday concerts, and psychedelic advertisements brought a new dimension and image to rock as a musical form. While the media focused on drug use and the untimely deaths of rock stars, the ordinary rock music fan was treated to an unparalleled feast of broad and diverse musical delicacies.

Some of the signal events in the mid-sixties transformation of rock occurred in Los Angeles, where rock fans were no longer forced to a choice between going to PJs to hear Trini Lopez, or to the Whiskey A Go Go to hear Johnny Rivers cover other people's tunes. Suddenly, in May 1966, Jim Morrison and the Doors and Van Morrison and Them cavorted onstage at the Whiskey A Go Go for a sixteen-night run. As Jim and Van sang *Gloria* together in a unique duet, there was little doubt that the rock music world was in the midst of a revolution. When Frank Zappa and the Mothers of Invention played the Whiskey, and a group of psychedelic dancers known as Vito and the Freaks took over the dance floor, it was obvious to everyone that all the old molds had been broken.

Chuck Berry's career in the rock music world was in another of transition during the mid-1960s. He was no longer a *Billboard* Hot 100 hit artist. Although *Nadine, No Particular Place to Go, You Never Can Tell* and *Little Marie* were *Billboard* Hot 100 hits in 1964, by 1965--1966 Chuck's music seemed dated and obsolete in the midst of the musical changes following the British Invasion. Although most rock acts of the late 1960s acknowledged a debt to

119

Chuck Berry In London   **Chess Int'l MGAR-9225 (LP—Holland)**

Chuck's music, he was increasingly placed in the oldies-but-goodies category. As a result, in the period from 1965 to 1970, although Chuck was one of many artists who performed in the new concert halls, he was considered a "nostalgic act." As a performer Chuck was no longer well known enough to close many rock shows. Yet, there were new audiences who discovered and appreciated his music. He also became a popular performer at the many rock festivals which occurred in the late 1960s. One of the ironies of the years from 1965 to 1970 is that Chuck made more money than ever before in his career, but had only one hit, *The Promised Land*, which reached number forty-one on the *Billboard* Hot 100 in January, 1965.

Since the lack of *Billboard* chart records was no longer critically important to Chuck, he instead worked diligently on expanding his songwriting skills. As a consequence, his albums from the mid- to late-1960s all reflect some highly experimental musical tendencies. This innovative bent was obvious in Chuck's attempt to interpret blues tunes. The search for a new sound surfaced on the album **Chuck Berry in London** (Chess 1495). On January 9, 1965, Chuck entered the Pye studios in London and recorded five songs for the album. The London sessions were completed on January 31, when Chuck cut three extraordinary songs. One of Chuck's original tunes from this session, *I Got a Booking*, was a remake of Little Walter's *Key to the Highway*. Chuck had observed Little Walter perform this tune in a number of Chicago clubs, and rewrote it with a rock-and-roll flair. Another unique song was W.C. Handy's *St. Louis Blues*. (This song was wildly applauded by European audiences in the mid-1960s as Chuck toured England and France. At the fabled Olympia Concert Hall in Paris, for example, he was brought back on stage for three encores.) The London sessions ended with the recording of *My Little Love Light*. In all, there were eight songs recorded in London, forming the nucleus of the **Chuck Berry in London** album. In addition, five songs were finished during sessions at the Chess studios, and one song, *Night Beat*, was an old tune from a February, 1958, session, previously issued on Chess LP 1488. When the album finally was released, it contained fourteen songs. It was common for English LPs to have fourteen to sixteen songs, whereas Chess albums contained eleven or twelve cuts. The album had a small note on the front, "Recorded in England," an attempt to merchandize the album to an American audience already mesmerized by the British sound and all things English.

Although the **Chuck Berry in London** album appeared to contain a great deal of commercially appealing material, initially Leonard Chess considered not releasing it at all. He believed that the LP lacked the type of music necessary to captivate a contemporary audience. In reality, the **Chuck Berry in London** LP showcased some of Chuck's strongest commercial material. One song, *Dear Dad*, which appeared briefly in the number ninety-five spot on the *Billboard* Hot 100 in April, 1965, was particularly important because it was Chuck's mid-sixties version of *Maybellene*. Another important change during the recording of this album was Chuck's decision to use a thin-bodied red Gibson guitar. This guitar added a new vitality to Chuck's music, and he was able to include a number of new instrumental riffs in his songs. It was ironic that *Dear Dad*, the most profound song on the album, was added at the last minute as a "filler" tune.

When Chuck rewrote *Let It Shine* and rerecorded it as *My Little Love Light* during the January 5, 1965 London sessions, he effectively incorporated the vocal backup of the Five Dimensions. Chuck had carried with him the memory of a similar arrangement of this song, which he'd heard when he was a young man attending the Antioch Baptist Church. Ray Charles had also previously rewritten and recorded the song, and Chuck's version also reflects Charles' influence. *My Little Love Light* was an interesting blend of black gospel music, combined with the soul of Ray Charles; yet, it went virtually unnoticed in the mid-1960s.

There was a great deal of tension in the air during the recording of **Chuck Berry in London**. Both Leonard Chess and Chuck Berry were perplexed by the inability of Chuck's records to register on the *Billboard* Hot 100. As a result, they began to argue over musical arrangements, the selection of songs, and the manner in which the LPs were packaged. This was a time when Chuck was particularly irritated with Chess Records for including "audience" overdubbing on some of his recordings. Chuck's antipathy extended to genuine live albums, however. As his popularity in Europe increased, Chess Records issued **Chuck Berry On Stage** in France; the album featured a French announcer, a live Parisian audience, and Chuck Berry shouting "Viva la Rock and Roll," "Ole," and "Ah, Paris." Additionally, a great deal of the controversy between Chess and Chuck can be traced to two albums. The first, **Twist with Chuck Berry** (Chess 1465), was issued in June, 1962, and there were critical reactions lamenting the fact that it was merely a repackaging of Chuck's old hits. This album was later reissued again under the title **More Chuck Berry** (Chess LP 1465). Chuck resented the first packaging, because it attempted to capitalize on the twist craze. The later reissue offered fourteen songs but was simply a rehashing of old tunes. Although two of these albums were issued in 1962--63 in an attempt to revive Chuck's career, their release instead led to irrevocable business and artistic differences with Leonard Chess.

The last record Chuck recorded for the Chess label before he signed with Mercury Records was **Fresh Berrys** (Chess 1498). This

Chuck Berry Twist   Chess 1465 (LP)

More Chuck Berry   Chess Int'l P-104 (LP–Holland)

album is a pleasant surprise, because Chuck used a traditional rock-and-roll musical approach fused with blues and calypso influences. *It Wasn't Me*, the lead off song on the album, is reminiscent of the 1950s, but the next number *Run, Joe*, an old Louis Jordan song, demonstrates calypso styling. *Every Day We Rock and Roll* is a remake of *Reelin' and Rockin'*, and it is a fine example of Chuck's continued ability to perform exciting rock songs. Chuck's propensity to experiment is demonstrated in such songs as Johnny Mercer's *One for My Baby (And One More for the Road), Ain't That Just Like a Woman*, in which Chuck reinterpreted versions by Louis Jordan and Fats Domino, and, finally, *Vaya Con Dios*. There were other songs on the **Fresh Berrys** album which were reminiscent of the 1950s. *Merrily We Rock and Roll, Wee Hour Blues*, and *My Mustang Ford* recaptured images of early rock-and-roll lyrics, and these songs were important ones in the continuing evolution of Chuck's songwriting talents. However, rock critics considered only one song an effective example of mid-1960s rock-and-roll: *Welcome Back Pretty Baby*. The song was picked by a number of Top 40 stations as the hit of the week, but it failed to catch on nationally. Since the English release of **Fresh Berrys**, *Welcome Back Pretty Baby* has been left off the album, and a harmonica-laced instrumental, *Sad Day-Long Night*, substituted. As a result, the original album issue is a very collectible item.

Despite cutting twenty-eight songs at the Pye and Chess Studios, 1965 was not a commercially successful year for Chuck Berry. Although the **Chuck Berry in London** album proclaimed that it was recorded in England, almost no one took the time to listen to it. The eleven original songs on the album were a varied set comprised of calypso, blues, rock, and pop influences. As a result, the album proved too eclectic for many rock music fans, and a number of critics complained about the lack of traditional rock music.

In 1965--1966, rock music's transition to folk-rock protest songs, typified by Barry McGuire's *The Eve of Destruction*, had made it difficult for many audiences to appreciate Berry's music. There was a developing pseudo-sophistication among rock music fans, and this led to concert and record products that reflected highly experimental material. Although notably innovative in his own way, Chuck refused to bend to prevailing folk-rock musical trends.

By 1967, the Summer of Love had descended upon San Francisco's Haight-Ashbury District. At the same time, Bill Graham, who opened the Fillmore Auditorium on November 6, 1965, began to experience enormous success in the rock music production field. One of Graham's booking strategies was to hire old blues and rock performers to play the Fillmore. As a result, from March 17 through

March 19, 1967, Chuck Berry performed at the Fillmore with the Grateful Dead, and Johnny Talbot and De Thangs. Prior to each show, Bill Graham spent a few minutes mentioning to the young audience the importance of Chuck Berry's contribution to rock-and-roll music. It was a pleasant gesture on Graham's part, but the audience was usually composed of impatient Grateful Dead fans. In the middle of Chuck Berry's first performance, the Dead's lead guitarist, Jerry Garcia, walked on stage to play backup guitar. Garcia's respectful move immediately evoked a more attentive response to Berry's music. Thus, the stage was set for a five-year period during which Chuck Berry was one of the most popular rock acts in ballrooms all over the United States.

Chuck returned to the Fillmore Auditorium from August 15--17, 1967, and shared the bill with the Steve Miller Blues Band, and the Charles Lloyd Quartet. Shortly after the concert began, Steve Miller joined Chuck for some guitar duets. The Fillmore Auditorium burst into cheers when Boz Scaggs emerged to add some vocal touches to the festivities. From December 26 to 28, 1967, Chuck shared the Fillmore stage with Jim Morrison and the Doors. It was a wild three nights, with Morrison delivering some of his best live performances in an attempt to upstage Chuck; the audience soon realized that Jim Morrison and Chuck Berry were engaged in a musical duel. As a lightshow flashed in the background, Chuck Berry rose to the occasion by delivering a nine-minute version of *Johnny B. Goode* which exhausted the ecstatic Fillmore crowd. A number of San Francisco area bands hoped to perform with Chuck, and this led to several more Fillmore Auditorium engagements for him. On December 29--30, 1967, local favorites like Big Brother and the Holding Company, and the Quicksilver Messenger Service were on the bill with Chuck at the Fillmore. Backstage, Janis Joplin and Chuck discussed the blues, the state of rock music, and the trend toward experimental electric music. Peter Albin of Big Brother and the Holding Company remembered that Janis and Chuck were so intent upon their conversation that each artist had to be virtually pushed onto the stage to perform.

In 1967, there were other important changes in Chuck Berry's career, principal among them being Chuck's departure from Chess Records in order to sign with Mercury for $150,000. Leonard Chess chided Chuck that he would see him in three years when his Mercury contract expired, a remark then basically made in jest, insofar as Chess and Chuck weren't talking to one another in 1967. It was a transitional period in which both men were undergoing radical changes. Chuck did eventually return to Chess Records, although he still harbored bitter feelings over money.

When Chuck agreed to sign with Mercury Records, a former

Chess Records executive, Johnny Sippel, was the person largely responsible for the contract negotiations. The main reason that Chuck signed with Mercury was the extraordinary amount of control he was given in the recording studio. During the negotiations, Quincy Jones was responsible for convincing Mercury Record executives to sign Chuck Berry. Jones believed that Chess Records had not fully developed Chuck Berry's potential as a blues and rock-and-roll superstar. The 1960s was a time of musical change in the rock music business, Jones reasoned, but he saw no reason why Chuck could not continue to write hit songs. As a result of Jones' encouragement, Chuck was able to write a number of new songs and develop more sophisticated recording techniques. Although Chuck Berry's Mercury albums were not critically acclaimed and did not sell very well, nevertheless, they represent excellent musical products.

Perhaps the best Chuck Berry album of the 1960s was **Chuck Berry in Memphis** (Mercury 21123). This was Chuck's second LP for Mercury, following a recut album of Chuck's old songs released as **Golden Hits** (Mercury 21103). The **Golden Hits** album was the worst LP in Chuck's lengthy career. The **Chuck Berry in Memphis** album, however, was an innovative LP with a strong cast of distinguished country and rock session musicians. During his last few years at Chess Records, Chuck had fallen into an uninspired and often tired musical sound, so that Mercury made the decision to record the **Chuck Berry in Memphis** LP at Sam Phillips' Sun Records studios, hoping for some revitalization. Mercury also provided a lush string section to augment Chuck's vocals. The album included seven original songs which were similar to Chuck's early Chess records. The inclusion of a dominant brass section in the remake of *Sweet Little Rock and Roller* was an effective musical idea. Another interesting song was Nat King Cole's *Ramblin' Rose*, through which Chuck was finally able to pay tribute to the vocalist who was the most influential in molding his own singing style. The use of a piano reminiscent of Jerry Lee Lewis' in a song entitled *I Do Really Love You* reflects another important change occurring in this album. In an attempt to capitalize on the popularity of old blues tunes, Mercury wisely included two excellent Chicago blues numbers. One was a remake of the tune Elmore James had made famous, *It Hurts Me Too*. In an odd twist, Chuck is listed as the writer on *It Hurts Me Too*. While he does add some new touches to the blues classic written by Mel London, nevertheless, it essentially remains the same song. When Chuck rewrote Johnny Lee (Sonny Boy) Williamson's *Good Morning Little Schoolgirl* and recorded it as *Our Little Rendezvous*, it was a completely new song. But *It Hurts Me Too* was not substantially altered. Another unique song on this album is *Check Me Out*. This song uses some modified *Johnny B. Goode* and *Carol* guitar riffs, but is essentially a blues tune. There is an uptempo feeling to this song, and it is one of the best original Chuck Berry songs in the 1960s. The diversity of the **Chuck Berry in Memphis** album is demonstrated in the final three songs: *Bring Me Another Drink*, which is a slow, drifting rhythm and blues tune; *Goodnight Well It's Time to Go*, which is a song that is a soulful rendition of the Spaniels old Vee Jay hit; and, finally, *So Long* which is a 1950s rhythm and blues type record with a brassy horn section.

Chuck's next Mercury album was also a very innovative one. After a number of lengthy discussions with a Mercury executive, a sophisticated live album was planned as the next Chuck Berry release. From August 15 to 17, 1967, Mercury Records set up an elaborate selection of sound equipment at Bill Graham's Fillmore Auditorium in San Francisco. The following month Mercury released **Chuck Berry Live at the Fillmore Auditorium** (SR61138). After a brief introduction by Graham, Chuck came on stage to perform one of the strongest concerts of his career. This album was a major turning point in Berry's musical style, as he finally recorded a blues-oriented LP. John Mayall and the Blues Breakers, Peter Green's Fleetwood Mac, and Chicken Shack were just a few English bands who were influenced by Berry's innovative live blues album. The Steve Miller Blues Band, featuring Boz Scaggs, provided the instrumental and vocal support for Berry's songs, and Mercury hoped that a vocal duet with Miller would increase record sales.

As he prepared to record the Fillmore album, Chuck checked into San Francisco's Civic Center Hotel, a small, inexpensive place behind the old Carousel Ballroom. Walking to Market and Van Ness streets to perform for Bill Graham, Chuck Berry was virtually an unrecognized, unnoticed figure. But when Chuck opened the Fillmore concert with an eight-minute medley of *Rockin' at the Fillmore*, (followed by *Everyday I Have the Blues*), he was an immediate success with the audience. He displayed a confident, aggressive stage presence, and he occasionally performed his duck walk amidst thunderous applause. The audience received Chuck warmly, and they were intrigued by his blues music. In particular, there was sustained applause for a bluesy version of Chuck Willis' *C.C. Rider*, and Charles Brown's *Driftin' Blues*. The inclusion of Willie Dixon's *Hoochi' Coochi' Man* brought the Fillmore crowd to its feet. It was the duet with Steve Miller on Elmore James' *It Hurts Me Too* that was the show's highlight, however. Unfortunately, **Chuck Berry Live at the Fillmore Auditorium** did not sell very well, and Chuck was pressured into performing his old hits in subsequent concerts. As a result, rather than heralding the blues phase of Chuck's career, the Fillmore album was Chuck's last serious attempt to interpret the blues. (Of the eleven songs performed on the live album, the only old Chuck Berry

A rock legend performing in the 1960s.

hit was *Johnny B. Goode*; Mercury Records was so unfamiliar with Chuck's hit material that *Johnny B. Goode* was misspelled.)

In 1967–1968, Chuck Berry was in demand for live performances in a number of new clubs. After playing at the Academy of Music in Brooklyn in 1967, Chuck appeared on WOR-TV in New York City in a television film entitled "From the Bitter End." The footage from this club appearance appealed to the folk-rock musical collectors of the late 1960s. Chuck also appeared on "Upbeat," a more traditional rock-and-roll show syndicated from WNEW-TV. In addition to these concerts, there were rave newspaper reviews for concerts in 1968 at New York's Generation Club, the Anderson Theater, and the Village Gate.

In 1968, Chuck returned to Bill Graham's Fillmore Auditorium for a concert with the Steve Miller Blues Band. Unlike the previous year's concert, Chuck sang mostly his old hits, but seemed generally disinterested in the audience's reaction to his music. The Fillmore crowd was amazingly quiet during Chuck's performance; there was little doubt that Chuck's old hits were intriguing to an audience used to endless electric guitar solos and highly experimental musical sounds. Chuck Berry's short songs were a refreshing break from the tedious drone of acid rock. As a result, Chuck intensified his concert schedule and increasingly ignored the recording studio.

The resurgence of Berry's live performances was a curious phenomenon in the late 1960s. The audiences who idolized Bob Dylan, the Beatles, and the Rolling Stones were becoming increasingly aware of the roots of rock music. Chuck Berry, as one of the most durable Founding Fathers of rock music, could fill his concerts with medleys of such hits as *Johnny B. Goode, Roll Over Beethoven, Rock and Roll Music, School Day* and *Maybellene*. This type of concert in turn revived the sales of Chuck's early Chess LPs. As a result, there were many disputes between Chuck and Mercury executives. A good example of these differences surfaced when Chuck suddenly appeared in Mercury's accounting department demanding an immediate check for his recordings. Mercury's accounting department attempted to explain to Chuck that royalty checks were issued every six months. When Chuck continued to argue over his royalties, Mercury simply issued a check. This story points up the basic differences between the Chess and Mercury labels. Leonard Chess routinely wrote out checks on demand, or often paid Chuck in cash; Mercury had carefully established corporate policies regarding royalty payments. Such monetary disagreements eventually spilled over into the artistic side of Chuck's life, and he found it increasingly difficult to record hit material.

One of the intriguing aspects of Chuck's career at Mercury centers around his unissued recordings, about which there has been very little publicity. In 1966, Mercury did not release *Campus Cookie*, because they did not believe that it was a commercially viable product. Mercury also did not release recordings of a number of Chuck's old hit songs. Even after Chuck rerecorded *Brown-Eyed Handsome Man, Almost Grown*, and *Around and Around*, Mercury executives left these songs off his future albums because they considered the remakes as inferior. In 1967, *Flying Home* became another unreleased studio cut. In 1968, an instrumental version of *Put Her Down*, and a slow version of *Concerto in B. Goode* were not immediately released to the general public; Chuck had hurriedly recorded and shipped them to Chicago, informing Mercury that they were for his new album!

In November, 1968, to capitalize on Chuck Berry's revived reputation as a dynamic concert performer, Mercury Records released **From St. Louis to Frisco** (SR61176). The album was a major disappointment, because he was not strong enough in either the blues or rock idiom. There were, however, a number of intriguing songs on this LP. *My Tambourine*, for example, was an earlier and cleaner version of Berry's 1972 million selling record *My Ding A Ling*. Another interesting song was *I Love Her, I Love Her*, which bore a striking resemblance to Elvis Presley's song *Suspicious Minds*. The twelve songs on this album were all original Chuck Berry compositions, but the spark and vitality of the 1950s and early 1960s was no longer to be found.

In June, 1969, Mercury released **Concerto in B. Goode** (SR-61223). This LP was recorded entirely at Berry Park, Chuck's home in Wentzville, Missouri, where he had installed elaborate recording equipment in 1968. The liner notes made reference to the number of Chuck Berry songs the Beatles had performed and recorded. Yet, the album had no connection with the Beatles, or with 1960s rock-and-roll. The first side contained four Chuck Berry originals, and included three excellent blues tunes: *My Woman, It's Too Dark in There*, and *Put Her Down*. The second side was a rambling and free-flowing eighteen-minute musical piece entitled *Concerto in B. Goode*. It was an indulgent and meaningless piece of music used to fill the album, which enjoyed no significant airplay at all. When Mercury Records announced that the single *It's Too Dark in There* backed with *Good Lookin' Woman* was not going to be released, there were renewed rumors of strife between Berry and Mercury.

Despite his problems with Mercury, Chuck continued to perform in a number of different clubs and concert halls.

In 1969, for example, Chuck toured extensively in the U.S. and Canada. He appeared with the Elvin Bishop group at Hunter College in New York City, and headlined a special performance in New

York's Central Park. When Bill Graham opened the Fillmore East in New York, Berry was one of the featured acts in this new rock showcase. In Hollywood, Chuck appeared in concert at the fabled Sunset Boulevard rock palace, the Whiskey A-Go-Go. A haven for the hip Hollywood set, the Whiskey was instrumental in the emergence of such 1960s rock groups as the Doors, Canned Heat, and the Mothers of Invention.

In August, 1969, the Woodstock Festival brought a new era to rock music. The mere mention of Woodstock evokes images of a generation nurtured on peace, love, and prosperity. Over 400,000 people endured three days of rain, thunderstorms, and generally unpleasant surroundings to hear such rock acts as the Who, Jimi Hendrix, Country Joe and the Fish, Joan Baez, Sly Stone, and many others in a much celebrated musical extravaganza. Woodstock was, in the end, only one of many rock festivals held between 1967 and 1971 (there were some 300 major outdoor rock concerts drawing more than three million people), but it did change the attitudes of the major record companies concerning their artists. At Warner Bros., for example, a decision was made to sign Van Morrison to a fifteen-year recording contract. This decision was surprising, because when Van's group, Them, recorded for London Records, they had only three minor hit records: *Gloria*, which was number seventy-one on the *Billboard* Hot 100; *Mystic Eyes*, which was thirty-three; and *Here Comes the Night*, which reached the number twenty-four position. On the strength of these early Them records, Van was scouted by a number of record companies. Because he had worked with an American producer and songwriter, Bert Berns, Van decided to move to New York City. Bert Berns owned Bang/Short Records, and he spent a considerable amount of time convincing Van to sign with his label. Eventually Van became a solo artist for Bang Records. With Bang he had only two hit records, and showed no potential for becoming a rock superstar. Warner, however, believed that Van was a quality artist who would add prestige to the Warner label. His record sales were of no concern to Warner's management, because they speculated that rock music was in the midst of an important transition.

The public's response to the rock music festivals of the late 1960s prompted the major recording companies like Warner Brothers to embark on a new style of merchandizing campaign. By advertising in small magazines and rock newspapers, Warner developed the reputation as the people's record label. Taking account of the impact of *Rolling Stone* magazine, Warner placed full-page ads suggesting that they were virtually giving their product away for only a few dollars. Most of these advertisements featured the Warner sampler albums which, like the rock music festival, offered single cuts by eleven on up to twenty-two different artists. It was a new means of merchandising rock music, and a highly successful one.

The major record companies also used the rock festival as a showcase for new talent, and soon Janis Joplin, Santana, Crosby, Stills, Nash and Young, and Grand Funk Railroad were major rock acts. Rock festivals likewise offered older artists like Little Richard, Big Mama Thornton, Lester Flatt, Earl Scruggs, and Chuck Berry a new forum for their music. It was yet another musical renaissance, creating new energies and reviving old musical directions.

The Monterey Pop Festival in June, 1967, was not the first, but it was the most significant early outdoor extravaganza. The brainchild of Alan Pariser, a Los Angeles promoter, Monterey Pop was supported by $10,000 loans from producer Lou Adler, Mamas and the Papas' vocalist John Phillips, folk duo Simon and Garfunkel, and pop rocker Johnny Rivers. The loans were to be repaid with gate receipts. The festival was set up as a nonprofit charity event, and virtually every major rock act in America was invited to perform. When Chuck Berry was contacted, he informed the Monterey Pop board of directors that he did not perform in charity concerts.

When the Monterey Pop Festival took place on June 16, 17, 18, such groups as the Paul Butterfield Blues Band, the recently formed Electric Flag, Big Brother and the Holding Company featuring Janis Joplin, and Canned Heat became best-selling recording artists. Columbia Records signed every act at the Monterey Pop Festival that did not have a recording contract. Had Chuck Berry elected to perform in Monterey, he might have revived his dormant record sales. Although Chuck had no difficulty in securing concert appearances, there is reason to believe that Monterey Pop might have helped promote his sagging LP and 45 releases. Johnny Rivers had million selling hits with *Memphis* and *Maybellene* in 1963--1964, and it was Rivers who took advantage of the Monterey concert setting to perform his versions of Chuck Berry's songs. Although Johnny Rivers has never been critically acclaimed for his cover records, nonetheless, his shrewd ability to choose classic rock-and-roll songs has resulted in more than thirty best-selling albums for him. Johnny Rivers realized, as Chuck Berry did not, that by playing the old rock classics at Monterey, he would again generate strong album sales.

One of the most successful concert productions of the era was the Miami Pop Festival of December 28--30, 1968. This was the first major festival to succeed outside of California, and it attracted more than 100,000 musical die-hards to the Miami-Fort Lauderdale area. A local race track, Gulfstream Park, was the site of the Miami Festival, and the three-day musical lineup included all types of music. Country Joe and the Fish, the Grateful Dead, the Iron Butterfly,

Procol Harum, Steppenwolf, Terry Reid, and Fleetwood Mac were the most significant rock acts. There were also pop artists like the Turtles, the Grass Roots, and Three Dog Night. The Paul Butterfield Blues Band, the James Cotton Band, and Booker T. and the MGs represented yet another form of music. Chuck Berry's performance at the Miami Pop Festival was one of the most energetic he had delivered in some time. The setting, the challenge of other top-level professional musicians, and the guaranteed concert fee prompted Chuck to sing, dance, and perform as he had in the late 1950s. After he finished *Johnny B. Goode*, the crowd accorded Chuck a standing ovation.

The 1969 Seattle Pop Festival was the second successful large-scale concert in the Pacific Northwest. In 1968, the Sky River Festival had inaugurated rock festivals in Seattle. The following year, Chuck Berry shared the stage with the Doors, Led Zeppelin, and Chicago. Jimmy Page of Led Zeppelin expressed the feelings of many musicians when he told a *Seattle Times* reporter that playing with Chuck Berry was one of the highlights of his musical career.

The festival season ended during the summer of 1969 with two rock extravaganzas: The Texas International Pop Festival, and New Orleans Pop. Chuck Berry performed at the New Orleans festival, held in Prairieville, Louisiana. Unlike the other major rock concerts, it drew only about 30,000 fans, and was an extremely orderly festival with only a few drug-related arrests. During the concert, there was a great deal of controversy over the more than 100 local law enforcement officers dressed as hippies, who searched through the crowd for drug pushers. Those who were booked were held on an excessive bail of $50,000; a number of people who were arrested complained to the judge that they had merely sold entire lids of marijuana for five dollars, simply to put gas in their cars. In the midst of the New Orleans Pop Festival, Chuck Berry flew into town, performed one night, and left in the early morning for another concert. It was obvious to Chuck that the New Orleans and the Toronto Rock and Roll Revival Show, featuring John Lennon's Plastic Ono Band, brought an end in 1969 to the festival phase of rock-and-roll music.

The festival years were important ones for Chuck and his music. Sales of the old Chess LPs increased due to the audience's nostalgic desire to hear *Johnny B. Goode, Sweet Little Sixteen*, and *Rock and Roll Music*. (The recent Mercury albums, however, languished in record store bins, and Chuck considered returning to Chess Records.) The festival years also helped extend Berry's influence upon a number of diverse musical artists in the 1960s. One example involves record producer Jon Landau, who persuaded the MC 5 to record

Chuck on the cover of *Rolling Stone*, June 1969.

Chuck's *Back in the USA*. The Motor City 5 was an excellent Detroit band, who were originally part of the Trans Love commune. Their manager, John Sinclair, was a member of the White Panther political party, and one of America's best known political radicals in the 1960s. Eventually, rock critic-turned-producer Landau persuaded the MC 5 to drop their political affectations, and to turn to recording solid rock-and-roll music. The MC 5 was signed to a recording contract with Atlantic, and an album entitled **Back in the USA**, featuring the Chuck Berry song as the hit single, did very well in counterculture circles. The MC 5, however, was an atrocious live band, and they were not well received in concert. After a disastrous European tour in 1972, the MC 5 retired from the entertainment business. The ironic aspect of this band's short-lived career is that they considered Chuck Berry's music the most political and revolutionary of all.

In 1968, the Beatles offered a similar tribute to Chuck's song *Back in the USA*. The Beatles issued a double album simply called **The Beatles**, but commonly known as the "White Album." It was released with a Berryesque tune, *Back in the USSR*, which had been inspired by *Back in the USA*, and written by Paul McCartney while in Rishikesh, India. The following year, the Beatles' **Abbey Road** album included a song called *Come Together*, which was closely adapted from Berry's *You Can't Catch Me*. Arc, Berry's music publisher, sued Apple Records and John Lennon and Paul McCartney for lifting the first two lyrical lines and the opening melody from *You Can't Catch Me* and incorporating it into *Come Together*. The suit was amicably settled when John Lennon agreed to record a number of Berry songs on a projected oldies album. Although another Beatle song, *Get Back*, was also Berry-inspired (by *Roll Over Beethoven*), there was no legal action over this song. When the Beatles broke up in 1970, there were seven unreleased Berry songs tucked away from previous recording sessions. This was an excellent indication of Chuck's influence upon the most popular group in rock music history.

As attention refocused upon Chuck Berry's career in the late 1960s, he became more cooperative during interviews with the rock press. On Friday, May 9, 1969, Chuck visited the University of California, Berkeley, Student Union lounge, and answered questions in an impromptu press conference. Chuck was scheduled to perform at UC, and the press conference was billed as a lecture. He quickly dispensed with his "lecture" and spontaneously answered questions from the audience. This was an unusual occasion, because Chuck was not known as a cooperative interviewee. Greil Marcus edited the material for *Rolling Stone* magazine, and the result was an excellent, in-depth article on rock music's master showman. Amidst a barrage of questions, Chuck selected his words carefully, recounting how he entered the music business, among other topics. A question on whether or not his musical style had changed since the advent of the Beatles prompted Chuck to remark: "I have not found it necessary to change my style in the last seven years." Chuck then pointed out that he wrote *Nadine* and *No Particular Place to Go*, which were 1964 hits, to evoke images of *Maybellene* and *School Day*. This was an interesting insight into Chuck Berry's approach to songwriting; he apparently believed that a basic reworking of ideas and themes which had already produced hits would result in new hit records.

The most revealing parts of the *Rolling Stone* interview were Chuck Berry's reflections on rock music. He stated his belief that rock-and-roll was an important means of personal communication, and he spent an inordinate amount of time lecturing his audience on peace, love, and race relations. He also talked about his autobiography, commenting that he had accumulated 220 pages of reflections on his years in the music business. Chuck bemoaned his decision to sign with Mercury Records, and informed the audience that he had kept in constant touch with Chess Records. When the interview terminated, there was little doubt that Chuck Berry would soon return to record for the Chess label. During the UC, Berkeley, interview, Chuck was the picture of a content person, and he spoke fondly of Berry Park in Wentzville, Missouri. "It's about a half a million dollar estate," Chuck said, " . . . it's a country club, pool, nightclub, motel . . . so it's very popular." Chuck Berry was obviously happy about the control that he was finally able to exert over his life.

The Mercury Records years had not been productive ones for Chuck Berry. Although some of his music was innovative and exciting, nevertheless, Mercury was never able to effectively market Chuck Berry's songs. There were also a number of arguments over money, and some Mercury executives believed that Chuck was no longer a productive artist. When Chuck returned to Chess Records, some changes had taken place at his old label. Shortly after Chuck separated from Chess, it was sold to the GRT tape corporation for $10 million. While this did not bother Chuck, nevertheless, it ended the small, family atmosphere at Chess Records. It was now part of a mammoth and impersonal corporation, and this made it more difficult to recapture the old Chuck Berry hit sound.

In September, 1970, Chuck returned to the Chess label with the release of an album appropriately called **Back Home** (LPS1550). The album was recorded in February, 1970 and featured nine original Chuck Berry compositions. The album's liner notes, by rock journalist Michael Lydon, hailed Chuck Berry as a pioneer artist who was returning with new material. The best song on the **Back Home** album was *Tulane*, the story of a young couple running a novelty store, who also sold drugs under the counter. In a tongue-in-cheek parody of the psychedelic lifestyle that he had observed in San Francisco's Haight-Ashbury district, Chuck wove the story of a counterculture business venture that goes awry. When Berry urged the young couple to "get a lawyer in the thick of politics," he made a rare political statement concerning America. In retrospect, *Tulane* was much like 1950s Berry songs which urged teenagers to get out into the streets. Critics recognized neither the message nor the sophistication of Chuck's lyrics, however. Perhaps the most intriguing aspect of the **Back Home** album is the manner in which Chuck reminisced about his own plight in the courts. In a song entitled *Have Mercy Judge*, he points out the double standard of justice for blacks, musicians, and young people. The remainder of the material on the **Back Home** album was directed to a blues audience. There was only one attempt to bring back the old songs, a tune entitled *I'm a Rocker*.

In the late 1960s and 1970s, another important change in the rock music business occurred when a New York promoter named Richard Nader bankrolled a series of "oldies-but-goodies" concerts. By featuring a large number of early rock musicians, these concerts brought about a 1950s musical revival. Soon, the television show "Happy Days" immortalized the music and helped to revive Chuck's dormant record sales. At the same time, Richard Nader complained that Chuck was very difficult to work with in a concert setting. The personal feuds between Chuck and Nader were legendary ones and, when Nader sent a film crew to Berry Park to film a sequence for the movie, "Let the Good Times Roll," Chuck was highly uncooperative. The movie director, Sid Levin, spent some time touring with Chuck in Oregon, and then he flew to St. Louis to film the short sequence at Berry Park. The result was a very uncomfortable experience for Levin and his crew. They were subjected to some of the volatile personal moods that Berry has been famous for in his career. When one cameraman finished shooting the final sequence, he hurt his eye and left Berry Park to find a doctor. When the camera crew returned to Berry Park, Chuck was standing at the chain-link fence holding a rifle. Chuck has reminisced about this incident as if it were a joke, and he tells the story of the Southern Sheriff who had run him out of a Louisiana town with a shotgun as a counterpoint. There was in fact strong symbolism to Chuck's story, and his brandishment of the gun: he was letting Richard Nader and Sid Levin know that Chuck Berry was now the sheriff.

As the 1970s dawned, Chuck Berry was a wealthy man who was assured of continued financial security through concert fees. Although his new records did not sell very well, nevertheless, the 1970s witnessed a resurgence of Chuck Berry's 1950s music. The demand was so great that Chess Records released the two LP set, **Golden Decade Volume 2** and **Golden Decade Volume 3** in 1973-- 1974, containing forty-eight songs and including virtually every important tune not already included on **Chuck Berry's Golden Decade** (Chess 1514D), which had been issued in March, 1967.

In sum, the period from 1965 to 1970 was an interesting one in Chuck Berry's life. He attempted to reassert his musical roots by turning out a number of excellent blues songs on his Mercury albums. When this music did not sell very well, Chuck shrewdly retreated to the oldies-but-goodies format and resurrected such hits as *Sweet Little Sixteen, Roll Over Beethoven, Carol,* and *Rock and Roll Music* for concert audiences. As he approached the 1970s, there was often trepidation in Chuck's voice when he discussed his future career.

CHAPTER 8

THE OLDIES FORMAT
AND SUPERSTAR RECOGNITION:
THE 1970S AND 1980S

The 1970s and 1980s were at last decades of superstar recognition for Chuck Berry. The oldies-but-goodies format dominated the music scene, so that many of Chuck's concerts featured his older songs. The demand for such songs as *Johnny B. Goode, School Day* and *Rock and Roll Music* made it difficult for Chuck to place new songs on the *Billboard* Hot 100. Yet, despite the lack of new chart records, virtually every important rock musician paid tribute to Chuck's enormous influence. Ian McDonald of Foreigner summed up the feeling of many musicians: "When I was 18 I was singing *Roll Over Beethoven* just like everyone else." Bill Wyman pointed out that when the Rolling Stones rehearsed in the early 1970s, they began each rehearsal by playing a number of Chuck Berry songs. George Thorogood paid Chuck Berry the ultimate professional compliment when he suggested that Chuck had written all the important rock songs. "Why should I write songs when Chuck Berry already wrote them all," Thorogood remarked. Elvis Presley reflected to a friend in Las Vegas in 1971: "Chuck Berry's *Johnny B. Goode* is my favorite concert song, because its lyrics remind me of home. I just wish I could express my feelings the way Chuck Berry does." The universal acclaim for Chuck's music in the early 1970s guaranteed continued movie, television, and concert appearances, Chuck's own musical output, in terms of original work, was not particularly memorable, however.

The best analysis of Chuck Berry's music in the 1970s was provided by Rolling Stones' bass guitarist Bill Wyman. "I really haven't bought his records in the last ten years," Wyman commented, "because they always seemed lazy attempts to rehash old material." Although Wyman emphasized that Chuck was still an exciting live act, he believed that Berry was no longer capable of writing and recording hit records. Wyman explained that Berry was too cost conscious, and as a result this led to a number of mediocre concerts. An example of this occurred in Monterey, California, in the early 1970s, when a San Francisco oldies band, Butch Whacks and the Glass

San Francisco Dues

Chess CH-50008 (LP)

Packs, backed Chuck in a concert. After Butch Whacks and the Glass Packs finished their set, Chuck walked on stage and motioned to the drummer to start a song. Since the pickup band had not previously met Chuck, they had no idea what songs he was going to perform. After a forty-minute set, Chuck invited a portion of the audience to dance on stage as he played *Sweet Little Sixteen*. Soon, almost a hundred people were dancing on the stage, and Chuck discretely exited the Monterey Fairgrounds. He was driving south on Highway 1 in his rental car when the concert ended. Chuck Berry's disinterest in his concert performances, and his use of mediocre pickup bands often lowered the quality of his appearances in the 1970s and 1980s.

Many of the albums released on Chess Records in the 1970s lacked new and innovative material. The lyrical direction and musical composition of Chuck's music was merely a restatement of old themes and ideas. A good example of this tendency was demonstrated in **The London Chuck Berry Sessions** (Chess CH60020) album. This LP combined a number of old songs with some hastily conceived new ones. The first tune, *Let's Boogie*, was an allegorical tale similar to many of Chuck's 1950s songs. The album also included live versions of *Reelin' and Rockin'*, *My Ding-A-Ling*, and *Johnny B. Goode*, recorded during a show at the Lanchester Arts Festival in Coventry, England. A novelty in this LP, *My Ding-A-Ling*, became a number one hit in England and the United States, and it was Chuck Berry's first legitimate gold record. In 1972, after three decades in the entertainment business, Chuck had finally reached the ultimate plateau with a gold record. Actually, Chuck first heard *My Ding A Ling* in 1954 when the Bees' version of *Toy Bell* was a hit on the *Billboard* rhythm and blues charts. The song was written by Fats Domino's band leader, David Bartholomew, and it was rewritten and recorded by Chuck in the mid-1960s as *My Tambourine*. Johnny Sippel of Mercury Records recalled that Chuck had performed the song for years, and he remembered hearing it played in the Chess studios. Irving Green, the president of Mercury Records, recollected that Chuck had included *My Ding A Ling* on a tape that he submitted to Mercury in 1954, when the label was reluctant to sign him. Everyone was surprised when *My Ding A Ling* sold two million copies, seventeen years after *Maybellene* was released as Chuck Berry's first 45 record.

In 1972, after his return from Mercury Records, Chuck's second Chess album, **San Francisco Dues** (Chess 50008), turned out to be one of the finest LPs in his career. In addition to writing the ten songs on the album, Chuck also produced it. In an attempt to revive Chuck's hit-making record successes of the 1950s, Chess Records employed Johnny Johnson as the piano player on this album. Johnson's piano was reminiscent of Fats Domino's New Orleans music, and this created an unusually exciting sound on many of the album's songs. Another innovative touch to **San Francisco Dues** was a change in recording location. Rather than using Chess' Chicago Studios, the album was recorded at the Lansing Sound Company, Lansing, Michigan. This studio had an outstanding reputation amongst Detroit and Chicago blues performers.

An example of the positive blues influence upon Chuck's recording techniques was demonstrated in the album's lead song, *Oh Louisiana*. This song was a combination of New Orleans rhythm and blues music with Chicago blues. The superior quality of Chuck's guitar playing was evident in a song entitled *Your Lick*. One of Chuck Berry's traits as a songwriter was to chronicle changes in American popular culture. In three original songs, *Lonely School Days, Viva Rock and Roll,* and *Festival,* Chuck reflected on the musical evolution in rock-and-roll during the 1960s. In *Festival,* Chuck also made some interesting references to Jimi Hendrix and Janis Joplin. In addition, this song reveals that Chuck viewed himself as a rock music survivor. Perhaps the most interesting song on **San Fransicso Dues**, however, was *Bordeaux in My Pirough*, a tribute to Chuck's friend Jean-Pierre Ravelli. The song combined a New Orleans musical flair with traditional rock-and-roll music, and blended the diverse music influences of Fats Domino, Rockin Sydney, Huey "Piano Smith," Doug Kershaw, Professor Longhair, and the Neville Brothers into a highly original Chuck Berry song. Despite this, the song failed to make the charts, and the album sold poorly. As a result, Chuck was forced to accept a rigorous concert schedule in order to continue to support his family and fund the changes he was making at Berry Park.

The early 1970s was an important period in Chuck's career. After Chess Records was purchased by GRT, there was a continual decline in his record sales. GRT was a large tape company which had little knowledge of the record business, failed to effectively merchandise Chuck Berry's music, and eventually went bankrupt. Despite his business problems in 1970 and 1971, Chuck emerged as a television personality, and he was a frequent guest on the Dick Cavett and Mike Douglas shows. This intensified TV exposure helped to increase Chuck's concert schedule, and he was making more money that any other time in his career.

As a result of new new-found TV fame, the Hilton Hotel in Las Vegas hired Chuck to play in its lounge. During one of Elvis Presley's engagements, a startled crowd watching Chuck perform suddenly saw Elvis and Sammy Davis, Jr. dance across the back of the stage. This was Elvis' way of letting people know that Chuck Berry was still an important musical influence. There were many other artists who

At the Olympia in Paris, February 1975.

A reflective moment in the 1970s.

continued to acknowledge Chuck's importance to the contemporary rock world. During a 1970 Madison Square Garden concert, for example, Mick Jagger, the lead singer in the Rolling Stones, remarked that Chuck Berry's records were played in rehearsal sessions to bring the Stones back to the basic structure of rock-and-roll music. When Jagger was questioned about the inclusion of Chuck Berry songs on the Stones' **Get Yer Ya-Ya's Out** album, he stated that *Carol* and *Little Queenie* were included to acknowledge Chuck as the driving force behind their music. The Berry influence, Jagger stated, was one of the reasons that the Stones were still a successful rock-and-roll band.

There were many other artists who used Berry's music for inspiration. When Creedence Clearwater Revival's lead singer, John Fogerty, wrote *Travelin' Band*, it was a tribute to Chuck Berry's lyrical and musical contribution to rock-and-roll. Another Creedence Clearwater Revival song, *It Came Out of the Sky*, was described by John Fogerty as having a Chuck Berry feeling. In the 1960s, Eric Burden and the Animals' *She'll Return It* was a remake of *Memphis, Tennessee*. John Kay and Steppenwolf also wrote and recorded a song entitled *Berry Rides Again*. These examples are indicative of Chuck's enormous musical influence in the development of rock music from the 1960s into the 1980s.

The dominant influence that Chuck had upon John Lennon was demonstrated on February 23, 1972, when John and Yoko Ono co-hosted the "Mike Douglas Show." Chuck Berry appeared with John on stage, and they sang *Memphis* and *Johnny B. Goode*. During the introduction, John referred to Chuck as "My hero." Lennon's affectionate reference to Berry as the father of rock-and-roll music was all but lost in the swirling controversy over Lennon's politics, and the well-publicized attempt by the U.S. government to deport him. Earlier in the 1970s, John Lennon listened constantly to Chuck Berry 45s and LPs, and he wrote a number of unpublished songs with Berryesque themes. A good example of Lennon's infatuation with Chuck's music occurred on the afternoon of October 28, 1971, as John sat on a shag rug in his seventeenth-floor suite in New York's St. Regis Hotel. For three hours, Lennon labored over a song about Chuck Berry and Bo Diddley. Finally, in a fit of rage, he flushed the small pieces of paper containing the song's lyrics down the toilet. No one knows exactly what Lennon's lyrics said about Chuck and Bo, but the song was obviously a tribute to two of rock music's pioneers. As he left the St. Regis Hotel for a night on the town, Lennon remarked to a close friend: "Elvis was my idol. Chuck Berry was my teacher."

One of the most significant expressions of John Lennon's admiration for Chuck Berry was the song *New York City*, recorded for

America's Hottest Wax   Reelin' (LP—bootleg)

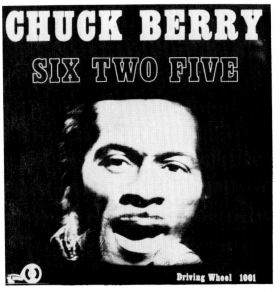

Six Two Five   Driving Wheel 1001 (LP—bootleg)

the album **Some Time in New York City**, a tribute to Berry's innovative musical genius. During the 1970s, Lennon was continually rethinking his music, the direction of his career, and the meaning of his life. Chuck Berry obviously remained an important intellectual influence on him during this period.

During a number of his interviews, John Lennon had urged the British people to recognize the talent and performing genius of Chuck Berry. As a result of Lennon's statements, Chuck began to appear more frequently in England and throughout Europe. The Hardrock Cafe in Copenhagen was one of Chuck's favorite performing venues. One of his best concerts was on July 22, 1972, when he performed on the BBC TV show, "Sounds for Saturday." When this program was aired, it was taped by Driving Wheel Records, which issued an excellent bootleg album entitled **Six Two Five**. The songs included from this forty-five-minute show were *Roll Over Beethoven, Sweet Little Sixteen, Memphis, Tennessee, South of the Border, Beer Drinkin' Woman, Let It Rock, Mean Old World, Carol, Liverpool Drive, Nadine, Bye Bye Johnny, Goodnight Sweetheart*, and *Johnny B. Goode*. The LP was so successful in Europe that it was reissued by Maybellene Records. Another interesting English bootleg LP is the **Rare Berries** album, issued on Kozmik Records. Although **Rare Berries** did not contain any unreleased songs, nevertheless it was an important item to English and European collectors, as it contained a number of difficult to find songs.

In 1980, Reelin Records issued another important bootleg called **Chuck Berry: America's Hottest Wax, Rare and Unreleased Tracks, 1955--1963**. The songs on this record originated from a session tape housed in the Chess Records studios, a tape apparently played by a number of people interested in its contents. When the Rolling Stones recorded in the Chess studios in the mid-1960s, for example, they listened to this tape and were impressed with the alternate cuts of *Sweet Little Sixteen, Reelin' and Rockin'*, and *Rock and Roll Music*. One of the most interesting songs on the album was a cut of *Brown-Eyed Handsome Man*, the same song that appeared on the Chess LP **On Stage**. On the bootleg LP, however, *Brown-Eyed Handsome Man* appears for the first time without a live audience. No one is precisely sure how the tape was eventually turned into a bootleg LP; it was pressed in Holland and suddenly surfaced in London record shops. One story alleges that Rolling Stones' guitarist Keith Richards loaned the tape to Reelin' Records, another suggests that the Dutch bootlegger paid a princely sum to a Chess Records underling for a copy. There is no way of verifying these stories. In a bizarre twist, Marshall Chess sold the rights to the LP to Charly Records and, in 1983, a legitimate version of this bootleg was released to the general public.

What **America's Hottest Wax** demonstrated was that Chuck Berry's best music was recorded in a blues vein, and that Leonard Chess recut many of the songs to appeal to a predominantly middle-class, white record-buying audience. In addition, Chess's profit-oriented approach prompted him to release only straight-ahead rock-and-roll numbers. While some have argued that the blues songs *were* released – as B sides to Chuck's records – nevertheless, there was no attempt to promote these songs. To Leonard Chess, Chuck Berry's blues music was simply filler to be thrown away on the B-side of hit record releases. To the average Chuck Berry fan, though, these blues songs were a delightful bonus at a time when it was extremely difficult to obtain good blues music. Thus, the average white, teen-age record buyer was perhaps first introduced to the blues in the 1950s when he or she played the flip side of one of Chuck's hit records.

By the 1970s, many unreleased Chuck Berry recordings were available on bootleg LPs or were issued by Chess Records on compilation albums. Yet, a number of Berry's songs remained unreleased due to their uneven quality. A good example of a substandard recording was Chuck's version of *It Ain't None of Your Business*, which sounded almost identical to a 1965 recording, *It's My Own Business*. Leonard Chess at least attempted to maintain product quality in merchandising Chuck's music, whereas Mercury Records released a number of very poor Berry records.

As a result of the compilation albums, which he disliked, Chuck refused a request to have his performance at the Montreux Jazz Festival included on a Chess LP entitled **Blues Avalanche** (Chess 2CH 60015). When Chuck performed at the Montreux Festival, he was backed by Lafayette Leake on piano, Fred Below, Jr., on drums, Louis Myers on guitar, and Willie Dixon on bass. During the Festival, Chuck performed *Everyday I Have the Blues*, with T-Bone Walker supplying the vocal. It is unfortunate that the music from this supergroup was not included on the Chess LP, but there are indications that the performances were below standard anyway. Since Chuck would not give his permission to use these songs, the double album was released with material by Bo Diddley, Muddy Waters, Koko Taylor, and T-Bone Walker. In the 1970s, Chess Records finally realized that they had missed an important market by not releasing and promoting many of Chuck's blues recordings. Consequently, **Golden Decade Volume 3** was released in 1974 as a double album, virtually a blues history of Chuck Berry's career.

Despite his problems with Chess Records, Chuck Berry's music continued to sell very well in European markets. The main reason for the return of Chuck's music was the advent of the first "Rock

Motorvatin'   Chess 9286 690 (LP—England)

and Roll Revival Show" in the United States. On October 18, 1969, Richard Nader's "Rock and Roll Revival Show" in New York's Madison Square Garden had drawn a sellout crowd. A very successful album from this concert led to a resurgence of oldies music in America and Europe. During the next five years, there were seventeen "Rock and Roll Revival Shows," and Chuck Berry headlined seven of these extravaganzas. This helped to revive the European concert and record-buying market, and Chuck spent much of the 1970s concentrating upon foreign engagements. In Sweden, Norway and Holland, the Chuck Berry sound was instrumental in the rise of a number of rock music bands. In Antwerp, Belgium, a young man who managed rock groups, Willy Pauwels, used Chuck Berry records to train his bands for public appearances. Throughout Europe, the Chuck Berry sound was the key to the development of rock-and-roll music. Naturally, Chuck benefited from his adulation: his record sales increased yearly. In 1977, an album issued in the United Kingdom entitled **Motorvatin'** contained twenty-two classic Berry songs from the 1950s and 1960s, and it entered the Top 10 LP charts in England. The **Motorvatin'** album produced a gold record for Chuck (who proudly hung it in his office at Berry Park), and is a good indication of Chuck's drawing power in Europe.

In 1972, while touring England, Chuck attempted to capitalize on his recent European popularity by recording an LP at London's Pye Studios. For a year, rumors swirled around the music business to the effect that the Rolling Stones would provide the backup music on Chuck's new album. It is impossible to verify whether or not Chuck and the Rolling Stones agreed on a joint album. In Paris, Chuck's admirer and close friend, Jean-Pierre Ravelli, was beseiged with requests from Berry and Stones fans for information on the album. Ravelli has refused to disclose if an album was in fact being considered, and whether or not there were differences between Chuck and Mick Jagger which prevented it. In public interviews, Chuck has often referred to Jagger in a scurrilous manner, which has prompted many critics to report a personality conflict between Chuck and Mick. The true story may never be known, but the evidence suggests that an album was in the planning stages. Perhaps the constant touring, recording, and attention to business which these rock-and-roll conglomerates engaged in made such an album an impossibility.

In order to meet the demand for a new Chuck Berry album, Chess Records decided to release a "live in concert" LP. In May, 1972, **The London Chuck Berry Sessions** (Chess 60020) was released to the general public. The album contained a live side, recorded at the Lanchester Arts Festival in Coventry, England, which included a seven-minute ten-second version of *Reelin' and Rockin'*, an eleven-minute-plus performance of *My Ding-A-Ling*, and an excellent version of *Johnny B. Goode*. This LP was one of Chuck's best-selling products, and rose to number eight on the *Billboard* album charts in November, 1972. It was not only a million-selling LP, but **The London Chuck Berry Sessions** remained on the charts for forty-one weeks. In England and on the European continent, it was also a best-seller. During this time, Chuck's reissue LP **Golden Decade** (Chess 2CH-1514) was also on the *Billboard* charts, reaching number seventy-two. These two albums finally reestablished Chuck as a best-selling recording artist.

By 1973, there was a noticeable change in Chuck's career direction, and in the quality of his music. He regained his form as an entertaining and energetic performer who could bring an audience to its feet with one well-performed song. This new-found energy was apparent on Saturday, August 3, 1972, when Chuck topped the bill in London's Wembley Stadium. The concert at the famed Wembley Stadium featured Little Richard, Bill Haley and His Comets, Jerry Lee Lewis, Bo Diddley, Lord Sutch, and Heinz and the Houseshakers. The Wembley show was filmed and released as a British movie entitled "The London Rock and Roll Show." The movie featured a lavishly attired Mick Jagger, who provided the commentary. After an unexplained series of events, the film was finally released over five years later, in 1978; unfortunately, it didn't play in American movie houses! "The London Rock and Roll Show" is an excellent historical document, and it demonstrates that Chuck Berry's performing skills remained as strong as ever in the 1970s.

The Wembley tour concluded a very successful summer for Chuck Berry, who had also performed in Montreux, Switzerland, for an enthusiastic crowd, and was well received that year in concerts in Germany. Chuck's close friend, Jean-Pierre Ravelli, persuaded him to record *Mean Old World*, which many critics consider one of Chuck's best blues tunes. Another interesting change in Chuck's performances was that he again began playing his old yellow Gibson guitar in concerts and during recording sessions.

The British press was particularly enthusiastic about Chuck Berry's performing skills, and he was lauded for long and carefully planned stage shows. The *New Musical Express* and *Melody Maker* were uncommonly kind in analyzing Chuck's guitar skills. The English rock press is a mercurial force, and they often attack a performer for no apparent reason. Chuck had been treated unkindly by the *NME* in the past, and he made an extraordinary effort to cooperate with that paper's interviewers. There was also a great deal of press coverage over the state-owned BBC TV network, and this helped to make Chuck Berry the most popular rock pioneer in England. The following year, in the United States, the English and European successes led to increased career opportunities.

In 1973, Chuck Berry received an unprecedented amount of television and film work. His career was further revived in the United States when he appeared on ABC-TVs "Dick Clark Presents the Rock and Roll Years." In addition, Chuck's music was featured on a popular cartoon movie entitled "Heavy Traffic." His appearance on the "Sonny and Cher Show," together with Jerry Lee Lewis, was the strangest engagement in 1973; he appeared uncomfortable and out of place with the Las Vegas glitter of Sonny and Cher. Chuck was also a frequent guest on the Merv Griffin and Mike Douglas shows. This mainstream television and movie success encouraged Chuck Berry to take some chances with his music. Although his record sales had fluctuated in the last decade, nevertheless, his live performances had generated a great deal of money. It was for this reason that Chuck began to consider new areas of music experimentation, even comparing himself to Jimi Hendrix: "He was like me in that he was different for his time," Chuck reminisced. The highly experimental nature of Hendrix's music was what Chuck admired the most. In 1973, Chuck's **Bio** album mixed blues, country, and basic rock-and-roll music. On some tracks, his musical support consisted of members of the Elephants Memory band; on two other cuts he employed studio musicians. It was a highly uneven, self-indulgent album, and there were too many instrumentally-oriented songs with country licks. Although *Rain Eyes* was an interesting country music piece, it failed to excite traditional Chuck Berry fans. When **Bio** was released in September, 1973, it was not a very successful album.

By the mid-1970s, Chuck Berry was no longer interesting, and was demonstrating a tendency to musical sloppiness in many live concerts. He had simply grown tired of performing the same set of songs. When he played with a solid blues band like Mark Naftalin's Rhythm and Blues Show, Chuck was still capable of exciting his audience. Despite the seesaw nature of Chuck's personal performances, he began to receive a number of important awards. He also began to receive some belated recognition for his pioneering work in rock music. On February 19, 1974, Chuck Berry appeared on TV with Lucie Arnaz on the "American Music Awards," and presented Charlie Pride with the "Best Country and Western Album" award. On August 9, 1975, Chuck was inaugurated into the CBS-TV Hall of Fame, and in 1976 he was presented with the American Music Conference National Music Award.

In 1975, the French newspapers reflected a revived hostility to Chuck's sloppy stage performances. Unlike his 1972 European tour, the 1975 tour of Great Britain, France, Holland, and Germany was not particularly well planned, and Chuck seemed intent upon playing only a forty-five-minute set and leaving the stage. One French

Photo courtesy Tore Jensen

Chuck in Sweden, 1976.

newspaper, *Paris Soir*, went so far as to suggest that Chuck retire. Although he was unusually cooperative with the French press, Chuck was not able to gain any favorable publicity. He attempted to charm the French press with a special news conference, but they acted like assassins in an hour-long question session. Another reason for Chuck's sloppy performances was that he had been secretly negotiating with Warner Brothers and ABC/Paramount for a new recording contract; during his European tour these negotiations fell apart, and Chuck was obviously preoccupied and dismayed over his inability to convince major recording companies to release his records.

In addition to his performing problems, Chuck had again grown disenchanted with Chess Records and indicated that he would like to leave the label. Since its purchase by a major tape manufacturing chain, Chess Records was no longer the small, vibrant, hit-making company of the 1950s and 1960s. There was a monolithic corporate structure which frustrated Chuck and impeded his art. Yet, he continued to turn out new albums. The LP **Chuck Berry 1975** (Chess 60032) was recorded with his daughter Ingrid Gibson Berry, but was a generally disappointing album. Originally, **Chuck Berry 1975** was to have been a double album. However, when it was released it was only a single LP, and it featured only three original songs written by Chuck Berry. The thirteen-song album was a strange affair; after it had been completed, ten of the songs were overdubbed with another guitar track played by Elliot Randall, who had not even been present at the original recording sessions. This artistically devastating move was the work of a new producer, Esmond Edwards, and it signalled one of the low points in Chuck's career. Edwards' production ideas had disco overtones, and he succeeded in making Chuck Berry's music sound absurd. This was the last straw for Chuck, and he notified Chess that he would not return to the label.

In 1976, Chuck retreated to his Berry Park Studios and recorded a number of new songs for a Warner Bros. album to be entitled **The Second Coming**. Chuck failed to reach agreement with Warner Bros., and the album remains stored at his Berry Park home. In fact, Chuck wrote his French friend, Jean-Pierre Ravelli, that Warner Bros. would release his new album on March 29, 1976. To add to Chuck's problems, his long-time guitar player, Billy Peek, left Chuck to tour with Rod Stewart. It was Peek's excellent backup guitar work which had made so many of Chuck's European tours so successful, and Peek's departure hurt Chuck's credibility among European audiences.

As new wave and punk rock music infiltrated rock-and-roll, Chuck Berry continued to survive and stand out as a figure instrumental in the rise of even such unlikely groups as the Sex Pistols. Sid Vicious of the Sex Pistols remarked that Chuck Berry's music was the main reason for the formation of the group. "We wanted to bring a modern version of Berry's music to a new generation of rockers," Vicious commented. As disco music became a popular part of the entertainment business, Chuck suddenly found that the late 1970s was fast becoming a decade of recycled pop, rock, country, and blues music. Although, in 1979, when even Chuck succumbed and recorded a disco version of *Havana Moon*, he was not happy with the changes in American music. He often jokingly remarked that if only the Everly Brothers could return to the *Billboard* Hot 100, everything would be right with the world again. This was Chuck's way of speaking out against the faddish music of the late 1970s. Despite his misgivings over the direction of American music and his inability to write hit records, Chuck Berry continued to maintain a busy schedule of personal appearances.

In the period from 1975 to 1983, Chuck Berry appeared on a number of TV shows. In addition to the "Midnight Special" and Don Kirshner's "Rock Concert," Chuck was a guest on the "Dinah Shore Show," the "Donny and Marie Osmond Show," "American Bandstand's 25th Anniversary Show," the "Merv Griffin Show," Chuck Barris' "Rah Rah Show," the "Sha Na Na Show," "Solid Gold," and the "Mike Douglas Show."

Another example of Chuck's celebrity status in the 1970s occurred when a Chuck Berry song was selected to accompany Voyager I and II spacecrafts as they took pictures of the solar system. When NASA orbited its satellites in outer space, the original Chess Records version of *Johnny B. Goode* was beamed back to earth. On January 30, 1981, to recognize Chuck's contributions to rock music, the American Music Awards presented Chuck with a pioneer award to commemorate his role as a Founding Father of rock music.

Perhaps the most important recognition of Chuck's musical greatness by his peers occurred on February 7, 1977, when Chuck Berry and two dozen well known musicians closed Dick Clark's Anniversary Show with a rousing version of *Roll Over Beethoven*. The honors continued to come in the late 1970s and, in 1978, the movie "American Hot Wax," which allegedly was the story of Alan Freed, featured Chuck Berry as one of the performing artists. In December, 1978, Keith Richards sat in Room 401 of the Royal Orleans Hotel playing Chuck Berry tapes as 80,000 people filed into the New Orleans dome to hear a Rolling Stones' concert.

On June 2, 1979, Chuck Berry sang *Carol*, among other songs, on the White House lawn. As President Jimmy Carter watched in amusement, Chuck substituted the words, "Oh, Amy" in the song. It was a nice moment in Chuck's career. Ironically, however, the Internal Revenue Service was at the same time investigating Chuck's

Leaving London's Heathrow Airport, 1975.

failures to report earnings and pay back income tax. Chuck was eventually indicted by the IRS for failure to report more than $100,000 in concert income in 1973, and he was presented with a tax bill of $374,982. The IRS charged that, on one occasion, Chuck had reported a concert income of $280, which was musician's scale. The reality was that the promoter paid Chuck $45,000 in cash. He then exchanged this money for cashier's checks, and he eventually opened certificates of deposit in a local bank. The IRS argued that this was an obvious attempt to launder the money and hide the source of his earnings. The IRS suggested that Chuck's refusal to sign receipts or standard contracts was another sign of nefarious business practices. In reality, this was standard procedure in Chuck Berry's business mind. He had been stiffed so many times by unscrupulous promoters that he no longer signed contracts or receipts. The IRS charged that Chuck earned more than $500,000 a year. (One of the most interesting revelations that the IRS made public was that Chuck Berry's net worth was $2.6 million.) Rock promoter Richard Nader testified for the federal government, Chuck pleaded guilty, and was sentenced in a California court. Chuck addressed the court and made a plea for a suspended sentence. He pointed out that his parents would find it difficult to accept his jail sentence. U.S. District Judge Harry Preger listened intently to Berry's plea, and he was ordered to serve 120 days in the Lompoc, California, Federal prison. In addition, Chuck was required to give benefit concerts and complete 1,000 hours of community work. Chuck was given thirty days to clean up his business, and he promptly embarked on a 12-day European concert tour.

When Chuck Berry entered the Lompoc Federal prison on August 10, 1979, he was intent upon completing his long-rumored autobiography. Lompoc prison was more like a country club than a Federal prison, and is perhaps most famous as the facility which housed most of the convicted Watergate felons. Almost immediately, a "Free Chuck Berry" movement sprang up inside Lompoc, and soon there were signs on the grounds, in the library, and mess hall. When he left Lompoc, Chuck Berry was fifty-three years old, and still a strong rock-and-roll concert attraction.

In 1979, ATCO Records signed Chuck Berry to a recording contract. He was given a great deal of latitude to produce his own records, but his time with ATCO was brief and only one album, entitled **Rockit**, was issued. This 1979 album included ten Chuck Berry originals, and a remake of *Havana Moon* with a disco beat. *Oh What a Thrill*, the 45 release from this album, did not make the *Billboard* Hot 100. **Rockit**, though, was an excellent album. Recorded at Berry Park, the popularity of disco music made it impossible for the LP to penetrate the *Billboard* charts.

157

A "Free Chuck Berry" poster inside California's Lompoc Prison, 1979.

On stage in Copenhagen, Denmark, January 25, 1973.

Bill Graham productions made an exceptionally nice gesture toward Chuck Berry in December, 1979, when they booked him into the Old Waldorf in San Francisco. The concert was billed as a "coming out party" after Chuck's brief jail term. Ingrid Gibson Berry was brought in to sing with her father, and there was a festive air in the small club.

From 1979 to 1981, Chuck continued to perform in as many places as possible, which often led to uneven concert performances. At the Seattle Blues Festival, for example, Chuck unplugged the bass guitar player's electric plug, because he was unable to follow his riffs. On May 8, 1981, Chuck played the Dixon May Fair in California, even though he refused to sign the contract. Mark Naftalin finally wrote Chuck's name on the contract, and he was paid for the night. After a tour of Japan, California, and Europe, Chuck made headlines when he was maced during a concert at the Olympia in Paris, France. Shortly after this incident, ATCO failed to renew Chuck's recording contract, and he found himself without a record company.

There is no doubt that Chuck Berry is one of the most significant figures in rock history. The music he produced during the 1950s forms the basis of modern rock-and-roll. It was basically his personality, and the publicity surrounding much of his career, that hurt Chuck more than any creative decline. No matter what indiscretion Elvis Presley committed, there was scarcely a murmur over it. Chuck Berry, on the other hand, had to constantly fight the press, the Federal government, and irate record companies. After a quarter of a century of controversy, the rock music life appears to have taken its toll on Chuck's creative energies. While he continues to be an outstanding performer, there is great uncertainty that he will ever again write and record hit records.

Great America Parkway, July 1984

CHAPTER 9

CHUCK BERRY TODAY:
NO MORE YESTERDAYS

After his initial string of hit records in the mid- to late-1950s, Chuck Berry's subsequent musical career has been characterized by a general lack of solid hit recordings. Although *Nadine* and *No Particular Place to Go* temporarily brought Chuck back to the *Billboard* Hot 100 in 1964, they could not match the power of songs like *Johnny B. Goode, School Day* and *Roll Over Beethoven* on the charts. Despite this, the half-dozen mammoth hits which Chuck had written and recorded guaranteed his place as a rock-and-roll musical pioneer and, for more than a quarter century, Chuck Berry has been one of the most electrifying live rock performers in history. As a rock-and-roll legend, Chuck is noted for his difficult, often obnoxious attitude toward journalists, disc jockeys, and concert promoters. He has a mercurial temperament which often results in poor concert reviews, overly critical album reviews, and generally disparaging remarks about his career.

Perhaps the most notorious personality quirk in Chuck Berry's professional life is his penchant for demanding larger concert guarantees. In 1964, for example, Chuck was booked into Hamburg, Germany's famous Star Club. The contract called for a $1,500 guarantee. As the club, made famous as the second home of the Beatles, filled up, Chuck believed that his fee was not commensurate with the huge throng gathering before him. He told Horst Fascher that he would not perform unless his fee was substantially increased. Fascher, who was once the Beatles bodyguard in the early Hamburg days, called Chuck's bluff: "If you don't perform for the agreed price," Fascher remarked, "I will announce to the crowd your decision and ask you to walk through the dance floor and out the front door." The idea of wading through an irate German crowd quickly altered Chuck's position. He not only performed, Fascher remembered, but he was perhaps the best American act to play the Star Club. Afterwards, Fascher and Chuck partied into the night and the incident was quickly forgotten. However, it does illustrate the tremendous changeability of Chuck's personality. Some very perceptive observations on Chuck's character and mood changes have been made by a well-known Italian-American singer who toured with Chuck in the late 1950s. He did not see any inconsistencies in Chuck's behavior or business attitudes: "Chuck was cheated, threatened and lied to during the early part of his career. He could never trust concert promoters. This created his suspicious nature, and it prompted Chuck to demand his concert fees in advance in cash." This singer, who continues to write hit songs in the 1980s, believed that Chuck was simply protecting his own interests. Many of Chuck's close friends rarely see the more contentious side of his character, and it offers an interesting insight into how the music business can evoke defensiveness and irritability in even the strongest personality.

One of the ways that Chuck Berry alleviates career pressures is to perform at Berry Park, or at the Rainbow nightclub in St. Louis, Missouri. An example of the psychological therapy Chuck's small club performances provide was demonstrated on August 22, 1972, when Chuck played for nearly three hours, instead of the usual forty-five minutes, to a delighted crowd. This set included old classics like *Johnny B. Goode, Maybellene, School Day*, and *The Promised Land*, but, in addition, Chuck performed *Mean Old Frisco, Beer Drinkin' Woman*, and *Everyday I Have the Blues*. It was an incredible set, and included thirty songs in all. The Rainbow nightclub is an important part of Chuck Berry's latter-day musical development, because it was there that he met two of the musicians who have been instrumental in his public performances in the 1970s and 1980s. In 1969, while performing in one of his "therapy concerts" at the Rainbow club, Chuck met a young guitarist named Billy Peek. For the next six years, Billy was a regular in Chuck Berry's band. The *New Musical Express*, England's premiere rock newspaper, was effusive in its praise of Peek's guitar work and, by 1975, a number of prominent musicians throughout Europe had made overtures to Peek. In 1972, a Las Vegas Chuck Berry engagement with Peek's guitar and Johnny Johnson's piano drew rave reviews from the press and fellow musicians. (One night, as Chuck was performing a crowd-rousing set, Elvis Presley walked into the side door of the Hilton International Lounge and watched backstage as Chuck performed for half an hour. As Elvis quietly left, he remarked to Red West: "You have just seen the King of Rock and Roll music.") Just as Chuck's backup musical aggregation began to take hold, Billy Peek was hired to back up Rod Stewart. Suddenly, Stewart began to perform Chuck's classic song, *Sweet Little Rock and Roller*, with such enthusiasm that reviewers frequently commented on his ability to match the Berry sound. It was in fact Billy Peek's guitar work which added a new dimension to Stewart's concerts in the mid- to late 1970s.

The Rainbow Club in St. Louis was also where Chuck met his

present bass player, manager, and musical compatriot, Jim Marsala. In 1976, Marsala's excellent bass techniques prompted Chuck to sign him as his travelling companion. With a whimsical look in his eye, Chuck often introduces Marsala as his manager, but the musical and personal friendship is equally important in Chuck's life. Marsala is one of a small number of people that Chuck personally trusts, and they make an excellent musical team. On the **Rockit** and **Tokyo Sessions** albums, Marsala adds strong musical accompaniment, and he often directs the backup bands used in concerts. Throughout his lengthy musical career, Chuck has demonstrated the ability to bring the best out in other musicians. In the 1950s, Chuck's piano-guitar duets with Johnny Johnson were classic, and his guitar-guitar interaction with Billy Peek and Jim Marsala continued this tradition in the 1970s and 1980s.

It was not until the 1970s that rock historians and journalists began to note that Chuck Berry's skill in playing off other instruments was reminiscent of Charlie Christian's guitar playing and Benny Goodman's clarinet riffs. Moreover, the innovative and technical skill of Chuck's music has never fully been recognized because Leonard Chess took the credit for the production work. While Chess' role was obviously an important one, nevertheless, Ron Malo, the sound engineer, and Chuck had an equally important role in the production of the record. As Bo Diddley remarked: "No one knows my music but me, and I produced all of my own records." Bo's statement is an accurate one, because the role of the producer was still almost a decade away in the early days at Chess Records. There are a number of examples of Chuck's technical and production skills, but one of the best is contained in the song *Let It Rock*. When this tune was released on the **Golden Decade, Volume 2 LP**, it was now minus Chuck's undubbed guitar, and instead, the piano was given a free-flowing solo. Chuck had alternated the piano and guitar solos to suit his mood. On the original release of *Let It Rock*, the piano is heard only faintly in the background, a mistake which Chuck believed had prevented the record from hitting the *Billboard* Hot 100.

In the Chess studios, Chuck often took off on a number of musical tangents. He also played both solo and rhythm guitar on most of the songs he recorded from 1958 until April, 1960. Some accounts of Chuck's Chess days mention a "mysterious" guitar player, usually identified as Bo Diddley, as one of the session players, but Bo Diddley has confirmed that he was not the guitarist on these recordings: the mystery man was Chuck Berry himself, playing both guitar parts. During the period from August, 1961 until January, 1964, Chuck would record a song without the solo guitar part. He would then go back and dub in an exquisite solo run before releasing the record. At Berry Park, Chuck often played a tape he was very proud of, a cassette containing his version of *It Don't Take But a Few Minutes*, recorded without the lead guitar. There is also an excellent bootleg tape of Chuck playing the instrumental background to the song *Things I Used to Do*. A great deal of Chuck Berry's innovative and original musical experimentation is unknown to his fans, and the tapes at Berry Park provide some very interesting insights into Chuck's extraordinary skills.

The Berry Park recording studio has been one of the principal assets in lending expression to Chuck's creative powers. He frequently holds private recording sessions or small concerts for friends. Howlin' Wolf turned up one night at Berry Park, and the veteran Chicago bluesman and Chuck turned the small gathering into a musical feast. At such relaxed gatherings, Chuck has often talked about his favorite musicians. Guitarist Steve Cropper was described as one of his most respected colleagues. Chuck also revealed that he loved Johnny Rivers' and Lonnie Mack's versions of *Memphis* but, on another occasion, mentioned that he did not care for Elvis Presley's version of the same song. He has always been intrigued by the sheer number of artists who have recorded his songs.

The obvious product of an inclination to try new things, coupled with the availability of one's own recording studio, is an abundance of unreleased recordings. By 1966, the recording studio at Berry Park was sophisticated enough to allow Chuck complete musical freedom. As a result, there were often tapes played only at Berry Park which demonstrated that Chuck still had hit record material available to the general public. Unfortunately, neither Mercury nor Chess inquired about the possibility of obtaining new songs. Many of the tapes, to be sure, hold rerecordings of old Berry tunes, but other efforts showcase old standards interpreted in a new way. The holdings at Berry Park also include an album recorded for Warner Bros. in 1976--1977, which was never released due to Chuck's inability to reach a contract agreement with Warner management. In addition to the songs which Chuck recorded at Berry Park, there is also a great deal of material from Chuck's St. Louis studio work. From 1976 to 1978, Chuck personally supervised the construction of a St. Louis recording studio, where he intended not only to record his own music but to expand into the business end of the recording industry. It was in this newly created St. Louis studio that Chuck began to perform unreleased instrumental tunes like *Floyd*, which sounded very much like *Deep Feeling*, and continued to experiment with old standards as like *Silver Threads, Vaya Con Dios,* and *Jambalaya.*

Since 1964, Chuck has often toured Europe. During a tour in the 1960s, he met a young French fan, Jean-Pierre Ravelli, and they

Great America Parkway, July 1984

have been close friends for two decades. Currently, Ravelli resides on the Rue de l'Abbe Groult in Paris; he visits Chuck for the month of August each year, flying with his wife, Monique, to Berry Park or to Chuck's Hollywood home. Their daughter, Carol Nadine, affectionately refers to Chuck as "grandpa." For a number of years, Ravelli operated a very successful Chuck Berry fan club. He also published a sensitive and often probing short biography of Chuck's life. As a result of their friendship, Chuck has arranged to play a large number of concerts in France and Western Europe. The strong support from French fans, and the almost fanatical acceptance of Chuck's music throughout Western Europe, has prompted some of the best concerts of Berry's career.

When Chuck delivered his first concert at the fabled Olympia Concert Hall in Paris on February 7, 1965, he was not prepared for the outpouring of emotion. As one fan remarked: "Chuck Berry is the reason that the French were able to understand rock and roll music." Another aspect of Paris which appealed to Chuck was its free racial climate. He could not only walk the streets virtually unnoticed, but he did not have the same disagreeable incidents with people which plagued his American tours. There was also a strong respect for Chuck's abilities as a blues musician throughout Europe. He was often asked to play obscure blues tunes, and Chuck surprised many audiences by readily agreeing to perform these songs.

One night after performing in a Paris concert, Chuck talked about the influence of Memphis Minnie upon his music. When he arrived in Chicago, Memphis Minnie was recording for Leonard Chess' Checker label. By the mid-1950s, she had returned to Memphis and Chuck was no longer able to benefit from her musical tutelage. However, sometime during the 1960s, Memphis Minnie invited Chuck to participate in a jam session. There is a tape which Chuck has played for a number of friends in which he is playing in an extended jam with Memphis Minnie. To this day Chuck will not acknowledge when the tape was made nor identify the songs contained on it; there is little doubt that Memphis Minnie was an important influence upon Berry's musical development.

An important change in Chuck's life occurred in 1973, when he purchased a Hollywood home. His frequent television and movie appearances, as well as the proximity to the West Coast record industry, made it imperative for Chuck to purchase a Southern California dwelling. Although he continues to spend a great deal of time in Berry Park, or near his family in St. Louis, Chuck is often seen walking down Santa Monica, Hollywood, or Sunset Boulevards in the heart of Hollywood. It was the royalties from his million-selling version of *My Ding-A-Ling* which enabled Chuck to purchase the

Hollywood home. Jean-Pierre Ravelli, Chuck's French friend, refers to the West Coast residence as "the palace," an indication of not only the financial prosperity but also the artistic recognition which Chuck finally received in the 1970s and 1980s. Much like Bo Diddley, Chuck is finally established as one of the most technically proficient guitarists in rock music.

As Chuck Berry's popularity continued to grow in Europe and as his lengendary guitar feats drew increased attention from the media, the record industry realized that no significant recording of Chuck Berry existed in European release. This was remedied in 1977 when England's Phonogram Record Company conceived and released the stylish LP **Motorvatin' (Chuck Berry – 22 Rock 'n' Roll Classics)**. The album, released on a European Chess label, was beautifully packaged, with a red Cadillac convertible on the cover. The twenty-two songs were Chuck's best known tunes, and the album was marketed through a no-expense-spared advertising campaign. The result was that it went platinum, and Chuck Berry proudly displays his awards for this European classic release at his Berry Park studios.

There were also strong signs of change in Chuck Berry's personal musical tastes. His private record collection was steadily enlarged by more and more discs by such artists as Ray Charles, Nat "King" Cole, Harry Belafonte, T-Bone Walker, Muddy Waters, and the Everly Brothers. In 1981, Chuck informed San Francisco disc jockey Gene Nelson that the Everly Brothers were still his favorite musical act. As he toured Europe in September, 1983, Chuck informed a close friend that he would love to have seen the Everly Brothers' concert in London's famed 6,000-seat Royal Albert Hall. It is this eclectic approach to music which has helped to mold Chuck Berry's extraordinary musical skills. There are few artists who could blend these diverse musical styles into a rock-and-roll format.

At the same time, there were also indications that Chuck's own musical fortunes were not on stable ground, at least in the area of recording. After almost a year of negotiating with ATCO in the late 1970s, he signed a recording contract. When the formal signing took place at the ATCO Records office at 75 Rockefeller Plaza in New York, Chuck and ATCO believed that he would soon come back on the charts. *Oh What a Thrill* was released as a single, and Johnny Johnson was brought in to play piano. A new executive producer, Doug Morris, was assigned to aid Chuck, who was ostensibly his own producer and was given extraordinary control over his own product. The songs for the **Rockit** LP were recorded at Berry Park, and it was not until May 20, 1979, that Chuck gave ATCO formal approval for the album cover design. The **Rockit** album was finally on its way to record stores, but it was not long before it was on its way to the cut-out bins. ATCO's overindulgence of Chuck was a mistake; the album was sloppy and overly disco-fied. The end result was a great deal of bitter controversy and disagreement over the direction of Chuck's music. ATCO refused to release any more of Chuck Berry's records. After that, from 1979 to 1985, at the very pinnacle of his performing career, Chuck was not even able to secure a record contract.

Although frustrated in his attempts to develop a long-term relationship with a "name" label, there have been many professional recording triumphs since 1979. Perhaps the best indication of Chuck's continued prowess was demonstrated in 1981, when he released an album in Japan entitled **The Tokyo Sessions**. Although this album was a recording of old songs, it was an excellent reinterpretation of his former work. Jim Marsala's fine bass and Ingrid Berry's backup vocal support helped to make the LP an exciting one. The Japanese musicians who backed up Chuck were, for the most part, solid jazz performers who easily made the transition to basic rock-and-roll music. Bear Family Records in Bremen, West Germany, and stores like Downhome Music in El Cerrito, California, quietly sell hundreds of copies of this album each year, and there is strong evidence that Chuck Berry record buyers continue to look for his product.

One of the problems with Chuck Berry's record output is that so many of his LPs are simply rehashings of old tunes, however, and many of those fall well below the quality of **The Tokyo Sessions**. A good example is the music from the Toronto Festival held on September 13, 1969, at the Varsity Stadium. Officially billed as the "Toronto Rock and Roll Revival," the show was skillfully promoted by Brower/Walker Enterprises, who sold a double soundtrack album of Chuck Berry's concert portion to Magnum Records in Germany. Eventually, the two LP **Chuck Berry, Live in Concert** was released, containing thirteen songs from the concert. It was a blatant attempt to capitalize on a concert that Melinda McCracken of the *Toronto Globe and Mail* described as one of the "rock n roll greats." The album's production was not top quality, and there was a listless transformation of the music to vinyl. As a result, many fans were not treated to the type of concert that Chuck was capable of giving in the 1960s, 1970s, and 1980s. This album did little, if anything, to further Chuck Berry's musical career, and it often discouraged record buyers from his other products.

There were also problems with bookings in the late 1970s and early 1980s. Bill Graham's organization no longer presented Chuck Berry in concert, and there were rumors of a serious disagreement between Berry and Graham. Nick Clainos' office at Bill Graham Productions would not confirm any rift, and would only comment that

Chuck was always welcome to perform for Bill Graham. By the early 1980s, Chuck often played to sold-out houses in country and western bars. It was not uncommon to find 2,000 drunken cowboys cheering for Chuck Berry in places like Turlock, California, as occurred in 1982. There were also state fairs and a number of small-town concerts in the early 1980s. However, during a large portion of 1982--1983 Chuck was not on the road. He did tour Europe in the fall of 1983, and performed selected weekend concerts in America. Despite everything, the lengthy tours were no longer a necessity because Chuck Berry's financial status and performing career were on solid ground in the 1980s. Still, he was bothered that he did not have a recording contract. In 1982, when he played at Caesar's/Tahoe in Lake Tahoe, Nevada, he was apparently preparing an album for commercial release. During an interview with KYA disc jockey, Gene Nelson, Chuck informed the San Francisco-based oldies DJ that he had recently completed a double LP. Three sides of the album were his own music. One side was blues, another was country, and the third side was rock-and-roll. There were new songs and a blend of old standards. The surprise on the album was the fourth side: original material written and recorded by Chuck's beautiful daughter, Ingrid Berry. Although the album was brilliantly conceived and recorded, Chuck could not find a company to press and distribute it. For almost two years, he hawked his product to the major record companies, but by 1984 he was considering a private deal with a distributor who would represent Chuck's own company. It was a frustrating time in Chuck's life, as he once again was not able to sell his music.

Finally, there were also some high points in Chuck's career in the midst of this general frustration. In 1982, the Nashville Songwriters Association International Hall of Fame inaugurated Chuck Berry into its prestigious ranks. On October 11, before a black-tie crowd at Nashville's Hyatt Regency Hotel, more than 600 writers and music industry figures turned out to see Chuck Berry, among others, hailed for important contributions to country music. Prominently mentioned in Berry's career was the success of the country-based song *Maybellene*. Brenda Lee paid tribute to Chuck's place in the music business, but Chuck himself was unable to attend the ceremony.

In assessing Chuck Berry's career, there can be no doubt that he is one of a half dozen figures who established rock music as the most creative force in the present-day popular music scene. Chuck's ability to infuse lyrics with relevant ideas about the direction of American culture is one of his most redeeming contributions. His talent lies in the ability to transform the everyday, the mundane — automobiles, hot dogs, coca colas, and young girls — into tunes and lyrics which

Thirty plus years later: a weary performer takes a much-deserved break (Lake Tahoe, California, 1982).

mirrored and bespoke the problems and frustrations of American teenagers at a time when technology, nuclear war, and a volatile world economy played havoc with the national psyche. In the end, it was Chuck Berry's music which provided reassurance for the old values. In *Back in the USA*, Chuck celebrated his return to American hamburgers and crowded freeways after a tour of Australia. There were other signs of his strong national attitudes in songs like *Johnny B. Goode*, which recounted the plight of anyone attempting to find their place in the rock music world of the 1950s and 1960s. *Sweet Little Sixteen, Carol,* and *Nadine* were teen-age refrains about adolescent problems that neither parents nor teen-agers could seem to solve in the 1950s and 1960s. It was on the basis of his singular interpretations of common experiences and problems that Chuck Berry became such an influential part of American culture.

DISCOGRAPHY & APPENDIXES

THE CHUCK BERRY DISCOGRAPHY

This discography is the product of twenty years of record collecting, research, and communication with Chuck Berry fans around the world. Due to the high and low points in Chuck's career, it has not always been easy to collect all of his recordings. Even more difficult to locate have been cover records, which have been purchased in six countries and through mail-order companies around the world.

Perhaps the most intriguing aspect of this Chuck Berry discography is that it demonstrates wide discrepancies in LP records in the United States and England. A good example of these differences is evident in **Golden Decade Volume 3**. The English edition contains one unreleased song, whereas the American issue does not have the same tune. Yet, the covers and general packaging appear to be identical. It is with these slight differences that this discography is concerned, as well as with the release, packaging, and distribution of Chuck Berry records in general.

The first section of this discography separates Chuck's recordings into lists of singles, EPs, LPs, and compilations issued in the United States. Then, there are sections listing releases in the U.K., France, Germany, Holland, Sweden, Belgium, China, Denmark, Italy, Japan, Poland, Portugal, and Spain. The discography attempts to analyze the recordings which each nation has released, and to thereby document the worldwide phenomenon known as Chuck Berry music. The search for rare Chuck Berry records has unearthed such things as a single issued in South Africa on Teal Records (TSP-41), *Nadine* backed with *No Particular Place to Go*, probably from 1964. There is also a single issued in India on the London label (HL-8712).

One of the most interesting parts in the discography is the bootleg record section. For those interested in doing more than just collecting bootlegs, whether Chuck Berry bootlegs or otherwise, see the introduction to Lee Cotten and Howard A. DeWitt's excellent book, *Jailhouse Rock: The Bootleg Records of Elvis Presley, 1970--1983* (Pierian Press, 1983), and an Appendix in the book *You Can't Do That: Beatles Bootlegs & Novelty Records, 1963--1980* (Pierian Press,

1981), both of which help place the bootleg record industry within the context of the modern record business.

In addition to the general discography, an attempt has been made to delineate some other aspects of Chuck Berry's career. The listing of cover records provides an important means of assessing Chuck's general influence upon rock-and-roll artists. The section dealing with Chuck's contributions to movie soundtracks is also an important historical precedent for arguing Chuck's worth as a rock-and-roll music pioneer. The listing of *Billboard* hit records in the U.S., and of charted songs in the U.K., further establishes the incredible creative legacy of Chuck Berry.

This discography would have been impossible to complete without the help of Rune Halland and Tormod Uleberg from Norway; Christer Lundberg and Johan Hasselberg from Sweden; Rob Vader from Holland; John Beecher from England; and Dieter Boek from West Germany. Mr. Boek kindly supplied me with many Germany LPs issued in the early 1970s. Perhaps my most significant and helpful ally, in one form or another, was France's Jean-Pierre Ravelli. He has not only kindly answered my letters over the last fifteen years, but he has gone out of his way to help increase my holdings of Chuck Berry records. Jean-Pierre Ravelli is a friend whom I can never fully thank.

Finally, I would like to thank Howard A. DeWitt for his input and suggestions on the discography. During his two weeks at my home in Drobak, Norway, he not only drank all the beer in my refrigerator, but he helped to shape the form and content of the discography. If you have any additions to the discography, please send them to: Morten Reff, Vestbyveien 62, N-1440 Drobak, Norway.

Good reading!
Morten Reff

NOTE

All songs in the various discographies which were recorded *but not written* by Chuck Berry have been identified with a plus sign (+) at the end of the song title.

U.S. SINGLES DISCOGRAPHY

CHESS

1604	*Maybellene/Wee Wee Hours* (1955)
1610	*30 Days/Together*
1615	*No Money Down/The Downbound Train* (1956)
1626	*Roll Over Beethoven/Drifting Heart*
1635	*Too Much Monkey Business/Brown-Eyed Handsome Man*
1345	*You Can't Catch Me/Havana Moon*
1653	*School Day/Deep Feeling* (instr.) (1957)
1664	*Oh Baby Doll/La Juanda*
1671	*Rock and Roll Music/Blue Feeling* (instr.)
1683	*Sweet Little Sixteen/Reelin' and Rockin'* (1958)
1691	*Johnny B. Goode/Around and Around*
1697	*Beautiful Delilah/Vacation Time*
1700	*Carol/Hey Pedro*
1709	*Sweet Little Rock and Roller/Jo Jo Gunne*
1714	*Run Rudolph Run+/Merry Christmas Baby+*
1716	*Anthony Boy/That's My Desire+* (1959)
1722	*Almost Grown/Little Queenie*
1729	*Back in the USA/Memphis, Tennessee*
1737	*Broken Arrow/Childhood Sweetheart*
1747	*Too Pooped to Pop+/Let It Rock* (1960)
1754	*Bye Bye Johnny/Worried Life Blues+*
1763	*I Got to Find My Baby/Mad Lad+* (instr.)
1767	*Jaguar and the Thunderbird/Our Little Rendezvous*
1779	*I'm Talking About You/Little Star* (1961)
1799	*Go Go Go/Come On*
1853	*I'm Talking About You/Diploma for Two* (1963)
1866	*Sweet Little Sixteen/Memphis, Tennessee*
	Reissue with dubbed "live" audience.
1883	*Nadine/O'Rangutang* (instr.)
1898	*No Particular Place to Go/You Two*
1906	*You Never Can Tell/Brenda Lee*
1912	*Little Marie/Go Bobby Soxer*
1916	*Promised Land/Things I Used to Do+*
1926	*Dear Dad/Lonely School Days* (slow version) (1965)
1943	*It Wasn't Me/Welcome Back Pretty Baby*
1963	*Lonely School Days* (fast version)/*Ramona Say Yes* (1966)
1963	*Ramona Say Yes/Havana Moon*
	Ramona Say Yes was issued twice on Chess 1963, first as a B-side, then as an A-side. *Havana Moon* is the same song as 1645.

CHECKER

1089	*Chuck's Beat/Bo's Beat+* (1964)
	These are extracts from Checker LP-2991, **Two Great Guitars**. Chuck and Bo Diddley play on each song, each of which is 2:55 long.

72643	*Club Nitty Gritty/Laugh and Cry* (1966)
72680	*Back to Memphis/I Do Really Love You* (1967)
72748	*It Hurts Me Too+/Feelin' It* (instr.)
72840	*St. Louie to Frisco/Ma Dear* (1968)
72963	*It's Too Dark in There/Good Lookin' Woman* (1969)
30143	*Maybellene/Sweet Little Sixteen*
30144	*School Day/Memphis, Tennessee*
30145	*Roll Over Beethoven/Back in the USA*
30146	*Rock and Roll Music/Johnny B. Goode*

CHESS

2090	*Tulane/Have Mercy Judge* (1970)
CH2131	*My Ding-A-Ling/Johnny B. Goode* (live) (1972)
CH2136	*Reelin' and Rockin'* (live)/*Let's Boogie* (1973)
CH2140	*Bio/Roll 'em Pete+* (live)
	Roll 'em Pete was recorded on February 3, 1972 in Coventry, England. The band was replaced by studio musicians in U.S. before release.
CH2189	*Shake Rattle and Roll+/Baby What You Want Me to Do+* (1975)

ATCO

7203	*Oh What a Thrill/California* (1979)

A NOTE ON U.S. CHESS SINGLES

The earliest Chess Record releases through number 1664 were originally issued with the silver-top blue Chess label. Afterward, releases had the blue Chess label as far as number 1799, when they began to use the black label with Chess in gold letters on top (in front of a special logo) as far as number 1963; then, Berry went to Mercury.

Reissues carried various versions of the label in the sixties: light blue with red edging on top of the Chess name in white; yellow/orange with a black line which surrounded the extreme edge and the center hole; the Gold Standard series. With the release of 2090, recordings had the light blue label. With CH2131, Chess began use of an orange label with a blue lining which surrounded the extreme edge, and a wider lining crossing the middle.

RE-RELEASES

The following titles were re-released in 1973 as part of the Chess Blue Chip Series (the label color was yellow):

9010	*Roll Over Beethoven/Nadine*
9020	*Maybellene/Rock and Roll Music*
9021	*Sweet Little Sixteen/Johnny B. Goode*
9030	*Memphis, Tennessee/School Day*

The following Chess recordings have been reissued on Eric Records:

224	*Johnny B. Goode/Carol*
225	*School Day/My Ding-A-Ling*
226	*Rock and Roll Music/Memphis, Tennessee*
227	*Roll Over Beethoven/Maybellene*
228	*Sweet Little Sixteen/No Particular Place to Go*

Re-releases with the original fifties' Chess number and blue label, but different B-sides:

1671   *Rock and Roll Music/House of Blue Lights+*
1700   *Carol/County Line*
                        Both B-sides are fifties' recordings, but were first issued in 1974 on the **Golden Decade Vol. 3** double-LP set.

The following titles were re-released in 1982 on the Chess label (Sugar Hill Records Ltd.):

CH-101   *Johnny B. Goode/Little Queenie*
CH-102   *Rock and Roll Music/Back in the USA*
CH-103   *Carol/Sweet Little Rock and Roller*
CH-122   *Maybellene/Almost Grown*
CH-123   *No Particular Place to Go/You Never Can Tell*
CH-133   *My Ding-A-Ling/Reelin' and Rockin'* (live)
                        These titles have a very good sound quality, which is not so common on singles, and CH-123 has the stereo versions.

A SPECIAL ISSUE

HIP POCKET
    HP-34   *Maybellene/Roll Over Beethoven* ('50s Chess recordings)
                        This is a special, very thin 4-inch "record" probably issued in the late sixties by Philco-Ford Corporation. It was part of a series created for single-play phonographs only. Mostly hits from the sixties were included, with Berry, and also Bo Diddley, among the artists.

A CHESS RARITY

CHESS
    CH-6145 019   *My Ding-A-Ling/Let's Boogie*
                        This is really a strange one! The number is the same as on the U.K. issue and also has the same B-side. The label is the U.S. light blue with red edging on the top of the white Chess name, which was used on all U.S. issues in the late sixties up until 1972, when they began using the orange label with a blue lining.
                        The single's label states that the songs are taken from the **London Chuck Berry Sessions** LP (CH-6310 122). Strangely enough, this is also the same number as the U.K. LP issue!

U.S. EP DISCOGRAPHY

CHESS

5118   **AFTER SCHOOL SESSION** (1957)
*School Day/Wee Wee Hours/Too Much Monkey Business/
Brown-Eyed Handsome Man*

5119   **ROCK AND ROLL MUSIC** (1957)
Rock and Roll Music/Blue Feeling (instr.)/*Oh Baby Doll/La
Juanda*

5121   **SWEET LITTLE SIXTEEN** (1958)
Sweet Little Sixteen/Rockin' at the Philharmonic (instr.)/
Reelin' and Rockin'/Guitar Boogie (instr.)

5124   **PICKIN' BERRIES WITH CHUCK BERRY** (1958)
Beautiful Delilah/Vacation Time/Carol/Hey Pedro

5126   **SWEET LITTLE ROCK AND ROLLER** (1958)
*Sweet Little Rock and Roller/Jo Jo Gunne/Johnny B. Goode/
Around and Around*

COMPILATION EPs

AUGUST

B-101   **DICK CLARK – AMERICA'S FAVOURITE – PRESENTS ALL
TIME HITS**
School Day
A record of uncertain origins, a special issue of some kind,
perhaps produced by Clark. Contains six tracks by six different
artists, all hits from 1957/58.

U.S. ALBUM DISCOGRAPHY

1957
CHESS
LP-1425

ROCK ROCK ROCK (soundtrack LP)
Maybellene/Thirty Days/You Can't Catch Me/Roll Over Beethoven
The Flamingos and The Moonglows are also featured on the album.

1958
CHESS
LP-1426

AFTER SCHOOL SESSION
School Day/Deep Feeling (instr.)*/Too Much Monkey Business/ Wee Wee Hours/Roly Poly* (instr.)*/No Money Down/Brown-Eyed Handsome Man/Berry Pickin'* (instr.)*/Together/Havana Moon/The Downbound Train/Drifting Heart*

CHESS
LP-1432

ONE DOZEN BERRYS
Sweet Little Sixteen/Blue Feeling (instr.)*/La Juanda/Rockin' at the Philharmonic* (instr.)*/Oh Baby Doll/Reelin' and Rockin'/ In Go* (instr.)*/Rock and Roll Music/How You've Changed/Low Feeling* (instr.)*/It Don't Take But a Few Minutes*
Low Feeling is actually *Blue Feeling* repeated under the new title; for some reason, it was retaped at half speed and one twelve-bar stanza omitted. What an idea!

1959
CHESS
LP-1435

BERRY IS ON TOP
Almost Grown/Carol/Maybellene/Sweet Little Rock and Roller/Anthony Boy/Johnny B. Goode/Little Queenie/Jo Jo Gunne/Roll Over Beethoven/Around and Around/Hey Pedro/ Blues for Hawaiians (instr.)

1960
CHESS
LP-1448

ROCKIN' AT THE HOPS
Bye Bye Johnny/Worried Life Blues+/Down the Road a Piece+/ Confessin' the Blues+/Too Pooped to Pop+/Mad Lad+ (instr.)*/ I Got to Find My Baby/Betty Jean/Childhood Sweetheart/ Broken Arrow/Driftin' Blues+/Let It Rock*

1961
CHESS
LP-1456

NEW JUKE-BOX HITS
I'm Talking About You/Diploma for Two/Thirteen Question Method/Away from You/Don't You Lie to Me+/The Way It Was Before/Little Star/Route 66+/Sweet Sixteen+/Run Around/ Stop and Listen/Rip It Up+

1962
CHESS
LP-1465

CHUCK BERRY TWIST
Maybellene/Roll Over Beethoven/Oh Baby Doll/Around and Around/Come On/Let It Rock/Reelin' and Rockin'/School Day/Almost Grown/Sweet Little Sixteen/Thirty Days/Johnny B. Goode/Rock and Roll Music/Back in the USA
Reissued in 1963 as **More Chuck Berry** (LP-1465), with different cover.

181

1963

CHESS
LP-1480

CHUCK BERRY ON STAGE

*Go Go Go/Memphis, Tennessee/Maybellene/Surfin'
Steel (Blues for Hawaiians) (instr.)/Rockin' on the
Railroad (Let It Rock)/Brown-Eyed Handsome Man
(alt. take)/I Still Got the Blues/Surfin' USA (Sweet
Little Sixteen/Jaguar and the Thunderbird/I Just Want
to Make Love to You+/All Aboard/Trick or Treat/The
Man and the Donkey/How High the Moon+ (instr.)*

Surfin' Steel has the original second guitar omitted
and the song is faded earlier.

All titles on this LP have the "live" audience
dubbed in. It has been rumored that the LP was recorded live in the Tivoli Theatre, Chicago, mostly because of the opening. Not true. However, one can hear
Berry's voice (and others, too) many times between
songs, and during songs (*Memphis* and *Surfin' Steel*) —
a dubbing job so good that it's probably the best fake
"live" album ever made.

1964

CHESS
LP-1485

CHUCK BERRY'S GREATEST HITS

*Roll Over Beethoven/School Day/Rock and Roll Music/
Too Much Monkey Business/Johnny B. Goode/Oh Baby
Doll/Nadine/Maybellene/Memphis, Tennessee/Sweet
Little Sixteen/Thirty Days/Brown-Eyed Handsome
Man*

CHECKER
LP-2991
LPS-2991

**TWO GREAT GUITARS – CHUCK BERRY & BO
DIDDLEY**

*Liverpool Drive/Chuck's Beat/When the Saints Go
Marching In+/Bo's Beat*

This is strictly an instrumental album. Berry is not
playing on *When the Saints . . .* , and Diddley is not
playing on *Liverpool Drive*. *Chuck's Beat* is eleven
minutes long, *Bo's Beat* is fourteen minutes long.

This was the very first Berry recording issued in
stereo, although Chuck had recorded songs in stereo
as early as 1960.

See the U.K. discography, Marble Arch LP MALS-
702, for more information.

CHESS
LP-1488
LPS-1488

ST. LOUIS TO LIVERPOOL

*Little Marie/Our Little Rendezvous/No Particular Place
to Go/You Two/Promised Land/You Never Can Tell/
Go Bobby Soxer/Things I Used to Do+/Liverpool Drive
(instr.)/Night Beat (instr.)/Merry Christmas Baby+ (alt.
take)/Brenda Lee*

*Our Little Rendezvous, Night Beat, Merry Xmas
Baby*, and *Brenda Lee* are *not* stereo recordings.

1965

CHESS
LP-1495
LPS-1495

CHUCK BERRY IN LONDON
My Little Love-Light/She Once Was Mine/After It's Over (instr.)/I Got a Booking/Night Beat (instr.)/His Daughter Caroline/You Came a Long Way from St. Louis+/St. Louis Blues+/Jamaica Farewell+/Dear Dad/Butterscotch (instr.)/The Song of My Love/Why Should We End This Way/I Want to Be Your Driver
　　Jamaica Farewell is complete only on the stereo issues of this LP. On the mono issues the song is faded. Compared to the U.K. issue, the U.S. one has an extra guitar added which is more audible in the stereo version.
　　A part of this LP was actually recorded in London.

CHESS
LP-1498
LPS-1498

FRESH BERRY'S
It Wasn't Me/Run Joe+/Everyday We Rock and Roll/One for My Baby+/Welcome Back Pretty Baby/It's My Own Business/ Right Off Rampart Street/Vaya Con Dios+/Merrily We Rock and Roll/My Mustang Ford/Ain't That Just Like a Woman+/ Wee Hour Blues
　　The U.K. issue of this LP has an instrumental, *Sad Day— Long Night*, instead of *Welcome Back Pretty Baby*.
　　See U.K. discography for information.

1967

CHESS
LPS-1514D

CHUCK BERRY'S GOLDEN DECADE (2 LP set)
Maybellene/Deep Feeling (instr.)/Johnny B. Goode/Wee Wee Hours/Nadine/Brown-Eyed Handsome Man/Roll Over Beethoven/Thirty Days/Havana Moon/No Particular Place to Go/ Memphis, Tennessee/Almost Grown/School Day/Too Much Monkey Business/Oh Baby Doll/Reelin' and Rockin'/You Can't Catch Me/Too Pooped to Pop+/Bye Bye Johnny/ Around and Around/Sweet Little Sixteen/Rock and Roll Music/Anthony Boy/Back in the USA
　　This LP only available with electronic stereo. It was reissued in 1972 with different fold-out cover.

MERCURY
MG-21103
SR-61103

CHUCK BERRY'S GOLDEN HITS
Sweet Little Sixteen/Memphis, Tennessee/School Day/May-bellene/Back in the USA/Johnny B. Goode/Rock and Roll Music/Roll Over Beethoven/Thirty Days/Carol/Club Nitty Gritty
　　These re-recordings of Berry's old hits (except *Club Nitty Gritty*, which was a new song) are just terrible! The way they are done exemplifies how best to destroy good songs!

MERCURY
MG-21123
SR-61123

CHUCK BERRY IN MEMPHIS
Back to Memphis/I Do Really Love You/Ramblin' Rose+/ Sweet Little Rock and Roller/My Heart Will Always Belong to You/Oh Baby Doll/Check Me Out/It Hurts Me Too+/Bring Another Drink+/So Long+/Goodnight, Well It's Time to Go+

MERCURY
MG-21138
SR-61138

LIVE AT THE FILLMORE AUDITORIUM, SAN FRANCISCO
Medley: *Rockin' at the Fillmore* (instr.) – *Everyday I Have the Blues+/C.C. Rider+/Driftin' Blues+/Feelin' It* (instr)/*Flying Home+* (instr.)/*Wee Baby Blues+/Johnny B. Goode*
　　This is strictly a blues album; Berry is backed by The Steve Miller Band.

1968
MERCURY
SR-61176

FROM ST. LOUIE TO FRISCO
*Louie to Frisco/Ma Dear/The Love I Lost/I Love Her, I Love
Her/Little Fox/Rock Cradle Rock/Soul Rockin'/I Can't Be-
lieve/Misery/My Tambourine/Oh Captain/Mum's the Word*

1969
MERCURY
SR-61223

CONCERTO IN B. GOODE
*Good Looking Woman/My Woman/It's Too Dark in There/
Put Her Down/Concerto in B. Goode* (instr.)
The title track is a nineteen-minute long instrumental.

1970
CHESS
LPS-1550

BACK HOME
Tulane/Have Mercy Judge/Instrumental (instr.)/*Christmas/Gun*
(instr.)/*I'm a Rocker/Flyin' Home* (instr.)/*Fish & Chips/Some
People*
On some issues of this LP, the record label has two different titles: Side 1: *Back Home*; Side 2: *Home Again*. Some
have *Home Again* on both sides.

1971
CHESS
CH-50008

SAN FRANCISCO DUES
Oh Louisiana/Let's Do Our Thing Together/Your Lick (instr.)/
*Festival/Bound to Lose/Bordeaux in My Pirough/San Francisco
Dues/Viva Rock & Roll/My Dream* (poem)/*Lonely School
Days* (fast version)
Viva Rock & Roll and *Lonely School Days* are from April
1966 recording session. Berry is playing piano on *My Dream.*

1972
CHESS
CH-60020

THE LONDON CHUCK BERRY SESSIONS
*Let's Boogie/Mean Old World+/I Will Not Let You Go/London
Berry Blues* (instr.)/*I Love You/Reelin' and Rockin'/My Ding-
A-Ling/Johnny B. Goode*
The first five tracks were recorded at Pye Studios in Lon-
don, February 5. The last three were recorded live at The
Lanchester Arts Festival in Coventry, February 3.
First printings of this LP had fold-out covers. Second
printings featured only single cover.
This LP might also have been issued as CH 6310 122; see
the very end of U.S. singles discography for information.

MERCURY
SRM 2-6501

ST. LOUIE TO FRISCO TO MEMPHIS (2 LP set)
Sides 1 and 2 are the entire LP, FILLMORE LPS-61138.
Side 3 and 4 as follows:
*St. Louie to Frisco/Ma Dear/Soul Rockin'/Check Me Out/
Little Fox/Back to Memphis/My Tambourine/Misery/It's Too
Dark in There/I Do Really Love You/I Can't Believe/My Heart
Will Always Belong to You/So Long+*

184

PICKWICK
SPC-3327

JOHNNY B. GOODE

*Johnny B. Goode/Memphis, Tennessee/Roll Over Beethoven/
Sweet Little Sixteen/School Day/Maybellene/Reelin' and
Rockin'/Rock and Roll Music/Back in the USA*
The Mercury version of *Reelin' and Rockin'* appears here
for the first time.

1973

CHESS
2CH-60023

CHUCK BERRY'S GOLDEN DECADE VOL. 2 (2 LP set)

*Carol/You Never Can Tell/No Money Down/Together/Mad
Lad* (instr.)/*Run Rudolph Run+/Let It Rock/Sweet Little
Rock and Roller/It Don't Take But a Few Minutes/I'm Talking
About You/Driftin' Blues+/Go Go Go/Jaguar and the
Thunderbird/Little Queenie/Betty Jean* (alt. take)/*Guitar
Boogie* (instr.)/*Down the Road a Piece+/Merry Christmas
Baby+/Promised Land/Jo Jo Gunne/Don't You Lie to Me+/
Rockin' at the Philharmonic* (instr.)/*La Juanda/Come On*
Run Rudolph Run appears on this LP for the first time.
The same goes for *Merry Christmas Baby*, which is the single
version.
Let It Rock is without Berry's solo guitar playing.
Go Go Go has the "live" audience dubbed in.

CHESS
CH-50043

BIO

Bio/Hello Little Girl Goodbye/Woodpecker (instr.)/*Rain Eyes/
Aimlessly Driftin'/Got It and Gone/Talkin' About My Buddy*
Berry is playing piano (and guitar) on *Rain Eyes* and *Got
It and Gone*.
The LP was issued both with fold-out cover and single
cover.

PICKWICK
SPC-3345

SWEET LITTLE ROCK AND ROLLER

*Sweet Little Rock and Roller/Check Me Out/Ramblin' Rose+/
Goodnight, Well It's Time to Go+/Carol/Oh Baby Doll/Back
to Memphis/It Hurts Me Too+/C.C. Rider+*
Issued with two different pictures on the front cover.

1974

PICKWICK
SPC-3392

WILD BERRYS

*I Do Really Love You/So Long+/It's Too Dark in There/My
Heart Will Always Belong to You/Bring Another Drink+/Good
Lookin' Woman/My Woman/Thirty Days/Put Her Down*
Good Lookin' Woman is misprinted as *Good Lovin' Woman*
on the back cover.

CHESS
2CH-60028

CHUCK BERRY'S GOLDEN DECADE VOL. 3 (2 LP set)

*Beautiful Delilah/Go Bobby Soxer/I Got to Find My Baby/
Worried Life Blues+/Roly Poly* (instr.)/*The Downbound Train/
Broken Arrow/Confessin' the Blues+/Drifting Heart/In Go*
(instr)/*Man and the Donkey/St. Louis Blues+/Our Little
Rendezvous/Childhood Sweetheart/Blues for Hawaiians* (instr.)/
Hey Pedro/My Little Love Light/Little Marie/County Line/
Viva Rock & Roll/House of Blue Lights*/Time Was*/Blue on
Blue** (instr.)/*Oh Yeah**
The songs marked with an asterisk (*) were unreleased ones
from the 1958--59 sessions. *Man and the Donkey* has the
audience dubbed in. *Beautiful Delilah* appears on this LP for
the first time in the U.S.
For further information, see also the U.K. LP discography.

PICKWICK **FLASHBACK** (2 LP set)
PTP-2061   This is a repackaging of Pickwick LPs SPC-3327 and
    SPC-3345. Different fold-out cover.
ARISTOCRAT **CHUCK AND HIS FRIENDS** (3 LP set)
(BROOKVILLE 1274) *Roll Over Beethoven/Memphis, Tennessee/Viva Rock & Roll/*
BR-100 *Bordeaux in My Pirough/You Never Can Tell/Lonely School*
Days (fast version)/*My Ding-A-Ling/Johnny B. Goode/Nadine/*
School Day/Sweet Little Sixteen/Maybellene/Rock and Roll
Music
    These three LPs were issued in a single cover. The first is
Berry, the second and third are by various other artists.

1975
CHESS **CHUCK BERRY**
CH-60032 *Swanee River+/I'm Just a Name/I Just Want to Make Love to*
You+/Too Late+/South of the Border+/Hi Heel Sneakers+/
You Are My Sunshine+/My Babe+/Baby What You Want Me
to Do+/A Deuce/Shake Rattle and Roll+/Sue Answer/Don't
You Lie to Me+
    This LP contains two songs from the **Bio** session, March
1973: *A Deuce* and *Sue Answer*. The rest are all new record-
ings.

1976
EVEREST **CHUCK BERRY'S GREATEST HITS**
Archive of Folk *Roll Over Beethoven/Johnny B. Goode/Sweet Little Sixteen/*
& Jazz Music *School Day/Maybellene/Rock and Roll Music/Ramblin' Rose+/*
FS-321 *Carol/C.C. Rider+/Memphis, Tennessee*
    These are Mercury recordings. Greatest hits?

1978
GUSTO **THE BEST OF THE BEST OF CHUCK BERRY**
GT-0004 *Johnny B. Goode/School Day/Reelin' and Rockin'/Rock and*
Roll Music/Sweet Little Sixteen/Maybellene/Roll Over Beet-
hoven/Brown-Eyed Handsome Man/No Particular Place to Go/
My Ding-A-Ling
    Chess recordings.
TRIP **CHUCK BERRY'S 16 GREATEST HITS**
TOP-16-55 *Maybellene/Roll Over Beethoven/Sweet Little Sixteen/School*
Day/Around and Around/Back in the USA/Too Pooped to
Pop+/Almost Grown/My Ding-A-Ling/Johnny B. Goode/Rock
and Roll Music/No Particular Place to Go/Nadine/Sweet Little
Rock and Roller/Carol/You Never Can Tell
    Chess recordings. It says *Reelin' and Rockin'* on the
record and label, but it is actually *Around and Around*.
MAGNUM **CHUCK BERRY LIVE IN CONCERT** (2 LP set)
MR-703 *Rock and Roll Music/Nadine/School Day/Wee Wee Hours/*
Medley: *Johnny B. Goode–Carol–Promised Land/Hoochie*
Coochie Man+/Sweet Little Sixteen/Memphis, Tennessee/Too
Much Monkey Business/My Ding-A-Ling/Reelin' and Rockin'/
Johnny B. Goode/Maybellene
    This is the Berry performance given as part of the "Rock &
Roll Revival" in Toronto, Canada, 1969. Some of the songs
are misspelled on the LP.
    Note that Berry performed *My Ding-A-Ling* live as early as
1969!

1979

ATCO SD 38-118	**ROCK IT** *Move It/Oh What a Thrill/I Need You Baby/If I Were/House Lights/I Never Thought/Havana Moon/Wuden't Me/California/ Pass Away* (poem) This is actually Berry's latest studio LP, recorded in 1979 at Berry Park with Johnny Johnson on piano.
UP FRONT UPF-199	**CHUCK BERRY ALL-TIME HITS** *Maybellene/Roll Over Beethoven/Sweet Little Sixteen/School Day/Back in the USA/My Ding-A-Ling/Johnny B. Goode/Rock and Roll Music/No Particular Place to Go* Chess recordings.

1981

STACK-O-HITS AG-9019	**ALIVE AND ROCKIN'** *Rock and Roll Music/Maybellene/Roll Over Beethoven/How High the Moon+* (instr.)*/Vacation Time* or *21 Blues/Chuck's Jam+* (instr.) *(One O'Clock Jump)/Reelin' and Rockin'/Sweet Little Sixteen/Childhood Sweetheart/I've Changed* Exactly the same compilation of tracks as on the Italian bootleg LP **La Grande Storia Del Rock**, with dubbed live audience. Different cover though. The liner notes on the back cover which indicate that the LP contains a "live" performance, recorded in Berry's prime, are untrue, except for *Maybellene* and *Roll Over Beethoven* (see Bootleg section for information). The sound quality is terrible. This particular LP might, itself, be a bootleg.
SSS INTER- NATIONAL SSS-36	**CHUCK BERRY LIVE** *Rock and Roll Music/Nadine/School Day/Wee Wee Hours/* Medley: *Johnny B. Goode–Carol–Promised Land/Hoochie Coochie Man+/Sweet Little Sixteen* Toronto "Rock & Roll Revival," 1969, again. Same songs as the first record of the MAGNUM MR-703 LP. The sound quality on this LP is not very good. Some song titles are also misspelled. On the front cover it says VOL. 1, but Vol. 2 never appeared. However, see the two Accord LPs following.

1982

ACCORD SN-7171	**TORONTO ROCK 'N' ROLL REVIVAL 1969 VOL. II** *Reelin' and Rockin'/Maybellene/Too Much Monkey Business/ My Ding-A-Ling/Memphis, Tennessee*
ACCORD SN-7172	**TORONTO ROCK 'N' ROLL REVIVAL 1969 VOL. III** Contains exactly the same songs as SSS-36, above. Vol. I of the Accord issues never appeared. Vol. II contains – except for *Johnny B. Goode* – the rest of the Magnum MR-703 LP, though not in the same order. There is also a German issue of the Magnum LP, and two LPs containing songs from the Toronto Festival were released in U.K. See the separate country discographies.

| CHESS | THE GREAT TWENTY-EIGHT (2 LP set) |
| CH-8201 | *Maybellene/Thirty Days/You Can't Catch Me/Too Much* |

THE GREAT TWENTY-EIGHT (2 LP set)

Maybellene/Thirty Days/You Can't Catch Me/Too Much Monkey Business/Brown-Eyed Handsome Man/Roll Over Beethoven/Havana Moon/School Day/Rock and Roll Music/ Oh Baby Doll/Reelin' and Rockin'/Sweet Little Sixteen/ Johnny B. Goode/Around and Around/Carol/Beautiful Delilah/ Memphis, Tennessee/Sweet Little Rock and Roller/Little Queenie/Almost Grown/Back in the USA/Let It Rock/Bye Bye Johnny/I'm Talking About You/Come On/Nadine/No Particular Place to Go/I Want to Be Your Driver

These twenty-eight songs are arranged in the sequence recorded and mastered from the original sessions tapes. The two LPs have a marvellous sound quality — no electronic stereo here! To quote from the writings on the cover: "Chuck Berry records are power-packed plastic, intense sonic creations that sparkle and cut with the brillance of diamonds." It couldn't have been better said! The LP has a fold-out cover with information on each song, when it was recorded, and who played on it. Apart from some mistakes, it's a very good compilation of Berry songs.

PROMO RADIO ISSUE
RR-82-26

"RETRO ROCK" — CHUCK BERRY — BROADCAST WEEK 6.21.82

Sounder — Opening Sounder/*Rock and Roll Music*/Commercial — Budweiser (George Thorogood singing and playing "This Bud's For You," Berry-style)/Commercial — Jensen/ Commercial — Lee/Local Avail/Medley: *Johnny B. Goode— Carol—Promised Land/Hoochie Coochie Man+/Reelin' and Rockin'/School Day/Too Much Monkey Business*/Commercial — Budweiser (unknown performing "This Bud's For You," Berry-style)/Local Avail/*My Ding-A-Ling*/Commercial — Budweiser/Commercial — Lee/Local Avail/*Memphis, Tennessee/ Maybellene*/Sponsor Billboard/Sounder

The Toronto Festival once again, only this time as a radio program. A female narrator binds it all together, though some of what she says is nonsense: *Johnny B. Goode* was not recorded and released in 1959! Despite this, an unusual and interesting issue for the collector. The LP comes in hard-paper white sleeve, and contains a Chuck Berry "Fact Sheet," primarily a transcription of what's said on the record.

AURA
A-1020

REELIN' AND ROCKIN'

Reelin' and Rockin'/School Day/My Ding-A-Ling/Too Much Monkey Business/Memphis, Tennessee/Maybellene/Nadine

Berry live again from the Toronto "Rock and Roll Revival," 1969.

PHOENIX 10
PHX-351

CHUCK BERRY

Wee Wee Hours/Johnny B. Goode—Carol—Promised Land/ Hoochie Coochie Man+/Sweet Little Sixteen/Memphis, Tennessee/School Day

Toronto Revival once again. Here Berry is heard talking between songs.

PHOENIX
PD-351

CHUCK BERRY (picture disc)

This is a picture disc of the above record, with the same songs. It has a color picture of Berry's face (mid-50s) on both sides. Also the same as front cover of PHX-351.

1983

PHOENIX 20
P20-630

20 HITS

Introduction/*In the Wee Wee Hours*/*Johnny B. Goode* (Part I)/
Johnny B. Goode (Part II)/*Carol*/*Hootchie Cootchie Man*+/
Sweet Little Sixteen/*Memphis* (Part I)/*Hail, Hail Rock 'N'
Roll*/*Blues*/*Rock 'N' Roll Music*/*Nadine*/*School Day*/*Memphis*
(Part II)/*Reelin' and Rockin'* (Part I)/*Reelin' and Rockin'* (Part
II)/*Maybellene*/*So Much Monkey Business*/*My Ding-A-Ling*
(Part I)/*My Ding-A-Ling* (Part II)

The songs are listed exactly as printed both on the cover and
the label. It looks interesting, but it's just the Toronto Revival
again. The repackager has mixed it around and printed "Part
I" and "Part II" on several tracks in order to make twenty
"cuts." As examples, *Blues* is just *Hoochie Coochie Man* remixed down to a minute-fifty seconds, utilizing the beginning
and the ending of the song. Berry's guitar solo on *School Day*
has been omitted for some reason, and *Hail, Hail Rock 'N'
Roll* is just *School Day* remixed a little to make it sound different. *My Ding-A-Ling* is shortened down to five minutes
eighteen seconds instead of the original track from the Festival,
which is over nine minutes long. And so on!

All Chess LPs from 1425 to 1485 were first released with the black label and silver
lettering. They have all been reissued several times with electronic stereo, using the prefix
letters LPS. These appeared first in the mid- and late 60s (light blue label with red edging
at the top of the white Chess name), then in the 70s with the orange label and the blue
lining. Many of the LPs were also issued with black-and-white covers in the 70s.

U.S. COMPILATION ALBUM DISCOGRAPHY

This is not intended to be a complete survey of American compilation albums featuring Chuck Berry cuts, as it's quite impossible to trace them all. The list does give a good idea of Berry's importance by his inclusion on many, many such releases, however.

1957

CHESS
LP-1425

ROCK ROCK ROCK (soundtrack album)
Maybellene/Thirty Days/You Can't Catch Me/Roll Over Beethoven
Also featured on the album are The Flamingos and The Moonglows.

1961

CHESS
LP-1461

MURRAY THE K'S BLASTS FROM THE PAST
Exact cuts not determined.

1962

CHESS
LP-1474

TREASURE TUNES FROM THE VAULTS
Sweet Little Sixteen

ATLANTIC
9068

HOUND DOG'S ORIGINAL ROCK & ROLL MEMORY TIME
Exact cuts not determined.

1963

ARGO
LP-4026

BLUES VOL. 1
Wee Wee Hours/Thirty Days

ARGO
LP-4027

BLUES VOL. 2
Worried Life Blues+

1969

CHESS
LP-1528

HEAVY HEADS VOYAGE 2
Exact cut(s) not determined.

CHESS
LP-1544

POP ORIGINS
Rock and Roll Music/Roll Over Beethoven/Memphis, Tennessee
Howlin' Wolf is featured with five songs; Bo Diddley has two; Lowell Fulson, Dale Hawkins, Muddy Waters and Little Milton have one song each.
A good compilation, but a terrible cover!

ROULETTE
R-25213

GOLDEN GOODIES VOL. 9
Maybellene
Chess recording.

ROULETTE
R-25214

GOLDEN GOODIES VOL. 8
School Day/Roll Over Beethoven
Chess recordings.

ROULETTE
SR-42027

REMEMBER HOW GREAT VOL. 1
Exact cuts not determined.

1970
CAPITOL
STBB-178

SUPER SOUL-DEES VOL. 3 (2 LP set)
Nadine
Chess recording. This one is listed principally because of
Berry's unusual presence on a Capitol record. The fold-out
cover is awful, a prime example of how not to package a recording. Of the seventeen black artists included, only eleven
are pictured on the inside (no Berry), and there are no liner
notes.

1970--1972/73
INCREASE	**CRUISIN' 1955**
INCM.2000	*Maybellene*
INCREASE	**CRUISIN' 1957**
INCM.2002	*School Day*
INCREASE	**CRUISIN' 1961**
INCM.2006	*Nadine*
INCREASE	**CRUISIN' 1956**
INCM.2001	*Roll Over Beethoven*
INCREASE	**CRUISIN' 1959**
INCM.2004	*Almost Grown*
INCREASE	**CRUISIN' 1965**
INCM.2010	*Sweet Little Sixteen*

All issued during 1970 and 1972--73 as part of a series
called "Cruisin' 1955-1967." Each is a re-creation radio program aired during the year indicated. Berry tunes featured are
all Chess recordings; the oddity is *Nadine*, which was recorded
in January 1964 but which appears on the album for 1961.

1972
CHESS/JANUS
(DJ only)

LP SAMPLER
Let's Boogie
A collection of tracks from various Chess LPs. There are
ten songs by ten different artists, including: The Dells, The
Gospel Six, Muddy Waters, Aretha Franklin, Bo Diddley, Jack
McDuff, Gloria Spencer, Harvey Mandel, and Rev. C.L.
Franklin. A very dull cover with no pictures of the artists.

1975
PICKWICK
SPC-3512

ONLY YOU – THE ORIGINALS
Reelin' and Rockin'/Johnny B. Goode
Mercury recordings. Originals? Except for two songs by
The Platters, there aren't any originals among the songs by
Jerry Lee Lewis, Fats Domino (live), Bill Haley or Berry!

1976
PICKWICK
SPC-3517

THE HAPPY DAYS OF ROCK 'N ROLL
Johnny B. Goode
Mercury recording. Twelve songs by twelve different artists, with more "originals" than Pickwick SPC-3512. Not
bad!

UNITED ARTISTS	**RHYTHM & BLUES CHRISTMAS**
UA-LA654-R	*Run Rudolph Run+*

A very good compilation of ten artists and ten songs. Great liner notes on each artist/song.

FESTIVAL	**AMERICA'S MUSICAL ROOTS**
FR-1008	*Wee Wee Hours/Blue Feeling* (instr.)

Chess recordings. This is really a good one. All songs are taken from the Chess files. Informative liner notes on inner sleeve. Besides Berry, artists include: Little Walter (two songs); Howlin' Wolf (two); Muddy Waters (two); "Sonny Boy" Williamson (two); Lowell Fulson (two); John Lee Hooker (two); Bo Diddley (two); Elmore James (one); and Memphis Slim (one).

1978?

TOP 50-2	**SUPER OLDIES OF THE 50'S VOL. 2**
GS-777	**THE BEST OF CHUCK BERRY**

This is a double LP set in a single cover. **Super Oldies** features twenty different artists, no Berry. The Berry LP has ten songs, which are the same as the first ten tracks on the Trip album (TOP-16-55), **Chuck Berry's 16 Greatest Hits**.

The Berry record (GS-777) has no label identification, other than the marking "Produced by F & G Marketing Inc. New York." The title and picture on front cover is the same as on the American Graffiti LP set, **Songs of American Graffiti and other Rock Favorites**. The back has the standard black-and-white picture of Berry with guitar. Here, the title is the same as on the record. A strange (cheap) album set, good candidate for sale in supermarkets.

GUSTO	**ROCK & ROLL SHOW**
GT-0002	*Sweet Little Sixteen/Reelin' and Rockin'/Roll Over Beethoven*

Chess recordings. This is one of those hard to understand issues. The front cover gives the impression that it's a "live" album, but all the songs are just 50s(?) recordings and some are even not the originals! Berry's are, though.

1982

ORIGINAL SOUND	**OLDIES BUT GOODIES VOL. 10**
OSR LP-8860	*Roll Over Beethoven*

Chess recording.

ORIGINAL SOUND	**OLDIES BUT GOODIES VOL. 11**
OSR LP-8862	*Maybellene*

Chess recording.

ORIGINAL SOUND	**OLDIES BUT GOODIES VOL. 12**
OSR LP-8862	*Sweet Little Sixteen*

Chess recording.

ROULETTE	**THE ORIGINAL ROCK 'N' ROLL HITS OF THE 50'S AND**
SR-59001	**60'S, VOL. 1**
	Roll Over Beethoven
ROULETTE	**THE ORIGINAL ROCK 'N' ROLL HITS OF THE 50'S AND**
SR-59002	**60'S, VOL. 2**
	You Can't Catch Me
ROULETTE	**THE ORIGINAL ROCK 'N' ROLL HITS OF THE 50'S AND**
SR-59003	**60'S, VOL. 3**
	Johnny B. Goode

ROULETTE SR-59004	THE ORIGINAL ROCK 'N' ROLL HITS OF THE 50'S AND 60'S, VOL. 4 *Maybellene*
ROULETTE SR-59005	THE ORIGINAL ROCK 'N' ROLL HITS OF THE 50'S AND 60'S, VOL. 5 *Sweet Little Sixteen*
ROULETTE SR-59006	THE ORIGINAL ROCK 'N' ROLL HITS OF THE 50'S AND 60'S, VOL. 6 *School Day*
ROULETTE SR-59007	THE ORIGINAL ROCK 'N' ROLL HITS OF THE 50'S AND 60'S, VOL. 7 *Rock and Roll Music*
ROULETTE SR-59011	THE ORIGINAL ROCK 'N' ROLL HITS OF THE 50'S AND 60'S, VOL. 11 *No Particular Place to Go*
ROULETTE SR-59013	THE ORIGINAL ROCK 'N' ROLL HITS OF THE 50'S AND 60'S, VOL. 13 *You Never Can Tell* All are Chess recordings.

Chuck Berry soundtrack albums are listed separately.

U.K. SINGLES DISCOGRAPHY

COLUMBIA
DB 3951   *School Day/Deep Feeling* (instr.) (1957)

LONDON
HLU 8275   *No Money Down/The Downbound Train* (1956)
HLN 8375   *You Can't Catch Me/Havana Moon* (1957)
HLU 8428   *Roll Over Beethoven/Drifting Heart*
HLM 8531   *Rock and Roll Music/Blue Feeling* (instr.)
HLM 8585   *Sweet Little Sixteen/Reelin' and Rockin'* (1958)
HLM 8629   *Johnny B. Goode/Around and Around*
HL 8677   *Beautiful Delilah/Vacation Time*
HL 8712   *Carol/Hey Pedro*
HL 8767   *Sweet Little Rock and Roller/Jo Jo Gunne*
HLM 8853   *Almost Grown/Little Queenie* (1959)
HLM 8921   *Back in the USA/Memphis, Tennessee*
HLM 9069   *Too Pooped to Pop+/Let It Rock* (1960)
HLM 9159   *Bye Bye Johnny/Mad Lad+* (instr.)

PYE INT'L
7N 25100   *I'm Talking About You/Little Star* (1961)

PYE INT'L
R&B Series
7N 25209   *Come On/Go Go Go* (1963)
7N 25218   *Memphis, Tennessee/Let It Rock*
7N 25228   *Run Rudolph Run+/Johnny B. Goode*
7N 25236   *Nadine/O'Rangutang* (instr.) (1964)
7N 25242   *No Particular Place to Go/Liverpool Drive* (instr.)
7N 25257   *You Never Can Tell/Brenda Lee*
7N 25271   *Little Marie/Go Bobby Soxer*
7N 25285   *Promised Land/Things I Used to Do+*

CHESS
CRS 8006   *I Got a Booking/Lonely School Days* (slow version) (1965)
CRS 8012   *Dear Dad/My Little Love Light*
CRS 8022   *It Wasn't Me/It's My Own Business*
CRS 8037   *Ramona Say Yes/Lonely School Days* (fast version) (1966)
CRS 8075   *Johnny B. Goode/Sweet Little Sixteen* (re-release)
CRS 8089   *No Particular Place to Go/It Wasn't Me* (re-release)

MERCURY
MF 958   *Club Nitty Gritty/Laugh and Cry* (1966)
MF 994   *Back to Memphis/I Do Really Love You* (1967)
MF 1057   *St. Louie to Frisco/Ma Dear* (1968)
MF 1102   *Back to Memphis/Roll Over Beethoven* (1969)

CHESS
6078 707   *Sweet Little Sixteen/Guitar Boogie* (instr.) (1971; re-release)
6145 007   Maxi Single: *Rock and Roll Music/Johnny B. Goode/School Day* (1972)
6145 012   Maxi Single: **Big Daddies**
        Johnny B. Goode (live)/*Down the Road a Piece+*
        Plus two songs by Bo Diddley.

6145 019	*My Ding-A-Ling/Let's Boogie*
6145 020	*Reelin' and Rockin'* (live)/*I Will Not Let You Go* (1973)
6145 027	*South of the Border+/Bio* (1973)
	(*South of the Border* legally issued; from the BBC 2 TV program "Six Two Five.")
6145 038	*Shake Rattle and Roll+/I'm Just a Name* (1975)
6198 080	Maxi Single: *Sweet Little Rock and Roller/No Particular Place to Go/Back in the USA* (1978; re-release)

HAMMER	**Chuck Berry Vol. 1**
HB-604	*Roll Over Beethoven/Johnny B. Goode/Carol/Memphis, Tennessee/Sweet Little Sixteen/Maybellene*
	Mercury recordings on a 33 rpm record. Carries the legend "The Big Six — Super Single."

PRT RECORDS
(Flashbacks)
FBS-18   *No Particular Place to Go/Sweet Little Sixteen* (1983)

OLD GOLD
OG-9296   *Memphis, Tennessee/No Particular Place to Go* (1983)

HAMMER   **Chuck Berry Vol. 2**
HB 610   *School Day/Rock and Roll Music/Sweet Little Rock and Roller/Reelin' and Rockin'/Back in the USA/Thirty Days* (1979)
    Mercury recordings on a 33 rpm record. Carries the legend "The Big Six — Super Single."

ATLANTIC
K-11354   *Oh What a Thrill/California* (1979)

U.K. EP DISCOGRAPHY

All the EPs listed below were released between 1963 and 1965.

LONDON	**RHYTHM AND BLUES WITH CHUCK BERRY**
REU 1053	*Maybellene/Wee Wee Hours/Thirty Days/Together*
LONDON	**REELIN' AND ROCKIN'**
REM 1188	*Reelin' and Rockin'/Rock and Roll Music/Sweet Little Sixteen/Guitar Boogie* (instr.)
PYE INT'L	**CHUCK AND BO – VOL. 1**
R&B Series	*Roll Over Beethoven/Our Little Rendezvous/(and two tracks*
NEP 44009	by Bo Diddley)
PYE INT'L	**CHUCK BERRY**
R&B Series	*Johnny B. Goode/Oh Baby Doll/School Day/Back in the*
NEP 44011	*USA*
PYE INT'L	**CHUCK AND BO – VOL. 2**
R&B Series	*You Can't Catch Me/No Money Down/(and two tracks by*
NEP 44012	Bo Diddley)
PYE INT'L	**THIS IS CHUCK BERRY**
R&B Series	*Bye Bye Johnny/Rock and Roll Music/Childhood Sweetheart/*
NEP 44013	*Broken Arrow*
PYE INT'L	**CHUCK AND BO – VOL. 3**
R&B Series	*Too Pooped to Pop+/It Don't Take But a Few Minutes/(and*
NEP 44017	two tracks by Bo Diddley)
PYE INT'L	**THE BEST OF CHUCK BERRY**
R&B Series	*Memphis, Tennessee/Roll Over Beethoven/I'm Talking About*
NEP 44018	*You/Sweet Little Sixteen*
PYE INT'L	**CHUCK BERRY HITS**
R&B Series	*Johnny B. Goode/Nadine/No Particular Place to Go/Memphis,*
NEP 44028	*Tennessee*
PYE INT'L	**BLUE MOOD**
R&B Series	*Driftin' Blues+/Lonely All the Time+ (Crazy Arms)/Things I*
NEP 44033	*Used to Do+/Fraulein+*
CHESS	**THE PROMISED LAND**
CRE 6002	*You Never Can Tell/Brenda Lee/Promised Land/Things I Used to Do+*
CHESS	**COME ON**
CRE 6005	*Come On/Reelin' and Rockin'/Around and Around/Don't You Lie to Me+*
CHESS	**I GOT A BOOKING**
CRE 6012	*I Want to Be Your Driver/St. Louis Blues+/Dear Dad/I Got a Booking*
CHESS	**YOU CAME A LONG WAY FROM ST. LOUIS**
CRE 6016	*You Came a Long Way from St. Louis+/His Daughter Caroline/My Little Love Light/Jamaica Farewell+*

U.K. COMPILATION EPs
FEATURING CHUCK BERRY SONGS

PYE	**HITMAKERS VOL. 1**
NEP 24215	*No Particular Place to Go*
PYE	**HITMAKERS VOL. 2**
NEP 24242	*Promised Land*
CHESS	**THE BLUES VOL. 2**
CRE 6011	*Wee Wee Hours*

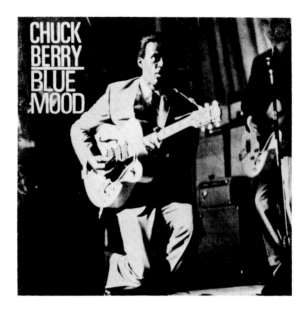

Blue Mood   Pye International NEP 44033 (EP)

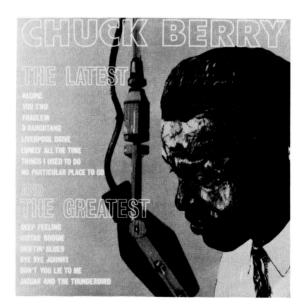

**The Latest And The Greatest
Pye International NPL-28031 (LP)**

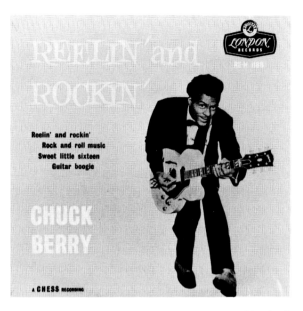

Reelin' And Rockin'   London REM 1188 (EP)

Chuck & Bo   Pye International NEP 44009 (EP)

U.K. ALBUM DISCOGRAPHY

1958

LONDON	**ONE DOZEN BERRIES**
HAM-2132	Contains the same tracks as on U.S. Chess LP-1432. Same front cover.

1960

PYE INT'L	**JUKE BOX HITS**
NPL-28019	Same as U.S. Chess LP-1456. Same front cover.

1962

PYE INT'L	**CHUCK BERRY**
R&B Series	*Maybellene/Down the Road a Piece+/Mad Lad+* (instr.)/*School*
NPL-28024	*Day/Sweet Little Sixteen/Confessin' the Blues+/Back in the USA/Johnny B. Goode/Oh Baby Doll/Come On/I Got to Find My Baby/Betty Jean/Around and Around/Almost Grown*

This LP was reissued on Pye Golden Guinea GGL-0352, same cover; and again in 1966 on Marble Arch MAL-611, this time minus four tracks and with a different cover.

1963

PYE INT'L	**CHUCK BERRY ON STAGE**
R&B Series	Contains the same songs as on U.S. Chess LP-1480, but
NPL-28027	*How High the Moon* is faded earlier. Same front cover.
PYE INT'L	**MORE CHUCK BERRY**
R&B Series	*Sweet Little Rock and Roller/Anthony Boy/Little Queenie/*
NPL-28028	*Worried Life Blues+/Carol/Reelin' and Rockin'/Thirty Days/ Brown-Eyed Handsome Man/Wee Wee Hours/Jo Jo Gunne/ Beautiful Delilah*

Although not the same compilation of tracks, this LP has the same front cover as U.S. Chess LP-1465.

1964

PYE INT'L	**THE LATEST AND THE GREATEST**
R&B Series	*Nadine/Fraulein+/Guitar Boogie* (instr.)/*Things I Used to Do+/*
NPL-28031	*Don't You Lie to Me+/Driftin' Blues+/Liverpool Drive* (instr.)/ *No Particular Place to Go/Lonely All the Time+ (Crazy Arms)/ Jaguar and the Thunderbird/O'Rangutang* (instr.)/*You Two/ Deep Feeling* (instr.)/*Bye Bye Johnny*

PYE INT'L	**YOU NEVER CAN TELL**
R&B Series	*You Never Can Tell/Diploma for Two/The Little Girl from*
NPL-28039	*Central/The Way It Was Before/Around and Around/Big Ben/ Promised Land/Back in the USA/Run Around/Brenda Lee/ Reelin' and Rockin'/Come On*

This LP was reissued in 1967 on Marble Arch MAL-702, same cover, but without *Around and Around* and *Come On.*

PYE INT'L	**TWO GREAT GUITARS – CHUCK BERRY & BO DIDDLEY**
R&B Series	Contains the same tracks as on U.S. Checker LP-2991, and
NPL-28047	same cover. *Not* available on stereo in U.K.

200

1965

CHESS CRL-4005	**CHUCK BERRY IN LONDON** Contains the same tracks as on U.S. Chess LP-1495, except that *Jamaica Farewell* is slightly different. See U.S. discography for information. Same cover; no stereo issued in U.K.
CHESS CRL-4506	**FRESH BERRY'S** Substitutes an instrumental, *Sad Day, Long Night*, in place of *Welcome Back Pretty Baby* on the U.S. Chess LP-1498. The two songs are actually the same, almost. On *Welcome Back . . .*, Berry is singing; on the instrumental a harmonica is playing the melody. Otherwise, the cuts have exactly the same backing, and are from the same recording session, September 1--2, 1965 (see the discography inside the cover of **Golden Decade Vol. 2**, LP set). Apart from this difference, the U.S. and U.K. albums have the same tracks, different covers, and no stereo in U.K.

1966

CHESS CRL-4548	**CHUCK BERRY'S GREATEST HITS** *No Particular Place to Go/It Wasn't Me/Thirty Days/My Mustang Ford/Too Much Monkey Business/Sweet Little Rock and Roller/Go Go Go/Johnny B. Goode/Maybellene/Brown-Eyed Handsome Man/Memphis, Tennessee/Sweet Little Sixteen/Bye Bye Johnny/Reelin' and Rockin'/You Came a Long Way from St. Louis+* *Go Go Go* is the "dubbed live audience" version.
MARBLE ARCH MAL-611	**CHUCK BERRY** See NPL-28024.

1967

MARBLE ARCH MAL-660	**CHUCK BERRY'S GREATEST HITS** This one contains the same songs as on U.S. Chess LP-1485, minus two tracks. Different cover.
MARBLE ARCH MAL-702	**YOU NEVER CAN TELL** See NPL-28039.
MARBLE ARCH MALS-702	**YOU NEVER CAN TELL** (Stereophonic) *You Never Can Tell/Diploma for Two/The Little Girl from Central/ The Way It Was Before/Around and Around* (alt. take)/**Big Ben/Promised Land**/Back in the USA/**Run Around**/Brenda Lee/Reelin' and Rockin'/Come On* (alt. take) This is a strange and a rare one. It has exactly the same cover as MAL-702, but on the label it says "stereophonic." This package includes twelve songs, as on the Pye LP NPL-28039, but the versions of *Around and Around* and *Come On* are different takes from any other issued. The two songs are not mentioned anywhere on the cover or label, but they are there, all right! The tracks in bold italic are in true stereo, the rest are monophonic. *The Little Girl from Central* is a little bit shorter on this stereo issue because of earlier fading.
MERCURY 20102 MCL 20102 SMCL	**CHUCK BERRY GOLDEN HITS** Contains the same tracks as on U.S. Mercury SR-61103. Same cover (?). Reissued in 1972 as **Back in the USA** (6336 216). Different cover.

MERCURY 20110 MCL 20110 SMCL	**CHUCK BERRY IN MEMPHIS** Contains the same tracks as on U.S. LP SR-61123. Same cover.
MERCURY 20112 MCL 20112 SMCL	**LIVE AT THE FILLMORE AUDITORIUM, SAN FRANCISCO** Contains same tracks as on U.S. LP SR-61138. Same cover.

1968

MERCURY 6851 002	**CHUCK BERRY MEDLEY** Side 1 is the same as side 1 on the **Fillmore** LP. Side 2 is the same as side 1 on the **In Memphis** LP. The cover is almost the same as on the **Memphis** LP.
MERCURY CMP-7029 (tape)	**FROM ST. LOUIS TO FRISCO** The same tracks as on the U.S. LP SR-61176, but only issued in tape format in U.K.

1969

MERCURY 20162 SMCL	**CONCERTO IN B. GOODE** Same tracks as on U.S. LP SR-61223. Same cover.

1970

CHESS 6310 113	**BACK HOME** Same tracks as on U.S. LP-1550. Same cover. Reissued in 1975 on Contour 6870 638, and again on Contour CN-2019. Both times with the title **I'm a Rocker** and different covers.

1971

CHESS 6310 115	**SAN FRANCISCO DUES** Contains same tracks as U.S. LP CH-50008. Same cover.

1972

CHESS 6310 122	**THE LONDON CHUCK BERRY SESSIONS** Same tracks as on U.S. LP CH-60020. Same fold-out cover.
CHESS 6641 018	**CHUCK BERRY'S GOLDEN DECADE** Same as U.S. LPS-1514D. Same fold-out cover.
PHILIPS INT'L 6336 216	**BACK IN THE USA** See LP **Golden Hits** (6336 215).
PHILIPS INT'L 6619 008	**ST. LOUIE TO FRISCO TO MEMPHIS** (2 LP set) Same tracks as on U.S. Mercury LP SRM-2 6501. Same fold-out cover.

1973

CHESS 6310 130	**ALL-TIME ROCK 'N' ROLL PARTY HITS** *Johnny B. Goode/Rock and Roll Music/No Particular Place to Go/Memphis, Tennessee/Nadine/Sweet Little Sixteen/Run Rudolph Run+/Reelin' and Rockin'/Maybellene/Carol/Little Queenie/School Day/Brown-Eyed Handsome Man/Roll Over Beethoven/Almost Grown/Bye Bye Johnny* As issued with number AVB-00208. Same cover.
CHESS 6499 650	**BIO** Same as U.S. LP CH-50043. Same fold-out cover.

CHESS	**CHUCK BERRY'S GOLDEN DECADE VOL. 2** (2 LP set)
6641 058	Contains the same tracks as U.S. LP 2CH-60023, but different fold-out cover.

1974
CHESS	**CHUCK BERRY'S GOLDEN DECADE VOL. 3** (2 LP set)
6641 177	This U.K. issue has the unreleased track *Do You Love Me+*, instead of *Time Was* on the U.S. LP. *Berry Pickin'* is on this U.K. issue instead of *Viva Rock & Roll*. Apart from that, the tracks are the same. Also same fold-out cover.

1975
CONTOUR	**I'M A ROCKER**
6870 638	See Chess LP-6310 113, **Back Home**. Different cover. Reissued with number CN-2019 and different cover.
CHESS	**CHUCK BERRY '75**
9109 101	Same tracks as on U.S. LP CH-60032. Also same cover, except for the " '75."

1976
PHILIPS	**SWEET LITTLE 16 – ROCK & ROLL HITS**
Sonic Series	Contains the same tracks as on Chess LP 6310 130, **All-**
SON-006	**Time Rock 'n' Roll Party Hits**. Slightly different cover.

1977
CHESS	**MOTORVATIN'**
9286 690	*Johnny B. Goode/Roll Over Beethoven/School Day/Maybellene/ Rock and Roll Music/Oh Baby Doll/Too Much Monkey Busi- ness/Carol/Let It Rock/Sweet Little Rock and Roller/Bye Bye Johnny/Reelin' and Rockin'/No Particular Place to Go/Thirty Days/Sweet Little Sixteen/Little Queenie/Memphis, Tennessee/ You Never Can Tell/Brown-Eyed Handsome Man/Nadine/ Promised Land/Back in the USA*
	Let It Rock is the one without Berry's solo guitar. A good compilation that actually was in the British Top 10 in March, 1977.
HAMMER	**20 GOLDEN HITS**
HMR-9003	Mercury tracks, but no more information available.

1979
ATLANTIC	**ROCK IT**
K-50648	Same as U.S. LP ATCO SD 38-118. Same cover.

1980
MERCURY	**CHUCK BERRY'S MODS & ROCKERS**
6336 635	*Roll Over Beethoven/Everyday I Have the Blues+/Back in the USA/Club Nitty Gritty/Hoochie Coochie Man+/Check Me Out/ Johnny B. Goode/It Hurts Me Too+/Misery/Carol/Wee Baby Blues+/Back to Memphis*
	This LP has very bad sound quality on some tracks. The bass sound is gone!

CHESS	**SPOTLIGHT ON CHUCK BERRY** (2 LPs)
(PRT Records)	*School Day/Sweet Little Sixteen/Carol/Route 66+/Back in the*
SPOT-1003	*USA/Rock and Roll Music/Promised Land/Let It Rock/Brown-*

Eyed Handsome Man/Maybellene/Around and Around/Run Rudolph Run+/No Particular Place to Go/You Never Can Tell/ Nadine/Roll Over Beethoven/Too Much Monkey Business/ Go Go Go/Reelin' and Rockin'/Memphis, Tennessee/Johnny B. Goode/Tulane/Come On/My Ding-A-Ling

The two LPs are issued in a single cover.

1981

EVEREST
CBR-1007

CHUCK BERRY LIVE

*School Day/Wee Wee Hours/*Medley: *Johnny B. Goode–Carol –Promised Land/Hoochie Coochie Man+/Sweet Little Sixteen/ Memphis, Tennessee/My Ding-A-Ling*

This is the Toronto Rock & Roll Festival, 1969, again, but here issued for the first time in the U.K. The sound quality is the best of all the Toronto albums, and you'll also hear Berry talking between songs. Pity they didn't issue the whole concert. *School Day* is misprinted on cover and label as *No Particular Place to Go Hail Hail Rock and Roll*!

1983

SPOT
SPR-8512

THE GREATEST HITS – CHUCK BERRY LIVE

Johnny B. Goode/Sweet Little Sixteen/Nadine/Wee Wee Hours/ Rock and Roll Music/Maybellene/Too Much Monkey Business/ School Day/My Ding-A-Ling

Toronto Festival once again. Here we get the single version of *Johnny B. Goode*, with which Berry ended the show. It is only included on the original U.S. Magnum LP, and on the Bellaphon LP issued in West Germany.

CHESS
(PRT Records)
CXMP-2011

CHESS MASTERS

Rock and Roll Music (demo)/*Childhood Sweetheart* (alt. take)/ *21* (unreleased)/*Let Me Sleep Woman+* (The Ecuadors)/*Do You Love Me+* (alt. take)/*21 Blues* (unreleased)/*One O'Clock Jump+* (instr.–unreleased)/*Reelin' and Rockin'* (alt. take)/ *Sweet Little Sixteen* (alt. take)/*Brown-Eyed Handsome Man/ Say You'll Be Mine+* (The Ecuadors)/*I've Changed* (unreleased)/ *13 Question Method* (alt. take)/*How High the Moon+* (instr.)

This is the legal issue of the bootleg LP **America's Hottest Wax** (Reelin' 001), which appeared in 1980. *Brown-Eyed Handsome Man* is the same version as on Chess LP-1480, but here without dubbed "live" audience. The same goes for *How High the Moon*, and here it is complete. See "Miscellaneous Record Facts" for more information on The Ecuadors.

CHESS
(PRT Records)
CXMD-4016

CHESS MASTERS – CHUCK BERRY (2 LP set)

Maybellene/Wee Wee Hours/Thirty Days/You Can't Catch Me/ Downbound Train/No Money Down/Brown-Eyed Handsome Man/Roll Over Beethoven/Too Much Monkey Business/Havana Moon/School Day/La Juanda/Rock and Roll Music/Oh Baby Doll/Sweet Little Sixteen/Reelin' and Rockin'/Johnny B. Goode/Around and Around/Beautiful Delilah/House of Blue Lights+/Carol/Jo Jo Gunne/Memphis, Tennessee/Sweet Little Rock and Roller

Two LPs in a single sleeve; dull cover.

PRT DOW 14	**DUCKWALKING** (10-inch LP) *School Day/No Particular Plact to Go/Promised Land/Reelin'* *and Rockin'/Sweet Little Sixteen/Memphis, Tennessee/* *Nadine/You Never Can Tell* Chess recordings. Great picture of Berry!
BULLDOG BDL-1051	**REELING ROLLIN' AND ROCKING** *Memphis, Tennessee/Too Much Monkey Business/My Ding-A-* *Ling/Reelin' and Rockin'/Johnny B. Goode/Maybellene/* *Nadine/School Day/Sweet Little Sixteen* Toronto Rock and Roll Revival. This has the single *Johnny B. Goode* version.
BREAKAWAY BWY-69	**TORONTO ROCK 'N' ROLL REVIVAL 1969, VOLUME II** Exactly the same issue as U.S. LP Accord SN-7171. Same songs and same cover. The only difference is that this particu- lar LP has very good sound quality.

1984

MAGNUM FORCE MFM-017	**REELIN' AND ROCKIN'** *Reelin' and Rockin'/School Day/Too Much Monkey Business/* *Memphis, Tennessee/Maybellene/Nadine/My Ding-A-Ling* Toronto Festival again.

U.K. COMPILATION ALBUMS

1964

PYE NPL-18108	**THE HIT MAKERS** *No Particular Place to Go* Includes primarily English artists.
PYE INT'L R&B Series NPL-28030	**THE BLUES VOLUME 1** *Worried Life Blues+*
PYE INT'L R&B Series NPL-28035	**THE BLUES VOLUME 2** *Thirty Days/Wee Wee Hours* These two LPs contain Chess artists. Probably very similar to the two U.S. Argo LP issues.

1965

PYE NPL-18115	**THE HIT MAKERS VOL. 2** *Promised Land* Includes primarily English artists.

1968

MARBLE ARCH MAL-804	**THE BLUES** *Worried Life Blues+* This LP contains only ten tracks, and not all are the same as on NPL-28030.

1969

FONTANA SFL-13120	**ROCK 'N' ROLL** *Rock and Roll Music/Sweet Little Rock and Roller/Sweet Little Sixteen/Roll Over Beethoven/Check Me Out* Mercury recordings. This LP was in the British Top 20 in 1969, a surprise because it includes some poor sound quality. To add to the poor quality, a dubbed-in "live" audience has been added to the Berry tracks. Jerry Lee Lewis is represented with three songs from the Hamburg Star Club LP; there are also four live songs by Fats Domino. The album was reissued in 1975 as Contour 6870 536, **Rock & Roll Greats**, and again as Contour CN-2014, both with covers different from the Fontana issue.

1974

CHECKER 6445 151	**CHESS GOLDEN DECADE VOL. 2 – 1956** *Roll Over Beethoven*
CHECKER 6445 201	**CHESS GOLDEN DECADE VOL. 5 – 1959/1961** *Let It Rock*
CHESS 6445 204	**CHESS GOLDEN DECADE VOL. 8 – 1965/1966** *You Came a Long Way from St. Louis+* The "Golden Decade" is a very good series consisting of nine albums, issued only in the U.K. All LPs have fold-out covers and great liner notes.

1975
CONTOUR
6870 527

CRAZY ROCK
Carol/Club Nitty Gritty
Mercury recordings.

1980
HMR-9007

GIANTS OF ROCK & ROLL
Side 1 is Fats Domino with ten tracks. Side 2 is Berry, with the same tracks as on U.S. Everest LP FS-321.

1981
CHESS
(PRT Records)
CXMP-2002

THE BEST OF CHESS/CHECKER–CADET
School Day

1982
HRL-004

THE HISTORY OF ROCK – VOLUME 4 (2 LP set)
School Day/Sweet Little Sixteen/Johnny B. Goode/Rock and Roll Music/Memphis, Tennessee/Come On/No Particular Place to Go/You Never Can Tell/Roll Over Beethoven/Maybellene
Part of a thirty-one double-album rock music series. Most artists have one side each. A very good compilation with liner notes and many great pictures, but the inclusion of *Come On* instead of the first issue of *Promised Land* is puzzling.

Soundtrack albums are listed separately.

FRENCH DISCOGRAPHY

SINGLES

CHESS
(Rock Revival)

169512	*Rock and Roll Music/I Just Want to Make Love to You+* (dubbed-in "live" audience)
169513	*Memphis, Tennessee/Brown-Eyed Handsome Man* (second version with dubbed-in "live" audience)
169514	*Maybellene/Little Queenie*
169515	*Roll Over Beethoven/School Day*
169516	*Johnny B. Goode/You Can't Catch Me*
169528	*Nadine/Carol*
169532	*Rip It Up+/No Money Down*
169550	*Tulane/Have Mercy Judge*

CHESS

CH25002	*Reelin' and Rockin'/Johnny B. Goode* (both live)
CH25006	*Bio/Hello Little Girl Goodbye*

MERCURY

6167 208	*Johnny B. Goode/Sweet Little Sixteen* Both the cover and label proclaim: "1958 Original Hits"; hardly credible that the originals would be on Mercury, but a nice sleeve.

VOGUE
(Chess)

101479	*Nadine/You Never Can Tell* (1981 re-issue)

EPS

BARCLAY

70668	*Nadine/Thirty Days/School Day/Bye Bye Johnny*
70739	*You Never Can Tell/No Particular Place to Go/Carol/Too Pooped to Pop+*
70790	*Dear Dad/Lonely School Days* (slow version)*/Promised Land/ Things I Used to Do+* Preceding EPs carry the legend "Eddy Mitchell Presents Les Rois du Rock."
70858	**CHUCK BERRY A LONDRES** *My Little Love Light/You Came a Long Way from St. Louis+/ Jamaica Farewell+/I Want to Be Your Driver*

ALBUMS

BARCLAY
80225

VOL. 1 CHUCK BERRY
Nadine/I'm Talking About You/Bye Bye Johnny/Roll Over Beethoven/Thirty Days/Sweet Little Sixteen/Maybellene/ Reelin' and Rockin'/Johnny B. Goode/Wee Wee Hours/Brown-Eyed Handsome Man/School Day

BARCLAY 80245	**VOL. 3 CHUCK BERRY** *You Never Can Tell/Carol/Little Queenie/Confessin' the* *Blues+/I Got to Find My Baby/Childhood Sweetheart/No* *Particular Place to Go/Almost Grown/Anthony Boy/Around* *and Around/Worried Life Blues+/Too Pooped to Pop+*
BARCLAY 80258	**VOL. 5 CHUCK BERRY A L'OLYMPIA** This is very similar to the U.S. Chess LP *On Stage*, but here they have dubbed Berry "live" from l'Olympia in Paris, 1965. The fake "live" appearance even has a French compere introducing Chuck, who shouts "Viva la Rock and Roll – Viva la Musica – Ole! – Ah, Paris" between songs. *Go Go Go* and *How High the Moon* are missing on this issue.
BARCLAY 80279	**VOL. 8 CHUCK BERRY A LONDRES** Same issue as U.S. LP **Chuck Berry in London**, Chess LP- 1495.
BARCLAY 80318	**VOL. 11 CHUCK BERRY** *Rock and Roll Music/Rip It Up+/Go Bobby Soxer/Too Much* *Monkey Business/No Money Down/Down the Road a Piece+/* *Our Little Rendezvous/Route 66+/Let It Rock/Little Marie/* *You Can't Catch Me/Beautiful Delilah/Come On/Brenda Lee* "Eddy Mitchell Presents Le Rois du Rock" precedes the volume number on all Barclay LPs.
CHESS 69502	**CHUCK BERRY ROCK REVIVAL** *Carol/Rip It Up+/Route 66+/Let It Rock/Dear Dad/I Want to* *Be Your Driver/Thirty Days/Nadine/Around and Around/* *Reelin' and Rockin'/Bye Bye Johnny/No Particular Place to* *Go/Sweet Little Sixteen/Down the Road a Piece+*
MERCURY 124033	**LE DISQUE D'OR DE CHUCK BERRY** Same as U.S. Mercury **Golden Hits**. Different cover. Reissued with no. 134033. Different cover.
MERCURY 124046	**CHUCK BERRY IN MEMPHIS** Same as U.S. LP issue. Different cover.
MERCURY 134082	**FROM ST. LOUIE TO FRISCO** Same as U.S. LP issue. Different cover. Reissued with no. 6463 016, same cover.
MERCURY 134.057	**LIVE AT FILLMORE, SAN FRANCISCO** Same as U.S. LP issue. Different cover. Reissued with no. 6463 016, same cover.
MERCURY 134.222	**CONCERTO IN B. GOODE** Same as U.S. LP issue. Different cover.
FONTANA 6430 022	**ROCK AND ROLL MUSIC** Same as U.S. Mercury LP **Golden Hits**. Different cover; but same cover (and songs) as U.K. issue **Back in the USA** (Philips 6336 216).
MERCURY 6619 008	**ST. LOUIE TO FRISCO TO MEMPHIS** (2 LP set) Same as U.S. double album. Different cover. Reissued later with yet another different cover.
CHESS CH 50001	**THE LONDON CHUCK BERRY SESSIONS** The same as U.S. and U.K. albums.

CHESS CH 50013	**ROCK 'N ROLL WITH CHUCK BERRY** (2 LP set) *Sweet Little Sixteen/Let It Rock/My Mustang Ford/Little Queenie/No Particular Place to Go/Memphis, Tennessee/Roll Over Beethoven/Around and Around/Sweet Little Rock and Roller/Nadine/Promised Land/Reelin' and Rockin'/School Day/ Thirty Days/Oh Baby Doll/Almost Grown/Carol/You Never Can Tell/Johnny B. Goode/Rock and Roll Music/Brown-Eyed Handsome Man/Little Marie/Too Much Monkey Business/Go Bobby Soxer*
CHESS CH 50014	**SAN FRANCISCO DUES** Same as U.S. and U.K. album.
CHESS CH 50024	**CHUCK BERRY'S GOLDEN DECADE VOL. 1** (2 LP set) Same as U.S. and U.K. album.
CHESS CH 50028	**CHUCK BERRY'S GOLDEN DECADE VOL. 2** (2 LP set) Same as U.S. album.
CHESS CH 50047	**CHUCK BERRY** (1975) Same as U.S. album.
MUSIDISC 30CV 1292	**LE ROI DU ROCK** (1975) *Johnny B. Goode/Oh Baby Doll/Maybellene/Brown-Eyed Handsome Man/You Can't Catch Me/Around and Around/Roll Over Beethoven/Memphis, Tennessee/Too Much Monkey Business/Thirty Days/Deep Feeling* (instr.)/*Nadine* Chess recordings.
MUSIDISC 30CV 1386	**PROMISED LAND** (1975) *Promised Land/Carol/Almost Grown/Let It Rock/You Never Can Tell/Reelin' and Rockin'/Little Queenie/Sweet Little Six-teen/It Don't Take But a Few Minutes/Rock and Roll Music/ Bye Bye Johnny/School Day* Chess recordings. Both Musidisc albums appeared again in 1976 as a double-album set, Festival 219, titled **Promise Land** (Terre Promise). Different cover.
MUSIDISC 30CV 1401	**BACK HOME** (1977) Same as U.S. Chess LP. Different cover.
IMPACT 6886 403	**CHUCK BERRY** (1980) *Sweet Little Sixteen/Carol/Soul Rockin'/Ramblin' Rose+/ I Can't Believe/Bring Another Drink+/Louie to Frisco/Sweet Little Rock and Roller/Little Fox/Oh Baby Doll/Wee Baby Blues+/Back to Memphis* Mercury recordings.
IMPACT 6886 407	**CHUCK BERRY VOL. 2** (1980) *Johnny B. Goode/Misery/School Day/I Love Her, I Love Her/ Check Me Out/Feelin' It* (instr.)/*Ma Dear/Fillmore Blues* (instr.)/*The Love I Lost/My Tambourine/Rock Cradle Rock/Rock and Roll Music* Mercury recordings.
IMPACT 6995 402	**SWEET LITTLE SIXTEEN** (2 LP set, 1981) *Hoochie Coochie Man+/Rock Cradle Rock/Oh Baby Doll/ School Day/Soul Rockin'/Johnny B. Goode/Oh Captain/Wee Baby Blues+/Ma Dear/Ramblin' Rose+/Misery/Sweet Little Sixteen/Thirty Days/The Love I Lost/I Can't Believe/Check Me Out/Louie to Frisco/Fillmore Blues* (instr.)/*It Hurts Me Too+/Sweet Little Rock and Roller/My Tambourine/Little Fox/I Love Her, I Love Her* Mercury recordings.

MODE	**MR. ROCK 'N' ROLL** (1981)
(Vogue)	Same songs as on U.S. Chess LP, **Greatest Hits** (1485).
509075	Different cover.

In 1977, the three **Golden Decade** double albums were issued as a boxed set in France, selling at cheap prices in supermarkets. No liner notes were included, and only a small picture of Berry was used on the cover (Musidisc CCV-2601).

Many of Berry's original U.S. LPs have been reissued in France, beginning in 1980 (with original covers):

CHESS
9124 214	**CHUCK BERRY IS ON TOP**
9124 215	**AFTER SCHOOL SESSION**
9124 216	**ONE DOZEN BERRY'S**
9124 217	**CHUCK BERRY ON STAGE**
9214 218	**ROCKIN' AT THE HOPS**
9124 220	**NEW JUKE BOX HITS**
9124 223	**FRESH BERRY'S**
	No stereo.
9124 225	**SAN FRANCISCO DUES**
9124 226	**ST. LOUIS TO LIVERPOOL**
	No stereo.
9124 227	**BACK HOME**

CHESS
(Vogue)
427008	**CHUCK BERRY'S GOLDEN DECADE** (2 LP set, no. 8)
427009	**CHUCK BERRY'S GOLDEN DECADE VOL. 2** (2 LP set, no. 9)
427010	**CHUCK BERRY'S GOLDEN DECADE VOL. 3** (2 LP set, no. 10)
515 023	**TWO GREAT GUITARS** (no. 23)
515030	**AFTER SCHOOL SESSION** (no. 30)
515031	**ONE DOZEN BERRYS**
515 032	**NEW JUKE-BOX HITS**
515 033	**ROCKIN' AT THE HOPS**
515 034	**ST. LOUIS TO LIVERPOOL**
	Stereo.
515 035	**THE LONDON CHUCK BERRY SESSIONS**
	No fold-out cover.
	All Vogue issues were part of the "Chicago Golden Years" series, and all had the original covers.

COMPILATION ALBUMS

There are dozens of compilation albums issued in France which feature Chuck Berry, but only a few are of any interest.

MERCURY	**LA FANTASTIQUE EPOPEE DU ROCK VOL. 1**
850 057	*Carol/Memphis, Tennessee/Maybellene*
MERCURY	**LA FANTASTIQUE EPOPEE DU ROCK VOL. 2**
134 093	*Johnny B. Goode/Club Nitty Gritty/Sweet Little Sixteen/ Thirty Days/Rock and Roll Music*
MERCURY	**LA FANTASTIQUE EPOPEE DU ROCK VOL. 4**
138000 MCY	*Roll Over Beethoven/Sweet Little Rock and Roller*

MERCURY
138001 MCY

LA FANTASTIQUE EPOPEE DU ROCK VOL. 5
Oh Baby Doll
   Despite the fact that these are Mercury albums, they are
actually good compilations, in that they have good pictures
and liner notes (in French). Issued in the late 60s.
   On Vol. 4, both sides of cover state that Berry does *So
Glad You're Mine* (the old Arthur Crudup tune); the label says
Marty Wilde does the song, which is correct.

FESTIVAL
ALB-203

32 ROCKERS AND ROLLERS (2 LP set)
Roll Over Beethoven/Let It Rock
   Chess recordings. A good compilation featuring Chess
artists.

MODE
(Vogue)
000365

CHESS RECORDS – ORIGINAL RHYTHM 'N' BLUES HITS
(1983)
Sweet Little Sixteen/Maybellene
   This is a three-album boxed set. Dull cover, no pictures of
artists, no liner notes.

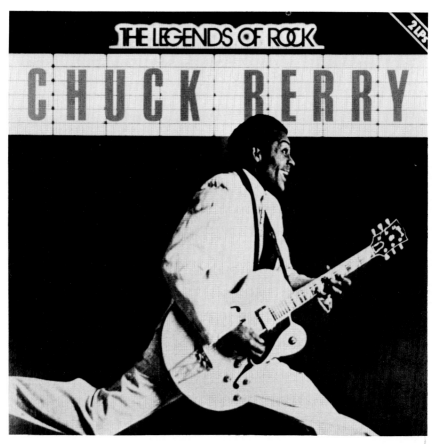

The Legends Of Rock   Chess 6.28500 DP (2 LPs)

WEST GERMAN DISCOGRAPHY

SINGLES

VOGUE
  DV 14547   *Lonely School Days* (fast version)/*Ramona Say Yes* (1966)

BELLAPHON
  BF 18108   *Johnny B. Goode/Sweet Little Sixteen* (1972; Chess reissue)
  BF 18214   *Bio/Roll 'Em Pete+* (1973)

All these singles have picture sleeves.

  My Ding-A-Ling and *Reelin' and Rockin'* (live) were also issued, but no information is available.

ALBUMS

  All the following albums were issued in the years from 1970 to date. The sequence of Bellaphon numbers is apparently unrelated to year of release, and no year appears on any of the issues. (Bellaphon is the trade name of Chess Records in West Germany.)

BELLAPHON   **THE BEST OF CHUCK BERRY** (2 LP set)
  BLST-6506   *Sweet Little Sixteen/Let It Rock/My Mustang Ford/Little Queenie/No Particular Place to Go/Memphis, Tennessee/Roll Over Beethoven/Around and Around/Sweet Little Rock and Roller/Nadine/Promised Land/Reelin' and Rockin'/School Day/Thirty Days/Oh Baby Doll/Almost Grown/Carol/You Never Can Tell/Johnny B. Goode/Rock and Roll Music/Brown-Eyed Handsome Man/Little Marie/Too Much Monkey Business/Go Bobby Soxer*
BELLAPHON   **CHUCK BERRY TODAY – BACK HOME**
  BLPS-19034   Same as U.S. Chess LP-1550. Same cover.
BELLAPHON   **SAN FRANCISCO DUES**
  BLPS-19055   Same as U.S. Chess LP CH-50008. Same cover.
BELLAPHON   **THE LONDON CHUCK BERRY SESSIONS**
  BLPS-19098   Same as U.S. Chess LP CH-60020. Same cover.
BELLAPHON   **BIO**
  BLPS-19 ?   Same as U.S. Chess LP CH-50043. Same cover.
BELLAPHON   **ORIGINAL OLDIES**
  BI-1547   *Roll Over Beethoven/Reelin' and Rockin'/Brown-Eyed Handsome Man/Too Pooped to Pop+/Around and Around/Bye Bye Johnny/Rock and Roll Music/Maybellene/Deep Feeling* (instr.)/*Anthony Boy/You Can't Catch Me/Back in the USA*
BELLAPHON   **ORIGINAL OLDIES VOL. 2**
  BI-1551   *Sweet Little Sixteen/Let's Do Our Thing Together/It Wasn't Me/Almost Grown/Your Lick* (instr.)/*St. Louis Blues+/Johnny B. Goode/She Once Was Mine/My Little Love Light/Dear Dad/Ain't That Just Like a Woman+/It's My Own Business*
                  Features one of the best cover pictures available on a Chuck Berry album.

BELLAPHON BI-1557	**ROCKIN' TOGETHER** *Reelin' and Rockin'/Tulane/Childhood Sweetheart/I'm a* *Rocker/Don't You Lie to Me+/Let's Do Our Thing Together* Berry is on side one, and Bo Diddley on side two. A mis- leading title as the two men do *not* rock "together."
BELLAPHON BI-15102	**CHUCK BERRY LIVE** Same as U.K. Pye International NPL-28027 (*How High the* *Moon* is faded earlier). Different cover.
BELLAPHON BI–15107	**ORIGINAL OLDIES VOL. 3** *Let It Rock/Nadine/No Money Down/Sweet Little Rock and* *Roller/Thirty Days/You Never Can Tell/Little Queenie/* *Memphis, Tennessee/Jo Jo Gunne/Brenda Lee/Guitar Boogie* (instr.)/*Route 66+*
BELLAPHON BI-15112	**BOXEN HITS** Same as U.S. Chess LP-1456. Different cover.
BELLAPHON BLS-5522	**24 OLDIES ORIGINAL** (2 LP set) Record 1 is the same as BI-1547. Record 2 is the same as BI-1551. Different fold-out cover.
FONTANA SPECIAL 6430 022	**ATTENTION!** Same tracks as U.S. **Golden Hits** (SR-61103). Mercury re- cordings. Different cover, but almost same cover as Philips issue in U.K., **Back in the USA** (6336 216).
ARIOLA 28 911 XAT	**THE STORY OF ROCK AND ROLL** Same tracks as U.S. LP Everest FS-321. Different cover. Mercury recordings.
BELLAPHON BLS-5573	**CHUCK BERRY LIVE IN CONCERT** (2 LP set) Same as U.S. Magnum LP MR-703. Different cover.
ATLANTIC 50648 Z	**ROCK IT** (1979) Same as the U.S. and U.K. issue.
KARUSSELL (MERCURY) 2872 103	**ST. LOUIE TO FRISCO TO MEMPHIS** (1980 ?) *Louie to Frisco/Flying Home* (instr.)/*Fillmore Blues* (instr.)/ *Check Me Out/Little Fox/Johnny B. Goode* (live)/*C.C. Rider+/* *Misery/Ma Dear/Soul Rockin'/My Tambourine/Back to* *Memphis* A single album release.
CHESS 6.24372 AP	**20 SUPER HITS** (1980) *Johnny B. Goode/Roll Over Beethoven/School Day/May-* *bellene/Rock and Roll Music/Oh Baby Doll/Too Much* *Monkey Business/Carol/Let It Rock/Sweet Little Rock and* *Roller/My Ding-A-Ling/Reelin' and Rockin'/No Particular* *Place to Go/Sweet Little Sixteen/Little Queenie/Brown-Eyed* *Handsome Man/Nadine/Too Pooped to Pop+/Back in the USA/* *Bye Bye Johnny*
CHESS 6.28500 DP	**THE LEGENDS OF ROCK** (2 LP set, 1980) *Maybellene/No Money Down/Too Much Monkey Business/* *You Can't Catch Me/Wee Wee Hours/Deep Feeling* (instr.)/*Roll* *Over Beethoven/Rock and Roll Music/Sweet Little Sixteen/* *Around and Around/Little Queenie/Johnny B. Goode/Almost* *Grown/Carol/Blues for Hawaiians* (instr.)/*Worried Life Blues+/* *Down the Road a Piece+/Driftin' Blues+/Let It Rock/Come* *On/I Got to Find My Baby/I Love You/Mean Old World+/* *Chuck's Beat* (instr., with Bo Diddley)

This is a good compilation of Berry tracks but, as usual on German issues, most of the old songs are destroyed by electronic stereo.

Sweet Little Sixteen is the unreleased take that appeared on the bootleg LP **America's Hottest Wax**; the Germans were actually the very first to issue this version legally.

Berry is also featured on the Bo Diddley set **Legends of Rock** (6.28524), on the cut *Bo's Beat*.

MERCURY
6463 044

ROCK! ROCK! ROCK 'N' ROLL! (1980)
Maybellene/Back in the USA/Johnny B. Goode/Rock and Roll Music/Carol/Sweet Little Sixteen/Roll Over Beethoven/Reelin' and Rockin'/Let It Rock/Sweet Little Rock and Roller/Oh Baby Doll/Goodnight, Well It's Time to Go+
The Mercury version of *Let It Rock* is here issued for the very first time. Compared to most of the other re-recordings of old hits, this is a good version. They have also included the Chess version of *Oh Baby Doll*, but in terrible electronic stereo.

CHESS
6.24472 AL

PROFILE – CHUCK BERRY (1981)
Memphis, Tennessee/Bye Bye Johnny/I'm Talking About You/Reelin' and Rockin'/Down the Road a Piece+/Let It Rock/Go Go Go/School Day/Sweet Little Sixteen/Havana Moon/Thirty Days/Confessin' the Blues+

CHESS
6.28584 DO

PORTRAIT – ORIGINAL ROCK 'N' ROLL HITS (2 LP set, 1982)
Sweet Little Sixteen/School Day/Oh Baby Doll/Brown-Eyed Handsome Man/Rock and Roll Music/Jo Jo Gunne/Sweet Little Rock and Roller/Roll Over Beethoven/Carol/Reelin' and Rockin'/Merry Christmas Baby+/Anthony Boy/Almost Grown/Johnny B. Goode/Little Queenie/Back in the USA/Let It Rock/Too Pooped to Pop+/Nadine/No Particular Place to Go/My Ding-A-Ling/You Never Can Tell/Little Marie/Promised Land/Dear Dad/Bye Bye Johnny
Another repackaging, "enhanced" with electronic stereo.

MERCURY
6463 129

MOTIVE (1982)
Roll Over Beethoven/Sweet Little Rock and Roller/Louis to Frisco/Back to Memphis/Wee Baby Blues+/Johnny B. Goode/Club Nitty Gritty/Sweet Little Sixteen/School Day/Feelin' It (instr.)/Let It Rock/Carol

MERCURY
6619 039

SWEET LITTLE ROCK AND ROLLER (2 LP set, 1982)
Maybellene/Back in the USA/Johnny B. Goode/Rock and Roll Music/Roll Over Beethoven/Reelin' and Rockin'/Club Nitty Gritty/Sweet Little Sixteen/School Day/Feelin' It (instr.)/Let It Rock/Carol/Concerto in B. Goode (instr.)/Sweet Little Rock and Roller/Little Fox/It's Too Dark in There/It Hurts Me Too+/Oh Baby Doll (Chess)/Goodnight, Well It's Time to Go+

RCA
NL-45338

TAKE OFF – LIVE IN TORONTO (1982)
Reelin' and Rockin'/Maybellene/Rock and Roll Music/My Ding-A-Ling/Too Much Monkey Business/Nadine/School Day/
Medley: *Johnny B. Goode–Carol–Promised Land/Sweet Little Sixteen*
From the 1969 Toronto Rock & Roll Festival.

KARUSSELL	**AUSGEWAHLTE GOLDSTUCKE** (1982)
(MERCURY)	*Sweet Little Sixteen/Carol/Soul Rockin'/Ramblin' Rose+/*
2876 035	*I Can't Believe/C.C. Rider+/Louie to Frisco/Little Fox/Wee*
	Baby Blues+/Ma Dear/My Tambourine/Back to Memphis

VINTAGE	**BACK IN THE USA** (1983)
F-50009	*Back in the USA/Good Lookin' Woman/Sweet Little Rock and*
	Roller/I Do Really Love You/Oh Baby Doll/Thirty Days/
	Goodnight, Well It's Time to Go+/Back to Memphis/My Heart
	Will Always Belong to You/Reelin' and Rockin'

Good Lookin' Woman is called *Good Lovin' Woman.*
They've probably taken it from the U.S. Pickwick LP **Wild Berry's**, where the mistake occurred for the first time. The LP has also been issued on Time Wind F-50009, same number and almost the same cover. This is also the same compilation of tracks issued in Denmark 1983 as a picture disc with the same number.

Many of Chuck Berry's original U.S. LPs have been reissued in Germany with original covers:

CHESS
515 023 AO	**TWO GREAT GUITARS** (with Bo Diddley)
515 030 AO	**AFTER SCHOOL SESSION**
515 031 AO	**ONE DOZEN BERRYS**
6.24722 AS	**THE LONDON CHUCK BERRY SESSIONS**
6.28595 DT	**AFTER SCHOOL SESSION/ONE DOZEN BERRYS** (2 LP set)
6.28596 DT	**ON STAGE/ROCKIN' AT THE HOPS** (2 LP set)

How High the Moon is not included on the **On Stage** LP.

COMPILATION ALBUMS

BELLAPHON	**4 ROCK GIANTS TALKS & HITS**
BI-15119	*Interview* (with Berry)/*Maybellene/Sweet Little Sixteen/*
	School Day

Chess recordings. Interview probably done at Wembley, England in 1972. More interviews and tracks with Jerry Lee Lewis, Bo Diddley, and Carl Perkins.

This LP was originally issued in Holland, 1972, on Sun/ Chess NQCS-1. Different cover. (See "Dutch Discography" for further information.)

BELLAPHON	**THE KINGS OF ROCK AND ROLL** (2 LP set)
BLS-5516	*Johnny B. Goode/School Day/Around and Around/No Particu-*
	lar Place to Go/Wee Wee Hours/Sweet Little Sixteen/Roll Over
	Beethoven/Reelin' and Rockin'/Dear Dad/Brown-Eyed Hand-
	some Man/Havana Moon/Rock and Roll Music

One side is Bill Haley, another is Little Richard, and Berry has two sides.

K-TEL	**THE GIANTS OF ROCK 'N' ROLL – DIE SUPER HITS DER**
TG-1367	**GROSSEN 4** (1982)
	Sweet Little Sixteen/Rock and Roll Music/Johnny B. Goode/
	Roll Over Beethoven

Chuck Berry, Bill Haley, Fats Domino, and Little Richard.

RCA   **THE GREATEST HITS OF ROCK 'N' ROLL** (2 LP set, 1982)
    NL-45337   *Too Much Monkey Business/Sweet Little Sixteen/Nadine/*
Maybellene/School Day
         The Berry songs are taken from the Toronto Rock & Roll
Revival, a fact not mentioned on the cover, itself a very dull
fold-out. Other artists on the set: Little Richard, Jerry Lee
Lewis, Bill Haley, and Roy Orbison.

Betty Jean/Down The Road A Piece
Funckler/Chess Int'l AR-45.179 (45)

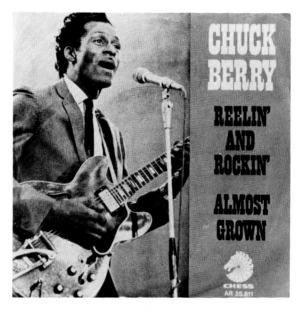

Reelin' And Rockin'/Almost Grown
Chess International AR-25.811 (45)

DUTCH DISCOGRAPHY

SINGLES

FUNCKLER--
CHESS INT'L
AR-45.082   *Roll Over Beethoven/Sweet Little Sixteen* (dubbed "live" audience)
AR-45.088   *Memphis, Tennessee/Go Go Go*
AR-45.096   *I Got to Find My Baby/Mad Lad+* (instr.)
AR-45.097   *Jaguar and the Thunderbird/Our Little Rendezvous*
AR-45.098   *Maybellene/Rock and Roll Music*
AR-45.111   *Nadine/Come On*
AR-45.119   *School Day/Johnny B. Goode*
AR-45.120   *Let It Rock/Too Much Monkey Business*
AR-45.123   *Reelin' and Rockin'/Carol*
AR-45.124   *No Particular Place to Go/Liverpool Drive* (instr.)
AR-45.126   *Fraulein+/Lonely All the Time+ (Crazy Arms)*
AR-45.133   *You Never Can Tell/Brenda Lee*
AR-45.140   *Little Marie/Go Bobby Soxer*
AR-45.143   *Promised Land/Things I Used to Do+*
AR-45.161   *Lonely School Days* (slow version)/*Dear Dad*
AR-45.179   *Betty Jean/Down the Road a Piece+*

This is the "Chuck Berry Songs Series," Volumes 1--16. All these singles were issued with picture sleeves in the mid-60s. The first issues did not carry the series title, which appeared on later volumes and reissues.

The first eleven singles were first issued on Funckler, the rest on Chess International. Volumes 1--11 were then issued again by Chess International. There are confusing combinations with Funckler printed on the sleeve and Chess International on the record.

MERCURY
127 260MCF   *Club Nitty Gritty/Laugh and Cry* (picture sleeve)

CHESS INT'L
AR-25.811   *Reelin' and Rockin'/Almost Grown* (1968 reissue; picture sleeve)

There are of course many more releases in Holland, on Mercury. For example, *My Ding-A-Ling* and *Reelin' and Rockin'* (live) were also issued, but no information is available.

EPs

FUNCKLER-- **THE BEST OF CHUCK BERRY**
CHESS INT'L   *Memphis, Tennessee/Roll Over Beethoven/I'm Talking About*
EPAR-6024   *You/Sweet Little Sixteen*
FUNCKLER– **FOUR FABULOUS FAVORITES**
CHESS INT'L   *Johnny B. Goode/Oh Baby Doll/School Day/Back in the USA*
EPAR-6024
FUNCKLER-- **CHUCK BERRY TIME**
CHESS INT'L   *Bye Bye Johnny/Rock and Roll Music/You Can't Catch Me/*
EPAR-6026   *No Money Down*

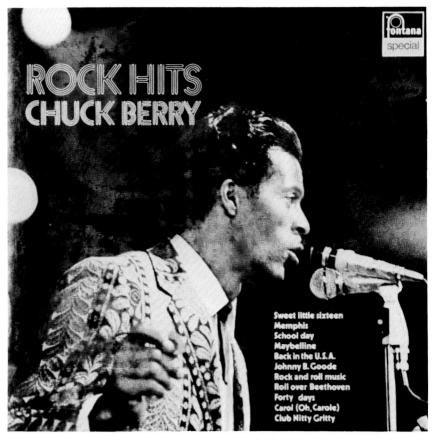

Rock Hits   Fontana Special 6430 022 (LP)

FUNCKLER-- CHESS INT'L EPAR-6028	**BRANDNEW BERRY BLOCKBUSETERS** *No Particular Place to Go/Fraulein+/Nadine/Lonely All the* *Time+ (Crazy Arms)* Again, some confusing combinations of Funckler and Chess International releases and packaging in the EP category.

ALBUMS

CHESS INT'L PAR-106 FUNCKLER MGCH-9218	**CHUCK BERRY ON STAGE** Same as U.K. Pye International issue. Different cover.
CHESS INT'L PAR-107 FUNCKLER MGCH-9219	**RHYTHM & BLUES RENDEZVOUS** Same tracks as U.S. Chess LP-1465. Different cover.
CHESS INT'L P-104	**MORE CHUCK BERRY** Same as U.K. Pye International NPL-28028. Different cover.
CHESS INT'L PAR-119	**JUKE BOX SPECIAL** Same as U.S. Chess LP-1456. Different cover.
CHESS INT'L MGAR-9223	**THE LATEST AND THE GREATEST** Same as U.K. Pye International NPL-28031. Different cover.
CHESS INT'L MGAR-9224	**ST. LOUIS TO LIVERPOOL** Same tracks as U.S. Chess LP-1488. Same cover, but no stereo. Reissued in 1973 on Chess CQ-20.062 in stereo.
CHESS INT'L MGAR-9225	**CHUCK BERRY IN LONDON** Same as U.K. Chess CRL-4005. Different cover, great picture.
CHESS INT'L PAR-031	**ROCKIN' WITH CHUCK** Same as U.S. Chess LP-1448. Different cover.

The albums above were issued in the mid-60s; PAR-031 appeared in 1968. Berry's early LPs were reissued in Holland in 1973/74, with original U.S. covers, starting with **After School Session** (Chess CQ-20.081). No more information is available.

FONTANA INT'L
(MERCURY)
858 002 FPY
	CHUCK BERRY GOLDEN HITS
	    Same as U.S. Mercury SR-61103. Different cover. Both content and packaging are terrible.
	    Reissued in 1972 on Fontana Special 6430 022 as **Rock Hits**. Different cover, but the same as U.K. Philips 6335 216, and the German and French issues (6430 022).

FONTANA INT'L (MERCURY) 858 ? FPY	**CHUCK BERRY IN MEMPHIS** Same as U.S. and U.K. issues.
FONTANA INT'L (MERCURY) 858 047 FPY	**CHUCK BERRY LIVE AT THE FILLMORE AUDITORIUM** Same as U.S. and U.K. issues. Same cover.
FONTANA INT'L (MERCURY) 134 082 MCY	**FROM ST. LOUIE TO FRISCO** Same as U.S. issue. Same cover.
FONTANA INT'L (MERCURY) 134 222 MCY	**CONCERTO IN B. GOODE** Same as U.S. and U.K. issues. Same cover.

CHESS HJC-171	**CHUCK BERRY'S GREATEST HITS** Same as U.S. Chess LP-1485, but different cover.
CHESS SPLO 3	**SPOTLIGHT ON CHUCK BERRY** *My Ding-A-Ling* (single version)/*No Particular Place to Go/ You Never Can Tell/No Money Down/Roly Poly* (instr.)/*Let's Boogie/Go Go Go/Reelin' and Rockin'* ('72 single version)/ *Carol/Run Rudolph Run+/Around and Around/Bye Bye Johnny/Wee Wee Hours/Berry Pickin'* (instr.)
CHESS SPLO 122	**CHUCK BERRY'S GREATEST HITS** No information available for titles and cover.
PHILIPS Success Series 9279 540	**ROCKIN' WITH CHUCK BERRY** *Sweet Little Sixteen/Memphis, Tennessee/Roll Over Beethoven/ Thirty Days/Carol/Nadine/Johnny B. Goode/Rock and Roll Music/School Day/Maybellene/Back in the USA/No Particular Place to Go*
PHILIPS Success Series 9279 541	**PORTRAIT OF CHUCK BERRY** *My Ding-A-Ling* (single version)/*Little Queenie/Let It Rock* (the lead guitar omitted)/*Too Pooped to Pop+/Bye Bye Johnny/Oh Baby Doll/Reelin' and Rockin'/Sweet Little Rock and Roller/Jo Jo Gunne/Run Rudolph Run+/Almost Grown*
CHESS 9283 004	**CHUCK BERRY GREATEST HITS** *Maybellene/Oh Baby Doll/Too Pooped to Pop+/Sweet Little Sixteen/Rock and Roll Music/Back in the USA/School Day/ Johnny B. Goode/Wee Wee Hours/Roll Over Beethoven/ Thirty Days/Memphis, Tennessee*
CHESS 9283 020	**MOTORVATIN'** Same as U.K. LP (9286 690). Same cover.
PHILIPS 6337 151	**ROCK LIONS – CHUCK BERRY** Same tracks as U.S. **Golden Hits** (Mercury SR-61103), but indicated only in small type. On the back of the cover are printed the U.S. and U.K. chart positions for each song (except *Club Nitty Gritty*). Fanciful liner notes state that Berry was born in 1931, and that *Roll Over Beethoven* was a hit in 1965!
RAINBOW 6063	**CHUCK BERRY GREATEST HITS VOL. 1** *Sweet Little Rock and Roller/Goodnight, Well It's Time to Go+/Oh Baby Doll/Thirty Days/Reelin' and Rockin'/Back in the USA/I Do Really Love You/My Heart Will Always Belong to You/Good Lookin' Woman/Back to Memphis*
RAINBOW 6068	**CHUCK BERRY GREATEST HITS VOL. 2** Same tracks as U.S. LP (Everest FS-321), but not in the same order. Different cover. Once again we get the Mercury recordings under the strange title of **Greatest Hits**, and in two volumes! Very dull covers. To make matters even worse, the two albums were issued in Belgium on Surprise Records as a three-LP boxed set. See the "International Discography" for more information.

Several more LPs were released in Holland during the 70s, such as **San Francisco Dues, Chuck Berry London Sessions**, and **Bio**, but no further information is available.

224

COMPILATION ALBUMS

SUN-CHESS
NQCS-1

ROCK SMUK (late 1972)

Interview (with Berry)/*Maybellene*/*Sweet Little Sixteen*/
School Day

Interview with Berry probably done in England, at
Wembley, August, 1972. Also has interviews and tracks by
Jerry Lee Lewis, Bo Diddley, and Carl Perkins. Songs are the
original 50s recordings.

READERS DIGEST
N82001 ND

GOLDEN GREATS OF THE 50'S AND 60'S (8 LP boxed set,
1981)

Maybellene/*School Day*/*Rock and Roll Music*/*You Never Can
Tell*/*Let It Rock* (lead guitar omitted)/*Memphis, Tennessee*/
No Particular Place to Go/*My Ding-A-Ling*

A very good compilation featuring sixteen artists, each on
one record side, with good pictures and liner notes. Pressed
and printed in Holland, probably for distribution in Northern
Europe. Unaccountably omitted *Johnny B. Goode*.

MASTERS
MA-0016983

20 GREATEST HITS (1982)

Roll Over Beethoven/*Back in the USA*/*Johnny B. Goode*/*Good
Lookin' Woman*/*School Day*/*Sweet Little Rock and Roller*/
Maybellene/*Oh Baby Doll*/*Rock and Roll Music*/*Thirty Days*/
Ramblin' Rose+/*Goodnight, Well It's Time to Go*+/*Carol*/*Back
to Memphis*/*C.C. Rider*+/*My Heart Will Always Belong to You*/
Sweet Little Sixteen/*Reelin' and Rockin'*/*Memphis, Tennessee*/
I Do Really Love You

Mercury recordings, with very bad sound quality.

BLACK TULIP
BT.555017

20 GREATEST HITS (1983)

Roll Over Beethoven/*Johnny B. Goode*/*Maybellene*/*Memphis,
Tennessee*/*Ramblin' Rose*+/*So Long*+/*Check Me Out*/*Oh Baby
Doll*/*Goodnight, Well It's Time to Go*+/*Bring Another Drink*+/
Sweet Little Sixteen/*School Day*/*Rock and Roll Music*/*Reelin'
and Rockin'*/*C.C. Rider*+/*Back in the USA*/*Sweet Little Rock
and Roller*/*Back to Memphis*/*My Heart Will Always Belong to
You*/*Good Looking Woman*

Mercury recordings with better sound quality.

In Holland, as in all other countries, Berry is featured on many other compilation
issues.

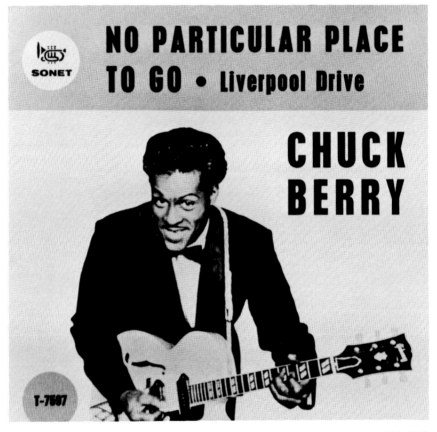

No Particular Place To Go/Liverpool Drive   Sonet T-7597 (45)

SWEDISH DISCOGRAPHY

SINGLES

PYE
  7N.25218

Memphis, Tennessee/Let It Rock
This has the same record number as the U.K. Pye International issue.

SONET
  T-7591
  T-7594

  T-7596
  T-7597
  T-7605

Nadine/O'Rangutang (instr.)
Roll Over Beethoven/Sweet Little Sixteen (dubbed-in "live" audience)
Maybellene/Rock and Roll Music
No Particular Place to Go/Liverpool Drive (instr.)
You Never Can Tell/Brenda Lee
All these singles were issued with picture sleeves, some also in colored vinyl.

CHESS INT'L
  AR-50.002
  AR-50.004
  AR-50.008
  AR-50.009

It Wasn't Me/It's My Own Business
Ramona Say Yes/Lonely School Days (fast version)
My Ding-A-Ling/Johnny B. Goode (live)
Reelin' and Rockin' (live)/*Let's Boogie*
All these singles had picture sleeves.

EPs

LONDON
  RE-5010
  RE-5014
  RE-5030

Same as U.K. Chess EP-5119
Same as U.S. Chess EP-5121
Same as U.S. Chess EP-5124

PYE
  NEP-5023

JUKEBOX HITS VOL. 1
Go Go Go/School Day/Rock and Roll Music/Sweet Little Sixteen

PYE
  NEP-5026

JUKEBOX HITS VOL. 2
Run Rudolph Run+/Johnny B. Goode/Memphis, Tennessee/Let It Rock

SONET
  SXP-6065

NO PARTICULAR PLACE TO GO
No Particular Place to Go/O'Rangutang (instr.)/*Nadine/Liverpool Drive* (instr.)

SONET
  SXP-6066

GOLDEN HITS VOL. 1
Memphis, Tennessee/Roll Over Beethoven/School Day/Back in the USA
"Original R&R Classics."

SONET
  SXP-6067

GOLDEN HITS VOL. 2
Johnny B. Goode/Oh Baby Doll/I'm Talking About You/Sweet Little Sixteen
"Original R&R Classics."

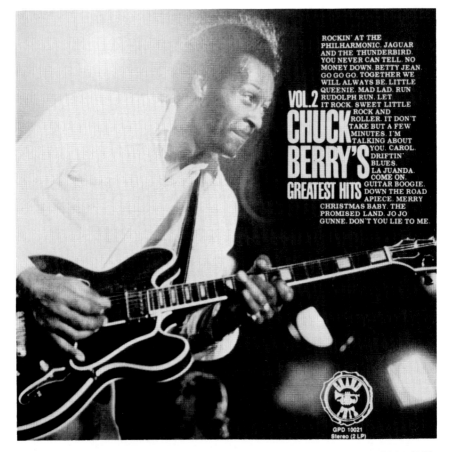

Chuck Berry's Greatest Hits, Vol. 2   Sonet GPD-10021 (LP)

CHESS INT'L	**GOLDEN HITS VOL. 3**
CHEP-900	*Carol/Jaguar and the Thunderbird/Around and Around/Let It Rock*
	"Original R&R Classics."
CHESS INT'L	**GOLDEN HITS VOL. 4**
CHEP-901	*Maybellene/Thirty Days/Reelin' and Rockin'/Sweet Little Rock and Roller*
	"Original R&R Classics."

Some of the Sonet and Chess International EPs had colored vinyl.

COMPILATION EPs

JUKEBOX	
JSEP-5552	*Down the Road a Piece+*
JSEP-5565	*Promised Land*
JSLP-5625	*Little Marie/Our Little Rendezvous*
JSLP-5630	*Sweet Little Sixteen*
	JSEP issues were 45 rpm, and contained four tracks. JSLP issues were 33 rpm, and contained six tracks.

ALBUMS

SONET	**ST. LOUIS TO LIVERPOOL**
GP-9912	Same as the U.S. Chess issue. Same cover, but no stereo.
SONET	**CHUCK BERRY'S GREATEST HITS** (2 LP set)
GPD-9967	Same as U.S. Chess LPS-1514D, but with another cover. A poor recording.
SONET	**CHUCK BERRY'S GREATEST HITS VOL. 2** (2 LP set)
GPD-10021	Same as U.S. Chess LP 2CH-60023, but different cover. A good recording.
SONET	**CHUCK BERRY'S GREATEST HITS VOL. 3** (2 LP set)
GPD-10032	Same as U.S. Chess LP 2CH-60028. Same cover.
FONTANA	**ROCK AND ROLL MUSIC**
6430 022	Same as U.K. Philips 6336 216. Same cover. Mercury recordings.
CHESS	**THE CHESS STORY VOL. 6 – CHUCK BERRY** (1973)
SPO-112	Same tracks as U.S. Chess LP-1485. Different cover. This is one in a series of ten albums from the Chess files distributed only in Scandinavia.
CHESS	**20 ORIGINALE ROCK 'N' ROLL HITS** (1975)
SP-19749	*Maybellene/Johnny B. Goode/Roll Over Beethoven/Too Much Monkey Business/Reelin' and Rockin'/Go Go Go/I'm Talking About You/Little Queenie/Around and Around/You Never Can Tell/My Ding-A-Ling/Shake Rattle and Roll+/No Particular Place to Go/Memphis, Tennessee/Come On/Sweet Little Sixteen/Rock and Roll Music/Sweet Little Rock and Roller/School Day/Bye Bye Johnny*
	The cover indicates "Made and Printed in England," but the label carries the "NCB" designation exclusive to Scandinavian issues.
CHESS	**THE GREAT TWENTY-EIGHT** (2 LP set, 1983)
SOSLP-74	Identical to the U.S. Chess issue. Same fold-out covers.

Berry's original U.S. Chess LPs were reissued in Scandinavia at the very end of the 70s with numbers identical to the ones mentioned in the "French Discography," starting with 9124 214, **Chuck Berry Is on Top**, and ending with 9124 223.

INTERNATIONAL DISCOGRAPHY

Compiling a complete Chuck Berry worldwide discography would be a prolonged and complicated endeavor; the recordings listed below represent only those in the compiler's personal collection, and obviously represent only a sampling of what exists.

AUSTRALIA

EPs

RCA VICTOR
20664

CHUCK BERRY (1982)
Sweet Little Sixteen/Reelin' and Rockin'/Johnny B. Goode/Memphis, Tennessee
Chess recordings. This maxi-single carries the legend "Collectors Originals Choice."

ALBUMS

RAINBOW
(Philips)
RDL-1506

ROCKIN' WITH CHUCK BERRY
Same as the Dutch issue. Same cover.

BELGIUM

SINGLES

SURPRISE
"GOLDEN 45's"
JTU 804-37
JTU 812-45
JTU 817-50

Memphis, Tennessee/Maybellene
Roll Over Beethoven/Johnny B. Goode
Rock and Roll Music/Sweet Little Sixteen
Mercury recordings. This is a series of fifty singles, all with picture sleeves, issued probably in the late 70s, consisting of artists from Berry to The Beach Boys and Glenn Miller.

ALBUMS

SURPRISE
JTU AL-39

GREATEST HITS
Same tracks as U.S. Everest FS-321. Different cover. Again, a misleading "greatest hits" package of Mercury recordings. At the end of the liner notes on the back of cover is printed: "On this album you will find a selection of his very greatest hits from the period 1955–1963, and boy, they sound as fresh as ever!" The "hits" are re-recorded, however. These songs were also issued in Holland on Rainbow LP 6068, but not in the same order. Different cover.

SURPRISE
JTU AL-48
	SWEET LITTLE ROCK AND ROLLER
	    Same tracks as on the Dutch album Rainbow LP 6063, but not in the same order. Different cover.
	    Also issued as two German albums (50009), and as a Danish picture disc.

SURPRISE TRI BOX 07	**CHUCK BERRY – GREATEST HITS** A three-LP set, consisting of the two Surprise albums above, plus an LP of recordings by various *other* artists.
VOGUE (CHESS) VMFP-521/3	**CHUCK BERRY** (1981) A three-LP boxed set: the two discs from Chess's **Golden Decade Vol. 1**, and a third LP containing the following songs: *Carol/You Never Can Tell/Run Rudolph Run+/Let It Rock/ Sweet Little Rock and Roller/Go Go Go/Guitar Boogie* (instr.)/ *Rockin' at the Philharmonic* (instr.)/*Roly Poly* (instr.)/*Viva Rock & Roll/Oh Year*
VOGUE (CHESS) VMFP-521	**THE BEST OF CHUCK BERRY** (1982) Exactly the same as the first record from the **Chuck Berry** boxed set above (**Golden Decade Vol. 1**), but different cover.

CHINA

ALBUMS

FIRST
S FL-1022
	CHUCK BERRY TWIST
	    This LP has the same tracks as the U.S. Chess LP-1465. It might be a bootleg, but the sound quality is as good as the U.S. one. The record is pressed on orange vinly. Some titles are misprinted: *Thirty Drys*, for example. The album is in a plastic-covered inner-sleeve with some Chinese printing and drawings. The label says "Stereo Record," and title and songs are printed both in English and Chinese.
	    The matrix numbers are the same as on the U.S. issue (11411/11412). An interesting record and a real collector's item!

DENMARK

ALBUMS

PD-50009	**BACK IN THE USA** (1983)
	    This is a picture disc containing Mercury tracks. The LP is interesting in that it appears to be the only picture disc featuring Berry's likeness. Pressed on red vinyl, with the same color picture of Berry on both sides, it comes in a clear plastic cover.
	    The album has the same number as the two German issues on Vintage and Time Wind, and the picture of Berry is the same as that used on those releases.
	    The disc is a good example of one which leads people around the world to judge Chuck Berry on the basis of his Mercury recordings, rather than on the far superior Chess originals.

AR-30013   **CHUCK BERRY** (late 1983)
                  Maybellene/Roll Over Beethoven/Too Much Monkey Business/
                  You Can't Catch Me/School Day/Rock and Roll Music/Sweet
                  Little Sixteen/Johnny B. Goode/Around and Around/Beautiful
                  Delilah/Carol/Run Rudolph Run+
                  A picture disc with Chess recordings, and a good one, too.
                  This has two different black-and-white pictures of Berry, one
                  on each side (early shots).

EAST GERMANY

ALBUMS

AMIGA   **CHUCK BERRY** (1982)
8 55 835   *Johnny B. Goode/Rock and Roll Music/Roll Over Beethoven/*
                  Reelin' and Rockin'/Sweet Little Sixteen/School Day/Feelin'
                  It (instr.)*/Oh Baby Doll/Maybellene/Carol/Sweet Little Rock*
                  and Roller/Club Nitty Gritty/Back in the USA/Little Fox/It's
                  Too Dark in There/Let It Rock
                  Mercury recordings.

ITALY

ALBUMS

CADET   **TWO GREAT GUITARS – CHUCK BERRY & BO DIDDLEY**
2991   Same issue as the U.S. Checker one.

CH 60020   **THE LONDON CHUCK BERRY SESSIONS**
                  Same as the second U.S. printing (without fold-out cover).

PHILIPS   **ROCK 'N' ROLL HITS** (1973)
9279 138   Mercury recordings again, from **Golden Hits** in U.S., and
                  also several other issues in Europe. The same cover as the
                  European ones: **Rock Hits** in Holland; **Rock and Roll Music**
                  in France and Scandinavia; **Back in the USA** in England. The
                  only interest, collector-wise, must be the Italian liner notes!

FROG   **CHUCK BERRY'S GOLDEN DECADE** (2 LP set, 1981)
ABRP-22011   Same as the second U.S. release. Almost the same fold-out
                  cover.

JOKER   **CHUCK BERRY VOL. 1 – ROLL OVER BEETHOVEN** (1982)
SM-3983   *Roll Over Beethoven/School Day/It Hurts Me Too+/Carol/C.C.*
                  Rider+/Bring Another Drink+/Oh Baby Doll/So Long+/Reelin'
                  and Rockin'/My Heart Will Always Belong to You/Back in the
                  USA/Sweet Little Rock and Roller
                  Mercury recordings. Great picture of Berry on front cover.

JOKER   **CHUCK BERRY VOL. 2 – MAYBELLENE** (1982)
SM-3984   *Maybellene/Good Lookin' Woman/I Do Really Love You/*
                  Memphis, Tennessee/My Woman/Rock and Roll Music/Thirty
                  Days/Ramblin' Rose+/Back to Memphis/Goodnight, Well It's
                  Time to Go+/Sweet Little Sixteen/Put Her Down
                  Mercury recordings.

JAPAN

ALBUMS

EAST WORLD
WTP-90072

CHUCK BERRY TOKYO SESSION (1981)
School Day/Roll Over Beethoven/Wee Wee Hours/My Ding-A-Ling/Memphis, Tennessee/Sweet Little Sixteen/Rock and Roll Music/Medley: Carol–Little Queenie/Bio/Johnny B. Goode
This LP is just marvelous in every way. It must be Berry's best "live" LP ever! Never heard him so good. He plays terrific guitar and the band is really good (Jim Marsala on bass and two Japanese musicians on drums and piano). Even if one has heard all the songs over and over again, these versions become new as a result of the enthusiasm of Berry and the band. Superb sound quality. The recordings were done under license of the Chuck Berry Communications System Inc., and are compiled from two Tokyo concert dates: April 27 and 29, 1981.

MERCURY
EVER-22

JOHNNY B. GOODE – CHUCK BERRY'S GOLDEN HITS (1982)
Same as U.S. release SR-61103. Different cover. Carries the legend "Ever Bright Collection."

CHESS
BT-5269

THE HISTORY OF CHUCK BERRY VOL. 1 (1982)
No more information available.

CHESS
BT-5270

THE HISTORY OF CHUCK BERRY VOL. 2 (1982)
No more information available.

CHESS
BT-5271

THE HISTORY OF CHUCK BERRY VOL. 3 (1982)
Too Pooped to Pop+/Bye Bye Johnny/I Got to Find My Baby/Our Little Rendezvous/Little Star/Come On/Nadine/No Particular Place to Go/Little Marie/Promised Land/My Ding-A-Ling

CHESS
PLP-834/6

VERY GOOD! – CHUCK BERRY'S 50 GREATEST ROCK & ROLL HITS
Maybellene/Wee Wee Hours/Thirty Days/You Can't Catch Me/No Money Down/Brown-Eyed Handsome Man/Roll Over Beethoven/Too Much Monkey Business/Havana Moon/School Day/Rock and Roll Music/Oh Baby Doll/Sweet Little Sixteen/Rock at the Philharmonic (instr.)/*Reelin' and Rockin'/Johnny B. Goode/It Don't Take But a Few Minutes/Around and Around/Beautiful Delilah/Carol/Anthony Boy/Jo Jo Gunne/Memphis, Tennessee/Sweet Little Rock and Roller/Run Rudolph Run+/Little Queenie/Almost Grown/Back in the USA/Let It Rock/Too Pooped to Pop+/I Got to Find My Baby/Don't You Lie to Me+/Worried Life Blues+/Bye Bye Johnny/Jaguar and the Thunderbird/Diploma for Two/Down the Road a Piece+/Confessin' the Blues+/I'm Talking About You/Route 66+/Rip It Up+/Come On/Rocking on the Railroad (Let It Rock)/Nadine/No Particular Place to Go/You Never Can Tell/Liverpool Drive* (instr.)/*Run Joe+/Jamaica Farewell+*
This is a terrific album. Great picture of Berry from mid-60s on front cover, and more pictures in the enclosed booklet. And as with every Japanese release, the lyrics to each song are printed as sung on the recording. *Rocking on the Railroad* is the dubbed version from the **On Stage** LP, a strange inclusion since the usual version is already on side D of the second LP. *Jamaica Farewell* is the complete U.S. issue.

MEXICO

ALBUMS

TREBOL
TI–70693   **COLLECTION CHUCK BERRY VOL. 1** (1983)
TI-70694   **COLLECTION CHUCK BERRY VOL. 2** (1983)
> Both are same as U.S. 2-LP set **The Great Twenty-Eight**, but here released as two separate albums with different covers. Vol. 1 has yellow front cover and Vol. 2 has blue; same drawing of Berry as on **The Great Twenty-Eight**, however.

POLAND

SINGLES

POLISH
POST-CARD DISC
R-0857-II   *Sweet Little Sixteen/Johnny B. Goode*
> This "record" is a thin square board with grooves on one side, pressed onto a color picture of a landscape. It comes in an orange paper bag (45 rpm size) with some Polish printing on the bag.

PORTUGAL

ALBUMS

DARGIL
FS-321   **CHUCK BERRY'S GREATEST HITS**
> Same as U.S. Everest LP, with same number and same cover. Portuguese liner notes on the back cover.

SPAIN

EPs

HISPA VOX
HX 007-54   **GRANDE EXITOS VOL. 1** (1965)
> *Memphis, Tennessee/Roll Over Beethoven/Rock and Roll Music/Johnny B. Goode*

HISPA VOX
HX 007-59   **GRANDE EXITOS VOL. 2** (1965)
> *School Day/Sweet Little Sixteen/Maybellene/Reelin' and Rockin'*

HISPA VOX
HX 007-61   **CHUCK BERRY** (1965)
> *Promised Land/Dear Dad/Carol/Nadine*

ALBUMS

PHILIPS
92 79 140

GIGANTES DEL POP — CHUCK BERRY — VOL. 51
No information about tracks available, but Mercury recordings again. The LP is one in a series of fifty-three albums containing songs by 60's groups and artists.

MERCURY
6841 151

HISTORIA DE LA MUSICA ROCK — 20 (1982)
Same as U.S. Mercry **Golden Hits**. Different cover.

YUGOSLAVIA

ALBUMS

PHILIPS
9279 140

ROCKIN' WITH CHUCK BERRY
Same as the Dutch issue with the same number and cover.

A GUIDE TO RECOMMENDED FOREIGN RELEASES

FRANCE

BARCLAY
80258

VOL. 5 CHUCK BERRY A L'OLYMPIA
Nearly the same LP as **Chuck Berry on Stage**, but on this one Berry is "live" at the Paris Olympia.
See "French Discography" for more information.

HOLLAND

SUN-CHESS
NQCS-1

ROCK SMUK
Interview with Berry, probably done at Wembley, August 1972. Available on this issue and also on the German LP
4 Rock Giants—Talks and Hits (Bellaphon BI-15119).
The interview is only a minute and thirty-eight seconds long.
For further information, see the Dutch and West German discographies.

JAPAN

EAST WORLD
WTP-90072

CHUCK BERRY TOKYO SESSION
This LP includes Berry live from Tokyo, 1981, and it's a must for every music lover around the world. It is Berry at his very best. A pity the distribution is limited. You might have problems finding this one, but don't hesitate if you do!
See the "International Discography" for more details.

WEST GERMANY

MERCURY
6463 044

ROCK! ROCK! ROCK 'N' ROLL!
Let It Rock
The very first appearance of the Mercury version, and it's a good one. Also available on two other German LPs: (6619 034) **Sweet Little Rock and Roller** (two-LP set) and (6463 129) **Motive.**

BELLAPHON
BLS-5573

CHUCK BERRY LIVE IN CONCERT (2 LP set)
This is actually the same LP set as the U.S. Magnum MR-703, but Germany is the only country outside the U.S. to issue this famous LP in its original form. The cover is not the same, however.

BOOTLEGS DISCOGRAPHY

KOZMIK
KZ-501

RARE BERRIES (U.K.)
Run Around/Roly Poly (instr.)/*Worried Life Blues+/Hey
Pedro/It Don't Take But a Few Minutes/Blue Feeling* (instr.)/
Sweet Sixteen+/Our Little Rendezvous/Deep Feeling (instr.)/
Merry Christmas Baby+ (single version)/*In Go* (instr.)/*How
You've Changed/Berry Pickin'* (instr.)/*Blues for Hawaiians*
(instr.)
    This LP was a rare one when issued somewhere between
1962--63 in England. An interesting compilation of tracks
with seven instrumentals. The sound quality is variable, but
generally poor.

DRIVING WHEEL
LP-1001

SIX TWO FIVE (U.K., 1972)
*Roll Over Beethoven/Sweet Little Sixteen/Memphis, Tennessee/
South of the Border+/Beer Drinkin' Woman+/Let It Rock/
Mean Old World+/Carol/Liverpool Drive* (instr.)/*Nadine/Bye
Bye Johnny/Goodnight Sweetheart+/Johnny B. Goode*
    This is a top quality LP, pressed on purple vinyl. It con-
tains the TV program "Sounds for Saturday" (45 minutes),
which Berry did for BBC 2 on March 29, 1972, transmitted on
July 22. Backing band: Rocking Horse. The sound quality is
excellent.
    South of the Border was issued legally in the U.K. on
Chess single 6145 027, with *Bio* as the B-side, probably in an
attempt to follow the success of *My Ding-A-Ling*.
    The LP was later reissued on Maybelline Records MBL-
676, on normal black vinyl.

REELIN'
001

AMERICA'S HOTTEST WAX (U.S., 1980)
    This is exactly the same LP which has now been legally
issued in England on Chess CXMP-2011, **Chess Masters**. The
bootleg was a real collectors' item when first issued in 1980,
containing what Berry fans had been waiting for for years: a
whole LP of largely unreleased tracks. The bootleg was first
available in a plain white cover, with liner notes on a paper
insert. At first, sound quality was not very good, but the record was reissued with a very good cover with many pictures,
and with excellent sound quality. The bootleg cover is actually
much better than on the later legal issue from Chess.

KOALA
KOA-14738

MEMPHIS (U.S., 1980)
*Reelin' and Rockin'/No Particular Place to Go/Thirty Days/
Sweet Little Sixteen/Little Queenie/Memphis, Tennessee/You
Never Can Tell/Brown-Eyed Handsome Man/Nadine/Promised
Land/Back in the USA*
    A peculiar bootleg designed for everyone unfamiliar with
the fact that all the original Chess recordings are readily avail-
able, and in much better sound quality.

LA GRANDE STORIA	**CHUCK BERRY** (Italy)
DEL ROCK	*Maybellene/Rock and Roll Music/Reelin' and Rockin'/Sweet*
GSR-64	*Little Sixteen/Childhood Sweetheart/Roll Over Beethoven/*

LA GRANDE STORIA **CHUCK BERRY** (Italy)
DEL ROCK *Maybellene/Rock and Roll Music/Reelin' and Rockin'/Sweet*
GSR-64 *Little Sixteen/Childhood Sweetheart/Roll Over Beethoven/*
How High the Moon+ (instr.)/*Chuck's Jam* (actually *One*
O'Clock Jump+) (instr.)/*I've Changed/Vacation Time* (or *21*
Blues)

Maybellene and *Roll Over Beethoven* are the same as on
the bootleg WINS 1010 and Radiola MR-1087. The rest are
from the bootleg **America's Hottest Wax** (Reelin' 001), only
this time with a dubbed-in "live" audience. A strange album,
but a nice fold-out cover with some great pictures of Berry.

The LP is the sixty-fourth in a series of a hundred covering
artists from the 50s, 60s, and 70s. Poor sound quality.

COMPILATION BOOTLEGS

TRADE MARK OF **TELECASTS – JOHN LENNON**
QUALITY *Memphis, Tennessee/Johnny B. Goode*
TMQ-71046 From U.S. TV's "Mike Douglas Show," January 1972,
Berry and Lennon sing two duets. Poor sound quality. The
songs are also available on CBM-3711, and on JL-517 (this
time with better sound quality).

WINS **RECORDED LIVE ON STAGE**
1010 *Maybellene/Roll Over Beethoven*
Carries the legend "Alan Freed's Rock N' Roll Dance Party
Vol. 1," and contains cuts by various artists recorded live on
radio in 1956. Release date of the LP is unknown. Berry's
two tracks are also featured on the next LP from Radiola.

RADIOLA **ROCK N' ROLL RADIO**
MR-1087 *Maybellene/Roll Over Beethoven*
This LP was issued in 1978. It might not even be a boot-
leg, but the sound quality is so poor that it sounds like one!

240

UNISSUED BERRY RECORDINGS

This is not meant to be any complete listing of songs, but gives a good impression of titles known to be in the files. Most of this information was provided by Jean-Pierre Ravelli.

CHESS

1956	*Brown-Eyed Handsome Man* (alt. take)
1957	*Wee Wee Hours* (alt. take)/*Someday Baby*/*Oh Baby*
1958	*Time Was* (alt. take)/*Hey Pedro* (alt. take)
1960	*Lucky So and So*/*Lucky So and So* (alt. take)/*Crying Steel* (instr.)
1961	*Nashville* (?)/*Go Go Go* (alt. take)
1964	*I'm in the Danger Zone*/*I'm in the Twilight Zone*/*The Little Girl from Central* (alt. take)/*Dust My Broom*+/*Mean Old World*+/*Spending Christmas*/*Adulteen*
1966	*His Daughter Caroline* (fast version)

The following titles exist *without* the dubbed-in "live" audience (from LP-1480):
All Aboard/*I Just Want to Make Love to You*+/*I Still Got the Blues*/*Trick or Treat*

MERCURY

1966	*Campus Cookie*/*Brown-Eyed Handsome Man*/*Almost Grown*/*Around and Around*
	All from the "Golden Hits" session.
1967	*Flying Home*+ (studio take)
1969	*Put Her Down* (instr. version)/*Concerto in B. Goode* (slow version)/untitled instrumental
	The whole LP **Concerto in B. Goode** was recorded at Berry Park Studios, so that many songs from that session remain unknown to the public.

CHESS

1970	*It Ain't None of Your Business*/*My Ding-A-Ling* (studio take)/untitled instrumental
	From the "Back Home" session.
1972	*Let It Rock*/*School Day*
	Two songs from the live performance in Montreaux, Switzerland; other songs were performed, but only these two were to be included on the 2 LP set **Blues Avalanche** (2CH-60015) from the above concert. Bo Diddley, Muddy Waters, Koko Taylor, and T-Bone Walker are on the album, but Berry withheld his songs.
1973	*You and My Country*/*Tell You About My Buddy* (short version)/*One Sixty Nine*/*Roll Away*
	All from the "Bio" session.
1974	*Turn the House-Lights On*/*Jambalaya*+/*The Song of My Love* (with Ingrid Berry)/*If I Was*/*Vaya Con Dios*+/*The Weight*+/*Johnny B. Blues* (instr.)/*Dust My Broom*+/*Together Again*+/*Here Today*/*Rockin'* (instr.)
	All from the "Chuck Berry '75" session. Planned for release on the abortive double-album set.
1976	*Floyd* (instr.)/*Silver Threads*+ (the old standard)

241

Chuck Berry's latest studio release, **Rock It** (1979), was recorded at Berry Park.

He also recorded songs which were meant to have been issued on Warner Brothers Records in 1976/77, but no LP appeared.

After the release of bootleg **LP America's Hottest Wax** in 1980, it revealed the existence of many unissued songs. Since Chuck Berry does so much recording at his own studios, it is probable that no complete listing of unissued songs and takes will ever appear.

MISCELLANEOUS RECORD FACTS

The songs in bold face italics are still available only on 45 rpm records:

CHESS
1697
    ***Vacation Time**/Beautiful Delilah* (U.K. London HL-8677)
    Also available on the American EP **Pickin' Berries with** . . .
    (Chess EP-5124), and in Sweden on London EP RE-5030.
1716
    ***That's My Desire**/Anthony Boy*
    Not issued in the U.K.
1926
    ***Lonely School Days** (slow version)/Dear Dad*
    Issued in U.K. coupled with *I Got a Booking* (Chess CRS-8006),
    and in Holland on Chess International AR-45.161.
1963
    ***Ramona Says Yes**/Lonely School Days* (fast version) (U.K. Chess
    8037)
    Issued in West Germany on Vogue DV-14547, and in Sweden
    on Chess International AR-50.004.

MERCURY
72643
    ***Laugh and Cry**/Club Nitty Gritty* (U.K. Mercury MF-958)
    Issued in Holland on Mercury 127 260MCF. Probably also
    issued in West Germany.

CHESS
2140
    ***Roll 'Em Pete**+/Bio*
    Issued in West Germany on Bellaphon BF-18214, but not
    issued in the U.K.
    ***South of the Border**+/Bio* (U.K. Chess 6145 027)
    Legally issued from the BBC 2 TV-program; also on the boot-
    leg LP **Six Two Five** (Driving Wheel 1001), or Maybelline
    MBL-676.

Chuck Berry has written one song especially for Bo Diddley:
CHECKER
1098
    ***Hey Good Lookin'**/You Ain't Bad* (U.K. Chess CRS-8000)
    Also available on Checker LP-2992, **Hey Good Lookin'**, and on
    the U.K. Chess LP CRL-4002.

Chuck Berry appears (guitar only) on two songs recorded by The Ecuadors in 1959:
ARGO
5353
    Let Me Sleep Woman+/Say You'll Be Mine+
    The songs were published by Chuck Berry Music, Inc., but
    Chuck didn't write them.

Before Berry signed with Chess in 1955, he was featured on a recorded by Joe
Alexander & The Cubans:
BALLAD Records
    AA 1008-X45
    Oh Maria+/I Hope These Words Will Find You Well+
    Recorded August 13, 1954; Berry on backing guitar only.

The following songs were issued only in the U.S.:
> *That's My Desire* (on Chess single 1716)
> *Jamaica Farewell* (the complete version, on Chess LPS-1495)
> *Welcome Back Pretty Baby* (on Chess single 1943, and LP/LPS-1498)

The following four LPs were issued also in stereo in the U.S.:
> **TWO GREAT GUITARS** (Checker LPS-2991)
> **ST. LOUIS TO LIVERPOOL** (Chess LPS-1488)
> **CHUCK BERRY IN LONDON** (Chess LPS-1495)
> **FRESH BERRY'S** (Chess LPS-1498)

The following songs were issued only in the U.K.:
> *Big Ben/The Little Girl from Central* (on the Pye International album NPL-28039, and on Marble Arch MAL/MALS-702)
> *Come On* (second version)
> *Around and Around* (second version) Available only on Marble Arch MALS-702.
> *Sad Day—Long Night* (the instrumental version of *Welcome Back Pretty Baby*, available on Chess LP CRL-4506)
> *South of the Border* (on Chess single 6145 027, and also on the bootlet LP **Drivin' Wheel** 1001, and on Maybelline MBL-676)
> *Do You Love Me* (the February 1959 version on the LP **Golden Decade Vol. 3**, Chess 6641 177)

Roll 'Em Pete+ was issued only on single in U.S. (Chess 2140), and on single in West Germany (Bellaphon BF-18214)

The U.K. LP **YOU NEVER CAN TELL** (Marble Arch MALS-702) contains several stereo tracks which are available nowhere else. (See the U.K. album discography for further information)

The song *Nadine* was recorded in stereo, but is only available in that form on two West German albums:
> **CHUCK BERRY – ORIGINAL OLDIES VOL. 3** (Bellaphon BI-15107)
> **THE BEST OF CHUCK BERRY** (Bellaphon BLST-6506; 2 LP set)

Fraulein+ and *Lonely All the Time+* (Crazy Arms) were issued on the U.K. EP Pye International NEP-44033, and on LP Pye International NPL-28031. Also available on some Dutch issues (see the Dutch discography).

The Mercury recording of *Let It Rock* is available only on three West German albums:
> **ROCK! ROCK! ROCK 'N' ROLL** (Mercury 6463 044)
> **SWEET LITTLE ROCK AND ROLLER** (Mercury 6619 039; 2 LP set)
> **MOTIVE** (Mercury 6463 129)

THE CHESS SESSIONS, 1955-1966

Individual songs which are labeled as "unreleased" are recordings that Chess Records did not immediately release to the general public in the U.S., principally because Leonard Chess felt they were commercially unsuitable. Many of the songs were later released, either in Europe or on future domestic albums. The three albums in Chess's Golden Decade series contain most of the important recordings in Chuck Berry's distinguished career.

MAY 21, 1955
Johnny Johnson, piano
Willie Dixon, bass
Jasper Thomas, drums
Jerome Green, maracas
Songs Recorded
Maybellene
Wee Wee Hours

SEPTEMBER, 1955
Johnny Johnson, piano
Willie Dixon, bass
Jasper Thomas, drums
Jerome Green, maracas
Songs Recorded
Together (We Will Always Be)
Thirty Days (To Come Back Home)

DECEMBER, 1955
Otis Spann, piano
Willie Dixon, bass
Eddie Hardy, drums
Songs Recorded
You Can't Catch Me
Down Bound Train
No Money Down
Roly Poly (instrumental) (Kalso, Roli Poli)
Berry Pickin' (instrumental)
I've Changed (Jasper Thomas, drums)

FEBRUARY, 1956
Johnny Johnson, piano
Willie Dixon, bass
Fred Below, drums
L.C. Davis, tenor saxophone
Unknown trumpet
Songs Recorded
Drifting Heart
Brown-Eyed Handsome Man
Brown-Eyed Handsome Man (unreleased)
Roll Over Beethoven
Too Much Monkey Business

OCTOBER, 1956
Jimmy Rogers, guitar
Johnny Johnson, piano
Fred Below, drums

Willie Dixon, bass
Song Recorded
Havana Moon

JANUARY, 1957
Johnny Johnson, piano
Willie Dixon, bass
Fred Below, drums
Songs Recorded
Deep Feelin' (instrumental)
School Day
La Juanda
Wee Wee Hours (unreleased)
Blue Feeling (instrumental)
Low Feeling
Rock and Roll Music (unreleased)
Wee Wee Hours

MAY, 1957
Lafayette Leake, piano
Willie Dixon, bass
Fred Below, drums
Songs Recorded
How You've Changed
Rock and Roll Music
Oh Baby Doll
13 Question Method (unreleased)
Some Day (unreleased)
Oh Baby (unreleased)
Twenty One (unreleased)
Twenty One Blues (unreleased)

FEBRUARY, 1958
Lafayette Leake and Johnny Johnson, piano
Willie Dixon, bass
Fred Below, drums
Songs Recorded
Sweet Little Sixteen (Surfin' USA)
Rockin' at the Philharmonic (instrumental)
Guitar Boogie (instrumental)
Night Beat
Time Was
Reelin' and Rockin'
Do You Love Me (unreleased)

Sweet Little Sixteen (unreleased)
Johnny B. Goode

APRIL, 1958
Personnel unknown: vocal/guitar,
2nd guitar overdubbed, piano,
clubs and drums*
Songs Recorded
Around and Around
Ingo (instrumental)
It Don't Take But a Few Minutes
Blues for Hawaiians (instrumental)
(also, *Surfin' Steel)*

MAY, 1958
Johnny Johnson, piano
G. Smith, bass
Eddie Hardy, drums
Unknown percussionist
Songs Recorded
Beautiful Delilah
Vacation Time
Carol
Oh Yeah (unreleased)
Hey Pedro
Time Was (unreleased)
House of Blue Lights (unreleased)
OCTOBER, 1958
Johnny Johnson, piano
Willie Dixon, bass
Fred Below, drums
Bo Diddley, guitar
Songs Recorded
Anthony Boy
Jo Jo Gunne
Sweet Little Rock and Roller
Memphis, Tennessee (Chuck Berry,
producer)

DECEMBER 12, 1958
Johnny Johnson, piano
Willie Dixon, bass
Fred Below, drums
Songs Recorded
Merry Christmas Baby
Run Rudolph Run

JANUARY, 1959
Johnny Johnson, piano
Willie Dixon, bass
Fred Below, drums
Songs Recorded
Little Queenie
That's My Desire

FEBRUARY, 1959
Johnny Johnson, piano
Willie Dixon, bass
Fred Below, drums
Vocals: The Moonglows

Songs Recorded
Do You Love Me (unreleased)
Almost Grown
Back in the USA
Blue on Blue (unreleased instrumental)

JULY, 1959
Johnny Johnson, piano
Willie Dixon, bass
Fred Below, drums
Equadors, vocals
L.C. Davis, trumpet
Songs Recorded
Betty Jean
County Line (unreleased)
Childhood Sweetheart
One O'Clock Jump (unreleased)
I Just Want to Make Love to You
Let It Rock
Too Pooped to Pop
Broken Arrow

DECEMBER, 1959
Johnny Johnson, piano
Willie Dixon, bass
Fred Below, drums
Equadors, vocals
Songs Recorded
Let Me Sleep Woman (unreleased)
Say You'll Be Mine (unreleased)

APRIL, 1960
Johnny Johnson, piano
Matt Murphy, guitar
Eddie Hardy, drums
L.C. Davis, tenor saxophone
Unknown, additional saxophone
Songs Recorded
Drifting Blues
I Got to Find My Baby
Don't You Lie to Me
Worried Life Blues
Our Little Rendezvous
Bye Bye Johnny
Jaguar and the Thunderbird
Run Around

MID-1960
Johnny Johnson, piano
Matt Murphy, guitar
Willie Dixon, bass
Eddie Hardy, drums
L.C. Davis, tenor saxophone
Songs Recorded
Diploma for Two
Little Star
The Way I Was Before
Away from You
Down the Road Apiece
Confessin' the Blues

*Speculation is that the overdubbed material is Chuck Berry's work.

Sweet Sixteen
13 Question Method (unreleased)
Stop and Listen
Still Got the Blues
Lucky So and So
Mad Lad
Crying Steel (unreleased instrumental)

JANUARY, 1961
Johnny Johnson, piano
Eddie Hardy, drums
Unknown clubs
Songs Recorded
Route 66
I'm Talking about You
Rip It Up

AUGUST, 1961
Johnny Johnson, piano
Eddie Hardy, drums
L.C. Davis, tenor saxophone
Martha Berry, vocals
Songs Recorded
Come On
Trick or Treat
All Aboard
Go Go Go
The Man and the Donkey
Adulteen (unreleased)

JUNE, 1963
Personnel unknown
Songs Recorded
Cranberries (unreleased)
How High the Moon (unreleased)

AUGUST 1, 1963
Johnny Johnson, piano
Eddie Hardy, drums
L.C. Davis, tenor saxophone
Songs Recorded
No Details
Nashville (unreleased)
Brown-Eyed Handsome Man (unre-
   leased)

JANUARY, 1964
Johnny Johnson, piano
Unknown second guitar (probably
   Bo Diddley)
Odie Payne, drums
Unknown saxophone
Unknown vocals
Willie Dixon, electric bass
Songs Recorded
Nadine
You Never Can Tell
Girl from Central High (unreleased)
Things I Used to Do
I'm in the Danger Zone (unreleased)

Faulein (unreleased)
Crazy Arms (unreleased)
Dust My Broom (unreleased)
O Rangutang (instrumental)

FEBRUARY 25, 1964
Lafayette Leake, piano
Odie Payne, drums
Unknown clubs
Willie Dixon, electric bass
Songs Recorded
Big Ben Blues (unreleased)
The Promised Land
Brenda Lee

MARCH 26, 1964
Paul Williams, piano
Odie Payne, drums
Unknown clubs
Songs Recorded
No Particular Place to Go
You Two
Liverpool Drive

AUGUST, 1964
Paul Williams, piano
Odie Payne, drums
Unknown clubs
Songs Recorded
Little Marie
Go Bobby Soxer

DECEMBER, 1964
Paul Williams, piano
Odie Payne, drums
Unknown, clubs and saxes
Songs Recorded
Lonely Schooldays
His Daughter Caroline
Dear Dad
I Want to Be Your Driver
Spending Christmas (unreleased)
The Song of My Love
Butterscotch

JANUARY 5, 1965, LONDON, ENGLAND
Instrumental personnel unknown
Five Dimensions, vocal support
Songs Recorded
After It's Over
Why Should We End This Way
You Came a Long Way from St. Louis
She Once Was Mine
Jamaica Farewell

JANUARY 31, 1965, LONDON, ENGLAND
Instrumental personnel unknown
Five Dimensions, vocal support
Songs Recorded
My Little Lovelight

247

I Got a Booking
St. Louis Blues

SEPTEMBER 1--2, 1965
Johnny Johnson, piano
Jasper Thomas, drums
Chuck Bernard, clubs
Peter John Hogan, harmonica
Songs Recorded
Run Joe
It's My Own Business
One for My Baby
Every Day We Rock and Roll
My Mustang Ford
Merrily We Rock and Roll
Vaya Con Dios
Wee Hours Blues
It Wasn't Me
Ain't That Just Like a Woman
Right Off Rampart Street
Welcome Back Pretty Baby
Loving You In Vain
Forgive Me

1965
Johnny Johnson, piano
Jasper Thomas, drums
Chuck Bernard, clubs
Peter John Hogan, harmonica
Song Recorded
Sad Day, Long Night (unreleased)

APRIL 13, 1966
Johnny Johnson, piano
Jasper Thomas, drums
Chuck Bernard, clubs
Songs Recorded
Ramona Say Yes
Viva Rock and Roll (unreleased)
His Daughter Caroline (unreleased)
Lonely School Days

CHUCK BERRY'S SONGS:
SOME SOURCES

The following list of songs offers examples of traditional blues, gospel, rhythm and blues, and pop tunes which Chuck Berry molded into his own special songs. In some cases, Chuck completely altered the original song, but in a number of instances he simply carried through the idea of the original tune into his own song.

BERRY'S SONGS   ORIGINAL SONG(S) & COMPOSER(S)

BERRY'S SONGS	ORIGINAL SONG(S) & COMPOSER(S)
After It's Over	*Baby What You Want Me to Do* (Jimmy Reed)
Ain't That Just Like a Woman	*Ain't That Just Like a Woman* (Louis Jordan, 1946; also, Fats Domino)
Blues for Hawaiians	*Floyd's Guitar Blues* (Floyd Smith; recording by Bill Doggett)
Broken Arrow	*Old MacDonald*
California	*Mendocino* (Sir Douglas Quintet)
Don't You Lie to Me	*Don't You Lie to Me* (Fats Domino; also, Johnny Young)
Downbound Train	*Ghost Riders in the Sky* (Sons of the Pioneers)
Havana Moon	*Calypso Blues* (Nat "King" Cole)
I Got a Booking	*Key to the Highway* (Little Walter)
I Want to Be Your Driver	*Let Me Be Your Chauffeur* (Memphis Minnie)
It Hurts Me Too	*It Hurts Me Too* (Elmore James)
Johnny B. Goode	*Strolling with Bones* (T. Bone Walker)
Jo Jo Gunne	*The Signifying Monkey*
Lonely All the Time	*Crazy Arms* (Ray Price)
Maybellene	*Ida Red* (Bob Wills and the Texas Playboys; also, The Louvin Brothers)
My Ding-A-Ling	*My Ding-A-Ling* (Dave Bartholomew) and *Toy Bell* (Dave Bartholomew; recording by The Bees)
My Little Love Light	*Let It Shine* (traditional gospel tune)
Night Beat	*Blues after Hours* (Pee Wee Crayton; also, Arthur Gunther) and *Farewell* (Moon Mullican)

BERRY'S SONGS	ORIGINAL SONG(S) & COMPOSER(S)
Our Little Rendezvous	*Good Morning Little Schoolgirl* (Johnny Lee "Sonny Boy" Williamson)
Reelin' and Rockin'	*Saturday Night Fish Fry* (Louis Jordan)
Sweet Little Sixteen	*Route 90* (Clarence Bon Ton Garlow)
Too Late	*Too Late* (Jimmy Wakely)

COVER RECORDS

As testimony to Chuck Berry's impact on the evolution of rock-and-roll, the following list enumerates some 850 cover versions of Chuck's songs by over 500 individuals and groups, principally from the United States and Europe. The most covered song is *Memphis, Tennessee* (120 times), followed by *Johnny B. Goode* (101), *Roll Over Beethoven* (73), *Maybellene* (62) and *Sweet Little Sixteen* (61). Other frequently covered songs include *Little Queenie* (33), *Rock And Roll Music* (32), *The Promised Land* (32), *Brown-Eyed Handsome Man* (30), and *Too Much Monkey Business* (26).

This listing represents the combined efforts of Morten Reff and Howard A. DeWitt, who have collected this information over a period of years. Despite even such concerted efforts, some artists have doubtless been overlooked, and the compilers would welcome any additions to this Appendix.

TERRY ADAM AND THE PANHANDLE
   MYSTERY
   Maybellene
DANNY ADLER
   Nadine
THE AD-LIBS
   Too Much Monkey Business
STEVE ALAIMO
   Sweet Little Sixteen
AGE ALEKSANDERSEN (Norwegian)
   The Promised Land (Live)
JOHNNIE ALLAN
   The Promised Land
THE AMBOY DUKES
   Maybellene
MAI-BRITT ANDERSEN (Norwegian)
   You Never Can Tell (Norwegian lyrics)
OLE ANDERSEN (Norwegian)
   The Promised Land
   Sweet Little Rock And Roller
THE ANGLO-SAXONS
   Brown-Eyed Handsome Man
THE ANIMALS
   Almost Grown (Live)
   Around And Around
   How You've Changed
   I Gotta Find My Baby (Live)
   Let It Rock (Live)
   Memphis, Tennessee
   Sweet Little Sixteen
   Too Much Monkey Business
PAUL ANKA
   Memphis, Tennessee

ANTOINE (French)
   My Ding-A-Ling
THE APPLEJACKS
   Too Much Monkey Business
THE ARCHIES
   Rock And Roll Music
LLOYD ARNOLD
   School Day
JAME ARP
   Let It Rock
THE ASTRONAUTS
   Almost Grown
   Around And Around
   Go Go Go
   Johnny B. Goode
   Memphis, Tennessee
   Roll Over Beethoven
   Sweet Little Rock And Roller
HOYT AXTON
   Maybellene

BABY RAY
   The Promised Land
LAVERN BAKER
   Memphis, Tennessee
THE BAND
   The Promised Land
THE BARBARIANS
   Memphis, Tennessee
BOBBY BARE
   Memphis, Tennessee
DAVE BARTHOLOMEW
   My Ding-A-Ling

COUNT BASIE
Memphis, Tennessee
THE BATS
Carol
THE BEACH BOYS
Johnny B. Goode (Live)
Rock And Roll Music
Sweet Little Sixteen (Surfin' USA)
THE BEAT KINGS
Roll Over Beethoven
THE BEATLES
I'm Talking About You
Little Queenie (Live)
Memphis, Tennessee
Rock And Roll Music
Roll Over Beethoven
Roll Over Beethoven (Live)
Sweet Little Sixteen
THE BEAT MIXERS
I'm Talking About You
HARRY BELAFONTE
Memphis, Tennessee
THE BEL AIRS
Roll Over Beethoven
BELLE EPOQUE
Memphis, Tennessee (1978)
PETER BELLI (Danish)
Johnny B. Goode
BENNY AND THE BEDBUGS
Roll Over Beethoven
ROD BERNARD
Memphis, Tennessee
No Money Down
The Promised Land
DAVE BERRY
Around And Around
Little Queenie
Memphis, Tennessee
JAN BERRY
Little Queenie
MIKE BERRY
Brown-Eyed Handsome Man
Johnny B. Goode
ROBERT BERTRAND
Memphis, Tennessee
BIG JORGEN & THE THUNDERBALLS
(Danish)
No Particular Place To Go
THE BIG THREE
Reelin' And Rockin'
BIG TOM & THE MAINLINERS
Johnny B. Goode
BIG WHEELIE AND THE HUBCAPS
Chuck Berry Medley
THE BLACK BATMAN (Danish)
Sweet Little Sixteen
THE BLACK BEATS (Danish)
Beautiful Delilah
BILL BLACK COMBO

Brown-Eyed Handsome Man
Carol
Johnny B. Goode
Maybellene
Memphis, Tennessee (Two versions)
Nadine
Little Queenie
Reelin' and Rockin' (Two versions)
Roll Over Beethoven
School Day
Sweet Little Sixteen
30 Days
BURT BLANCA & THE KING CREOLES
Carol
Maybellene
Memphis, Tennessee
Rock And Roll Music
Sweet Little Sixteen
BLOMMAN (Swedish)
Little Marie (Swedish lyrics)
THE BLUES BAND
Don't You Lie To Me
Nadine
THE BLUES PROJECT
I Want To Be Your Driver
You Can't Catch Me
THE BLUE STARS
School Day
THE BOGEY BOYS
You Can't Catch Me
THE BOOGIE KINGS
Let It Rock
Let It Rock (Live)
Sweet Little Rock And Roller (Live)
PAT BOONE
Memphis, Tennessee
Sweet Little Sixteen
THE BOPPERS (Swedish)
The Promised Land
DAVID BOWIE
Around And Around
NERO BRANDENBURG (German)
My Ding-A-Ling
TERESA BREWER
School Day
BILLY BRIDGE
Bye, Bye Johnny
BRINSLEY SCHWARZ
Run Rudolph Run (Live)
DONNIE BROOKS
Memphis, Tennessee
JIM BROWN
Maybellene
JOE BROWN
Sweet Little Sixteen (Live)
RUFUS BROWN
Sweet Little Sixteen
ROY BUCHANAN
Reelin' And Rockin'

252

BUDDY AND THE HEARTS
Let It Rock
30 Days
SANDY BULL
Memphis, Tennessee
THE BULLS
Johnny B. Goode
THE BUNCH
Nadine
Sweet Little Rock And Roller
ERIC BURDON
Have Mercy Judge
Too Late
SONNY BURGESS
Brown-Eyed Handsome Man
Memphis, Tennessee
School Day
ANGY BURRI & THE APACHES (Swiss)
Promised Land
School Day
Tou Never Can Tell
JAMES BURTON
Johnny B. Goode
BYFANARA (Swedish)
No Particular Place To Go
THE BYRDS
Roll Over Beethoven

AL CAIOLA
Memphis, Tennessee (Instrumental)
RAY CAMPI
You Can't Catch Me
CAN BALS (UK)
Nadine
Sweet Little Sixteen
FREDDY CANNON
Memphis, Tennessee
Too Much Monkey Business
THE CARROLL BROTHERS
Johnny B. Goode
Reelin' And Rockin'
JOE E. CARTER'S GROUP (Danish)
Too Much Monkey Business
BEN CASH
Memphis, Tennessee
BOB CATHEY
Johnny B. Goode
CAT MOTHER AND THE ALL NIGHT
    NEWSBOYS
Sweet Little Sixteen
CCS
School Day
THE CHALLENGERS
Maybellene (Instrumental)
Memphis, Tennessee (Instrumental)
THE CHAMBERS BROTHERS
Johnny B. Goode
CHUBBY CHECKER
Johnny B. Goode

Maybellene
JOHN CHESTER AND THE CHESSMEN
Bye Bye Johnny
THE CHILDREN (Danish)
Memphis, Tennessee
Rock And Roll Music
Roll Over Beethoven
ERIC CLAPTON
Little Queenie
DAVE CLARK FIVE
Memphis, Tennessee
Reelin' And Rockin'
Rock And Roll Music
Roll Over Beethoven
Sweet Little Sixteen
JIMMY CLARK
The Promised Land
THE CLIDOWS (Danish)
Memphis, Tennessee
Our Little Rendezvous
EDDIE COCHRAN
Sweet Little Sixteen
MAT COLLINS & HIS BEAT BAND
Johnny B. Goode
Memphis, Tennessee
COL. JOYE & JOY BOYS
Sweet Little Sixteen Twist
THE COMPTON BROTHERS
Brown-Eyed Handsome Man
Nadine
JIMMY CONE
Sweet Little Sixteen
THE CONNECTION
Rock And Roll Music
THE CONTENDERS
Johnny B. Goode
LOUISE CORDET
Around And Around
THE CORONADOES
Johnny B. Goode
THE MIKE COTTON SOUND
Around And Around
THE COUNT BISHOPS
Carol
Dear Dad
Johnny B. Goode
DON COVAY
Memphis, Tennessee
MICHAL COX
Sweet Little Sixteen
BILLY CRASH CRADDOCK
The Promised Land (1977)
BOBBY CRAFFORD
Johnny B. Goode
Memphis, Tennessee
THE CREAM
Too Much Monkey Business
CROSS COUNTRY
Rock And Roll Music

C.S.A. (British)
Little Queenie
KING CURTIS
Memphis, Tennessee (Instrumental)
LEE CURTIS & THE ALL STARS
Memphis, Tennessee
MAC CURTIS
Maybellene

TED DAIGLE
Sweet Little Sixteen
KIKKI DANIELSON AND VISEX
40 Days
MERCY DEE
(Come Back) Maybellene
THE DELTA CROSS BAND
Come On
THE DELUXE BLUES BAND
Let It Rock
Maybellene
No Money Down
JOHN DENVER
Johnny B. Goode (1979)
BO DIDDLEY
Memphis, Tennessee
DION DIMUCCI
Johnny B. Goode
THE DISCOTHEQUE ORCHESTRA
Roll Over Beethoven (Instrumental)
HELENE DIXON
Roll Over Beethoven
DR FEELGOOD
Beautiful Delilah
BILL DOGGETT
Memphis, Tennessee
JOE DOLAN
Sweet Little Rock And Roller
MICKEY DOLENZ
Johnny B. Goode
THE DOVELLS
Maybellene
Roll Over Beethoven
THE DOWNLINERS SECT
Beautiful Delilah
(Don't You Lie To Me)
Guitar Boogie
Our Little Rendezvous
Too Much Monkey Business
EDDY DRAKE
The Promised Land
JUDGE DREAD
My Ding-A-Ling

JACK EARLS
Roll Over Beethoven
T.O. EARNHEART
Around And Around
Back In The U.S.A.
THE EASYBEATS

Little Queenie
DAVE EDMUNDS
Dear Dad
It's My Own Business
Jo Jo Gunne
Let It Rock (Live)
No Money Down (Live)
The Promised Land
Run Rudolph Run
Sweet Little Rock And Roller
You Can't Catch Me
THE ELECTRIC LIGHT ORCHESTRA
Roll Over Beethoven (Two versions)
BERN ELLIOTT & THE FENMEN
I'm Talking About You
THE ENEMYS
Too Much Monkey Business
TORRY ENGHS (Norwegian)
Johnny B. Goode
The Promised Land
BARRY ENNIS
School Day
THE EVERLY BROTHERS
Maybellene
THE EXOTIC GUITARS
Memphis, Tennessee

THE FABOLOUS JOKERS
Memphis, Tennessee
THE FABULOUS SILVERTONES
Wee Wee Hours
THE FACES
Memphis, Tennessee
ADAM FAITH
Little Queenie
DON FARDON & HIS GANG
Johnny B. Goode
Memphis, Tennessee
Roll Over Beethoven
(Route 66)
DONNA FARGO
Johnny B. Goode
CHRIS FARLOWE & THE THUNDER-
BIRDS
Reelin' And Rockin'
THE FAROE BOYS (Danish)
Sweet Little Sixteen
FATS & HIS CATS
Sweet Little Sixteen
CHARLIE FEATHERS
Roll Over Beethoven (Live, 1973)
NARVEL FELTS
Maybellene (Live)
MICKEY FINN AND THE BLUE MEN
Reelin' And Rockin'
THE FIRESTONE BAND
The Promised Land
Roll Over Beethoven
THE FIVE EMPREES

Johnny B. Goode
THE FLAIRS
Roll Over Beethoven
THE FLAMING GROOVIES
Little Queenie
Sweet Little Rock And Roller
FLATT & SCRUGGS
Memphis, Tennessee
THE FLYING BURRITO BROTHERS
Roll Over Beethoven
THE FLYING SAUCERS
Johnny B. Goode
FOGHAT
Maybellene
Run Rudolph Run
WAYNE FONTANA & THE MIND-
BENDERS
I'm Talking About You
Jaguar And The Thunderbird
Memphis, Tennessee
Too Much Monkey Business
THE FRED BANANA BAND
Johnny B. Goode
FREDDIE AND THE DREAMERS
Johnny B. Goode
AL FREED
Carol
THE FROST
Rock And Roll Music
FUMBLE
Let It Rock (Rockin' On The Railroad)
No Money Down
BILLY FURY
Sweet Little Sixteen

THE GADABOUTS
Too Much Monkey Business
GREGG GALBRAITH
Memphis, Tennessee
LEIF GARRETT
Johnny B. Goode
GARY & THE NITE LITES
Sweet Little Sixteen
GENE AND THE GENTS
Sweet Little Sixteen
DANYEL GERARD
Memphis, Tennessee
LITTLE GERHARD (Swedish)
Johnny B. Goode
GERRY & THE PACEMAKERS
Maybellene
Reelin' And Rockin'
STEVE GIBBONS BAND
Tulane
GARY GLITTER
School Day
IAN GOMM
Come On
CHARLIE GRACIE

Too Much Monkey Business
PER "ELVIS" GRANBERG (Norwegian)
Johnny B. Goode
Memphis, Tennessee
TROND GRANLUND (Norwegian)
Almost Grown
Beautiful Delilah
Memphis, Tennessee
Sweet Little Sixteen
THE GRATEFUL DEAD
Johnny B. Goode
THE GREAT DAMES OF ROCK & ROLL
(British)
Maybellene
Nadine
JOHN GREER
Maybellene
MAX GREGER & HIS ORCHESTRA
Memphis, Tennessee
GUITAR MAC
Johnny B. Goode
HARDROCK GUNTER
Memphis, Tennessee
HELMUT GUNTHER & HIS ORCHESTRA
Sweet Little Sixteen (Instrumental)

BILL HALEY & HIS COMETS
Johnny B. Goode
Rock And Roll Music
ROY HALL
Little Queenie
JOHNNY HALLIDAY (French)
Carol
Maybellene
Nadine
Rock And Roll Music
Roll Over Beethoven
Sweet Little Sixteen
30 Days
THE BOB HAMMER BAND
Roll Over Beethoven
JOHN HAMMOND
Brown-Eyed Handsome Man
Maybellene
Nadine
No Money Down
HARD ROCK CIRCUS
Maybellene
Roll Over Beethoven
HAPPY HARRIS
Rock And Roll Music
EMMYLOU HARRIS
You Never Can Tell
ALEX HARVEY & HIS SOUL BAND
Reelin' And Rockin'
DALE HAWKINS
Johnny B. Goode
RONNIE HAWKINS
Let It Rock (1979)

PAYCHECK
Maybellene (1981)
Roll Over Beethoven (1981)
TOM JONES
Johnny B. Goode
Memphis, Tennessee
THE NEW JORDAL SWINGERS
(Norwegian)
Little Queenie
Maybellene
Memphis, Tennessee (Norwegian lyrics)
JUSSI & THE BOYS (Finnish)
Sweet Little Sixteen

THE KEIL ISLES (Australien)
Maybellene (Live)
JOHNNY KENSON
Memphis, Tennessee
Reelin' And Rockin'
GREG KHIN
Around And Around (Live)
SID KING & THE FIVE STRINGS
Maybellene (Live)
KINGFISH
Around And Around
THE KINKS
Beautiful Delilah
Too Much Monkey Business
BAKER KNIGHT
Reelin' And Rockin'
THE KNIGHTS
School Day
FRED KNOBLOCK
Memphis, Tennessee
BUDDY KNOX
Maybellene (1957)
Roll Over Beethoven (1973)
Sweet Little Sixteen (1973)
THE KOPPYKATS
Roll Over Beethoven
KJELL KRAGE (Swedish)
My Ding-A-Ling (Swedish lyrics)
JIM KWESKIN JUG BAND
Memphis, Tennessee

SLEEPY LA BEEF
Roll Over Beethoven
Too Much Monkey Business
You Can't Catch Me
LARRY LAKE
Johnny B. Goode
RONNIE LANE
You Never Can Tell
DON LANG
School Day
Sweet Little Sixteen
THE LANGLEYS
Memphis, Tennessee
KIM LARSEN & YANKEE DRENGENE

(Danish)
Havana Moon
JAMES LAST
Back To Memphis
Memphis, Tennessee
Rock And Roll Music
VIC LAWRENS
You Never Can Tell
BILLY LAWRIE
Roll Over Beethoven
RODNEY LAY & THE WILD WESTS
Reelin' And Rockin'
THE DAVE LEE SOUND
Little Queenie
DICKEY LEE
Nadine
JACK LEE
30 Days
THE LEGENDS
Rock At The Philarmonic
LENNIE & THE HAWKS (Norwegian)
You Never Can Tell
JOHN LENNON
Sweet Little Sixteen
You Can't Catch Me
KEN LEVY & THE PHANTOMS
Around And Around
Johnny B. Goode
Sweet Little Sixteen
GARY LEWIS & THE PLAYBOYS
Sweet Little Rock And Roller
JERRY LEE LEWIS
Brown-Eyed Handsome Man
Johnny B. Goode (Four versions)
Little Queenie (Two versions)
Maybellene
Memphis, Tennessee (Two versions)
No Particular Place To Go
Roll Over Beethoven (Three versions)
Sweet Little Sixteen (Three versions)
MARGARET LEWIS
Roll Over Beethoven
LES LIONCAUX (French)
Nadine
LITTLE JOE (French)
Little Queenie
LITTLE TONY (Italian)
Johnny B. Goode
THE LIVERPOOL BEATS
Little Queenie
Memphis, Tennessee
Roll Over Beethoven
THE "LIVING" GUITARS
Maybellene
Memphis, Tennessee
Roll Over Beethoven
School Day
JOHNNY LONG & HIS ORCHESTRA,
(Vocal by LEM JOHNSON AND

THE LONG SHOTS)
Maybellene
THE LONG HAIRS
Go Go Go
TRINI LOPEZ
Wee, Wee Hours
THE LOVIN' SPOONFUL
Almost Grown
JIM LOWE
Maybellene
JANNE LUCAS (Swedish)
Memphis, Tennessee
Roll Over Beethoven
MATT LUCAS
Maybellene
BOB LUMAN
Brown-Eyed Handsome Man
Maybellene
Memphis, Tennessee
JACKIE LYNTON
I'm Talking About You (1963)

LONNIE MACK
Memphis, Tennessee
JOHNNY MADDOX
Memphis, Tennessee
MAHAGONY RUSH
Johnny B. Goode
RAY MANZAREK
Downbound Train
STUART MARGOLIN
Brown-Eyed Handsome Man
THE MARK IV
Brown-Eyed Handsome Man
RALPH MARTERIE
Maybellene
MATCHBOX
It Don't Take But A Few Minutes
THE MAX FIVE (Danish)
Memphis, Tennessee
MC-5
Back In The U.S.A.
SCOTTY MC KAY
Brown-Eyed Handsome Man (1960)
THE MEDLEY SINGERS (Danish)
Carol
EDDIE MEDUZA
Oh What A Thrill
Roll Over Beethoven
Sweet Little Rock And Roller (Live)
MIKE MELVIN (Dutch)
Johnny B. Goode
Sweet Little Sixteen
THE MEMPHIS BEND
It's My Own Business
Maybellene
THE MIDNIGHT COWBOYS
The Promised Land
THE MIDNITERS

Johnny B. Goode
MIKE RAT & THE RUNAWAYS
Around And Around
Johnny B. Goode
THE MILKSHAKES
Jaguar And The Thunderbird
MISS MILLER
Memphis, Tennessee
EDDY MITCHELL (French)
Almost Grown
Brown-Eyed Handsome Man
Bye, Bye Johnny
I'm A Rocker
Johnny B. Goode
Maybellene
Memphis, Tennessee
No Particular Place To Go (Two versions)
Roll Over Beethoven
BOB MOLINO & THE NUTROCKERS
I'm A Rocker
CURLY MONEY
Little Queenie
THE ZOOT MONEY BIG ROLL BAND
Sweet Little Rock And Roller
SAMMIE MOORE
No Particular Place To Go
STEVE MOORE
40 Days
JOHNNY MOPED
Little Queenie
DERRICK MORGAN
My Ding-A-Ling
CHUCK LEE MORTON (Norwegian)
Johnny B. Goode (Bootleg)
THE MIKE MORTON CONGREGATION
Roll Over Beethoven ,
MOUNTAIN
Roll Over Beethoven
MUD
Bye Bye Johnny (Live)
MARIUS MULLER (Norwegian)
Roll Over Beethoven

THE NASHVILLE TEENS
Let It Rock
NEAL AND THE NEWCOMERS
Reelin' And Rockin'
RICK NELSON
I'm Talking About You
SANDY NELSON
Johnny B. Goode
School Day
Memphis, Tennessee
MICHAEL NESMITH
Nadine
THE NEW ADVENTURES
Come On
THE NEW RIDERS OF THE PURPLE
SAGE

School Day (Live)
You Never Can Tell
THE NIGHT ROCKERS
Almost Grown
TED NUGENT
Carol (Bootleg)

OLA & THE JANGLERS (Swedish)
Reelin' And Rockin'
THE ANDREW OLDHAM ORCHESTRA
Memphis, Tennessee (Instrumental)
ROY ORBISON
Memphis, Tennessee
BUCK OWENS
Johnny B. Goode
Memphis, Tennessee

JOEY PAIGE
Roll Over Beethoven
PAPA JOE'S MUSIC BOX
Memphis, Tennessee
GRAM PARSONS
Almost Grown
40 Days
JOHNNY PAYCHECK
see GEORGE JONES AND JOHNNY
PAYCHECK
TRACY PENDARVIS
Johnny B. Goode
School Day
CARL PERKINS
Brown-Eyed Handsome Man
Maybellene (1978)
Roll Over Beethoven
TOM PETTY AND THE HEARTBREAKERS
Jaguar And The Thunderbird (Bootleg)
THE PHANTOMS
Johnny B. Goode
Reelin' And Rockin'
'Round And 'Round
Sweet Little Sixteen
RAY PILGRIM
Brown-Eyed Handsome Man
THE PIRATES
Johnny B. Goode
THE PLYMOUTH ROCKERS
Around And Around
Brown-Eyed Handsome Man
WES POTTS
Memphis, Tennessee
KEITH POWELL
Too Much Monkey Business
ELVIS PRESLEY
Brown Eyed Handsome Man (Bootleg)
Johnny B. Goode (Two versions)
Memphis, Tennessee
No Particular Place To Go (Bootleg)
The Promised Land
Rock And Roll Music (Bootleg)

School Day
Too Much Monkey Business (Two
versions)
THE PRETTY THINGS
(Don't You Lie To Me)
Oh, Baby Doll
THE PRINCETON FIVE
Roll Over Beethoven

THE QUADS
Little Queenie
QUARTZ
Roll Over Beethoven

MIKAEL RAMEL (Swedish)
No Particular Place To Go (Swedish lyrics)
THE RAMONES
Jaguar And The Thunderbird
THE RATTLES
Bye, Bye Johnny
I'm Talking About You
Johnny B. Goode
Memphis, Tennessee
Roll Over Beethoven
THE RAVERS
Memphis, Tennessee
Rock And Roll Music
Too Much Monkey Business
RAY AND THE DARCHAES
Carol
JOHNNY REB
Maybellene
THE REDCAPS
I'm Talking About You
TEDDY REDELL
Back In The U.S.A.
REDWING
Bye Bye Johnny
Carol
DEAN REED (East German)
Sweet Little Sixteen
JERRY REED
Johnny B. Goode
Maybellene
Memphis, Tennessee
The Promised Land
School Day
THE REGENTS
Bye, Bye Johnny
THE REMAINS
Johnny B. Goode (Live)
REMEMBER THIS (British group, Danish
recordings)
Memphis, Tennessee
Rock And Roll Music
REO SPEEDWAGON
Rock And Roll Music
JOEY REYNOLDS & THE CARPENTARS
Memphis, Tennessee
JOEY REYNOLDS & THE PHONEES
Memphis, Tennessee (Ya Got Me By

The Calls Ma Bell)
CHARLIE RICH
School Day
CLIFF RICHARD
Little Queenie
Reelin' And Rockin'
30 Days (40 Days)
KEITH RICHARDS
Run Rudolph Run
JONATHAN RICHMAN AND THE
MODERN LOVERS
Back In The U.S.A.
BILLY LEE RILEY
Johnny B. Goode
Memphis, Tennessee (Instrumental)
Rock And Roll Music
Roll Over Beethoven
Sweet Little Sixteen
30 Days
DICK RIVERS
Johnny B. Goode
Sweet Little Sixteen
JOHNNY RIVERS
Brown-Eyed Handsome Man
Bye Bye Johnny
Johnny B. Goode
Maybellene
Memphis, Tennessee (Two versions)
The Promised Land
THE RIVIERAS
Little Donna (An exact copy of *Rock
And Roll Music*)
THE ROADRUNNERS (German)
Beautiful Delilah
MARTY ROBBINS
Maybellene
DUKE ROBILLARD & THE PLEASURE
KINGS
It's My Own Business
DICKIE ROCK & THE MIAMI
Rock And Roll Music
THE ROCK AND ROLL REVIVAL
Sweet Little Sixteen
ROCK FOLKET (Swedish)
Johnny B. Goode
Memphis, Tennessee
No Particular Place To Go
ROCK-JERRY (Swedish)
Maybellene
ROCKPILE (With Dave Edmunds)
Oh What A Thrill
ROCK RAGGE (Swedish)
Memphis, Tennessee
Reelin' And Rockin'
ROCKSLAGET (Swedish)
Johnny B. Goode
Memphis, Tennessee
Sweet Little Sixteen
ROCKY SALVATION AND THE
SATELLITES
Johnny B. Goode
Rock And Roll Music

TOMMY ROE
Brown-Eyed Handsome Man
Carol
Maybellene
PUGH ROGERFELDT (Swedish)
Reelin' And Rockin' (Swedish lyrics)
JAN ROHDE (Swedish)
I'm Talking About You
Rock And Roll Music (With the Rohde
Rockers; two versions)
Sweet Little Sixteen (With the Rohde
Rockers)
Roll Over Beethoven (With the Rohde
Rockers)
THE ROLLING STONES
Around And Around
Beautiful Delilah
Bye, Bye Johnny
Carol (Two versions)
Come On
Don't Ya Lie To Me
(Down The Road A Piece)
I'm Talking About You
Let It Rock
Little Queenie
Memphis, Tennessee
(Route 66)
You Can't Catch Me
LINDA RONSTADT
Back In The U.S.A.
ROSCOE AND HIS LITTLE GREENMEN
Roll Over Beethoven
THE ROUTERS (Instrumental; **Songbook**
LP)
Bye, Bye Johnny
Go Go Go
Johnny B. Goode
Maybellene
Memphis, Tennessee
No Particular Place To Go
Rock And Roll Music
Roll Over Beethoven
School Day
Sweet Little Sixteen
Too Much Monkey Business
Wee, Wee Hours
You Never Can Tell
THE ROYAL TEENS
Rock And Roll Music
RUBEN & THE JETS
Almost Grown
THE RUBINOOS
The Promised Land
TOM RUSH
Too Much Monkey Business
BOBBY RUSSELL
Roll Over Beethoven
BOBBY RYDELL
Little Queenie

Nadine
MITCH RYDER
Brown-Eyed Handsome Man
RYNO ROCKERS (Swedish)
The Promised Land
INGER-LISE RYPDAL (Norwegian)
Roll Over Beethoven

DOUG SAHM & AUGIE MEYERS
Carol
FRANK SALINAS
Johnny B. Goode
SAMMET (Swedish)
Johnny B. Goode
TOMMY SANDS
Maybellene
CARLOS SANTANA
Havana Moon
SANTO & JOHNNY
School Day (Instrumental)
SAVOY BROWN
Little Queenie
THE SCORPIONS
Bye, Bye Johnny
Rockin' At The Philharmonic
SCREAMIN' LORD SUTCH
Bye Bye Johnny
Johnny B. Goode
Roll Over Beethoven
SON SEALS
Johnny B. Goode
THE SEARCHERS
Maybellene
Sweet Little Sixteen
THE SENSATIONS
Sweet Little Rock And Roller
THE SHADOWS
Johnny B. Goode
Memphis, Tennessee
THE SHAKERS (Swedish)
Around And Around
(Surfin' USA)
Too Much Monkey Business
Roll Over Beethoven
School Day
Sweet Little Rock And Roller
30 Days
DEL SHANNON
Memphis, Tennessee
ROCKY SHARP AND THE REPLAYS
Too Much Monkey Business
RAY SHARPE
Almost Grown
No Money Down
The Promised Land
Wee Wee Hours
TONY SHERIDAN
Johnny B. Goode
THE SHIRELLES
Johnny B. Goode (Live)
SHORT LIST (British)

Down Bound Train
Havana Moon
Maybellene
SHORTY AND THEM
Carol
SHOWADDY WADDY
Rock And Roll Music
SHU-BI-DUA (Danish)
Johnny B. Goode
No Particular Place To Go
Roll Over Beethoven
SHUSHA
Johnny B. Goode
THE SILICON TEENS
Memphis, Tennessee
Sweet Little Sixteen
THE SILVER TORES
Let It Rock
CARL SIMMONS
Rock And Roll Music
GENE SIMMONS
Rock And Roll Music (Good Ole'
Country Music)
SIMON AND GARFUNKEL
Maybellene
SIR HENRY AND HIS BUTLERS
Johnny B. Goode
Sweet Little Rock And Roller
You Never Can Tell
MACK ALLEN SMITH
Maybellene (1973)
Memphis, Tennessee (1973)
The Promised Land (1973)
WARREN SMITH
Roll Over Beethoven (1978)
SMOKESTACK LIGHTNING
Nadine
SNIPERS (French)
Come On
THE SONICS
Roll Over Beethoven
JOE SOUTH
Little Queenie
BERND SPIER
Memphis, Tennessee
THE SPOTNICKS (Swedish)
Memphis, Tennessee (Instrumental)
BRUCE SPRINGSTEEN
Around And Around (Live)
Back In The U.S.A. (Live)
Little Queenie (Live)
No Money Down (Live)
Sweet Little Sixteen (Live)
You Never Can Tell (Live)
STACK
Johnny B. Goode
ANDY STAR
Round And Round
CHARLIE STARR

Memphis, Tennessee
STARSHIP
Johnny B. Goode
STATUS QUO
Bye Bye Johnny
Carol
SHAKIN' STEVENS AND THE SUNSETS
Little Queenie
Maybellene
ROD STEWART
Sweet Little Rock And Roller
SKIP STEWART
Sweet Little Rock And Roller
SAM STOCKARD
The Promised Land
WARREN STORM
Roll Over Beethoven
MAL STOVER
Memphis, Tennessee
BILLY STRANGE
Memphis, Tennessee
THE STRANGERS
Bye, Bye Johnny
THE STREAPLERS (Swedish)
Johnny B. Goode
You Never Can Tell (Swedish lyrics)
NAT STUCKEY
Around And Around
Roll Over Beethoven
GENE SUMMERS
Memphis, Tennessee (1976)
THE SURFARIS
Memphis, Tennessee (Instrumental)
JAN HARPO SVENSSON (Swedish)
Roll Over Beethoven (Swedish lyrics)
KENNETH SWANSTROM (Swedish)
Johnny B. Goode
THE SWINGING BLUE JEANS
Around And Around
Johnny B. Goode
THE SYNDICATE OF SOUND
Almost Grown
Maybellene

THE TAIFUNES
Memphis, Tennessee
CARMOL TAYLOR
Back In The U.S.A.
CAROL TAYLOR
Roll Over Beethoven
JAMES TAYLOR
The Promised Land
JOHNNY TAYLOR
Roll Over Beethoven
TED "KINGSIZE" TAYLOR
Broken Arrow
Memphis, Tennessee
Sweet Little Sixteen
VINCE TAYLOR

Memphis, Tennessee
Sweet Little Sixteen
TEDDY AND THE TIGERS (Finnish)
Brown-Eyed Handsome Man
TOM TEDESCO
Memphis, Tennessee (Instrumental)
LOS TEEN TOPS (Mexican)
Johnny B. Goode
Maybellene
School Day
TEN YEARS AFTER
Sweet Little Sixteen (Live)
THE 13th FLOOR ELEVATOR
Roll Over Beethoven
RUSTY THOMAS
Maybellene
THORLEIFS (Swedish)
No Particular Place To Go (1981)
GEORGE THOROGOOD
I'm A Rocker
It Wasn't Me
Johnny B. Goode
Nadine
No Particular Place To Go
THREE DOG NIGHT
Too Much Monkey Business
BR. THUE (Norwegian)
Guitar Boogie
Johnny B. Goode
TIELMAN BROTHERS (Dutch)
Sweet Little Sixteen (1976)
MITCHEL TOROK
No Money Down
PETER TOSH
Johnny B. Goode
PAT TRAVERS
Maybellene
DAVE TRAVIS
Johnny B. Goode
THE TROGGS
Jaguar And The Thunderbird
Little Queenie
Memphis, Tennessee
No Particular Place To Go
ERNEST TUBB
30 Days
GLYN TUCKER w/IAN LOWE &
    THE TORNADOS (Australien)
Carol
MAUREEN TUCKER
Around And Around
TANYA TUCKER
Brown-Eyed Handsome Man
TUSENFRYD (Norwegian)
Around And Around (Norwegian lyrics)
CONWAY TWITTY
Johnny B. Goode
Maybellene
Memphis, Tennessee

Reelin' And Rockin'
30 Days
TYGGEGUMMIBANDEN (Danish)
Rock And Roll Music

STAN URBAN
Little Queenie
URIAH HEEP
Roll Over Beethoven (Live)

LOS VALENTINOS
Memphis, Tennessee (Instrumental)
BOBBY VEE
Brown-Eyed Handsome Man
Little Queenie
Memphis, Tennessee
School Day
Sweet Little Sixteen
THE VELAIRES
Roll Over Beethoven
THE VENTURES
Memphis, Tennessee (Instrumental;
    two versions)
Roll Over Beethoven
VIKINGARNA (Swedish)
You Never Can Tell
GENE VINCENT
Maybellene
Roll Over Beethoven
THE VIOLENTS
Sweet Little Sixteen
KARE VIRUD (Norwegian)
Johnny B. Goode (Norwegian lyrics)
Roll Over Beethoven (Norwegian lyrics)
Sweet Little Sixteen (Norwegian lyrics)
SYLVIA VRETHAMMER (Swedish)
You Never Can Tell (Swedish lyrics)

JOHNNY WARD (Swedish)
Memphis, Tennessee
GERAINT WATKINS
I Got To Find My Baby
GENE WATSON & THE ROCKETS
School Day
PAT WAYNE & THE BEACHCOMBERS
Bye, Bye Johnny
Roll Over Beethoven
OTTO WEISS & HIS HAMMOND ORGAN
Rock And Roll Music (Instrumental)
FREDDY WELLER
The Promised Land
J.P. WEST (Norwegian)
Come On

Too Much Monkey Business
WHEELS (Swedish)
No Particular Place To Go
The Promised Land
AL WHITE AND HIS HI-LITERS
Johnny B. Goode
WALLY WIGGINS
Maybellene
THE WILD ANGELS
Johnny B. Goode
Let It Rock
Little Queenie
Memphis, Tennessee
Roll Over Beethoven
30 Days (40 Days)
Too Much Monkey Business
CHUCK WILLIAMS & THE FIRE BAND
Brown-Eyed Handsome Man
JERRY WILLIAMS
Let It Rock (Rockin' On The Railroad)
Nadine
No Money Down (1978)
Sweet Little Sixteen (Two versions)
BOB WILLS
Memphis, Tennessee
J. FRANK WILSON & HIS CAVALIERS
School Day
EDGAR WINTER
Back In The U.S.A. (Rick Derringer,
    vocals)
JOHNNY WINTER
Johnny B. Goode
30 Days
RON WINTERS
Back In The U.S.A.
WAYNE WORLEY
It's My Own Business
Memphis, Tennessee
The Promised Land

THE YARDBIRDS
Too Much Monkey Business (Live)
RUSTY YORK
Brown-Eyed Handsome Man
THE "YOU KNOW WHO" GROUP
Reelin' And Rockin
GEORGE YOUNG
Johnny B. Goode
JESSE COLIN YOUNG
Sweet Little Sixteen
THE YOUNGBLOODS
Too Much Monkey Business (Bootleg)

There are three Chuck Berry "Songbook" LPs:

BILL BLACK'S COMBO **Plays Chuck Berry** (HI Rec. SHL-32017)
JIM & JESSE **The Great Chuck Berry Songbook — Berry Pickin' in the Country**
  (EPIC BN-26176)
THE ROUTERS **Play the Chuck Berry Songbook** (WARNER BROS. WS-1595)

Seven groups or artists have recorded enough Berry songs to fill an entire album:

THE ANIMALS	8 songs
THE BEATLES	8 songs (including two on bootlegs)
DAVE EDMUNDS	9 songs
JOHNNY HALLYDAY (French)	10 songs
JERRY LEE LEWIS	8 songs
EDDY MITCHELL (French)	10 songs
THE ROLLING STONES	15 songs (including three on bootlegs, and three recorded but not written by Chuck Berry)

BERRY-INFLUENCED SONGS
& TRIBUTE SONGS

Parenthetical notes indicate the nature of the Chuck Berry musical influence or exact song resemblance. A short list of non-musical influences follows, together with a summary of the "tribute" songs contained in the main list.

THE ANIMALS
She'll Return It (Memphis, Tennessee)

EDDIE BARKDALL AND THE CORVETS
Scramble
THE BEACH BOYS
Do You Remember (one verse to Chuck)
Fun, Fun, Fun
Surfin' USA (Sweet Little Sixteen)
THE BEATLES
Back in the USSR
Come Together
Get Back
EDDIE BELL
Johnny B. Goode in Hollywood
EDDIE BISHOP
What Did He Say (instrumental)
THE BLASTERS
American Music
Marie, Marie
This Is It (Berry guitar riffs)
JOHNNY BURNETTE
Sweet Suzie

FREDDY CANNON
Little Autograph Seeker (Sweet Little Sixteen)
TONY CASANOVA
Boogie Woogie Feeling (guitar solo)
Showdown
MISS CHUCKLE CHERRY
My Pussycat (the female answer to *My Ding-A-Ling*)
CHRISTIE
Put Your Money Down
EDDIE CLEARWATER (the left-handed "Chuck Berry")
Boogie Woogie Baby
Cool Water
Hey Bernadine
Hillbilly Rock
I Wouldn't Lay My Guitar Down
A Real Good Time
Twist Like This
2 x 9

JAMIE COE (song written by Bobby Darin)
Summertime Symphony (Sweet Little Sixteen)
JEFFERSON "RAMBLIN' MAN" COUNTY
City Billy (Johnny B. Goode)
CREEDENCE CLEARWATER REVIVAL
It Came Out of the Sky
Travellin' Band (this is also a tribute to Little Richard)

JIMMY DANE
Tattle Tale (guitar solo)
Please Have Mercy (guitar solo)
RAYVON DARNELL
Don't Want You Maybellene
DETROIT
Can't Tear It Up Enough
MINK DeVILLE
Love Me Like You Did Before (guitar riffs)
BOB DYLAN
Subterranean Homesick Blues (Too Much Monkey Business

DUANE EDDY
Movin' and Groovin' (instrumental; uses the intro of *Brown-Eyed Handsome Man)*
DAVE EDMUNDS
From Small Things Big Things Come (song written by Bruce Springsteen)
Get Out of Denver (Tulane; song written by Bob Seger)
I Knew the Bride
ELEPHANTS MEMORY
Chuck and Bo
ESTUS
Truckin' Man
EVERLY BROTHERS
Be Bop A Lula (guitar riffs)
Rip It Up (guitar riffs)
This Little Girl of Mine (guitar riffs)

THE FABULOUS THUNDERBIRDS
My Babe

THE FANTASTIC BAGGY'S
Surfin' Craze (Surfin' USA)
FIVE MAN ELECTRICAL BAND
Money Back Guarantee

LEIF GARRETT
Surfin' USA (Sweet Little Sixteen)
DAVID GATES
Swingin' Baby Doll
CHARLIE GRACIE (song written by
Dave Travis)
All Change
JOHN GREER
Come Back Maybellene (the answer
to *Maybellene*)

ROLF WICKSTROEM HJARTSLAG
(Swedish)
No Particular Place to Go
62-ars Amazon
HUMBLE PIE
Natural Born Bugie (tribute)

JAN & DEAN
Philadelphia P.A. (Surfin' USA)
Skateboarding (Memphis, Tennessee)
BILL JENKINS
Poni-Tails & Bobby-Sox
JOHNNY & THE JAMMERS (Johnny
Winter — 1960)
Schoolday Blues
JOHNNY & THE ROCCO'S
Rough Cut (Berry guitar riffs)

SLEEPY LaBEEF
Flying Saucers Rock & Roll
(guitar riffs)
Tore Up (guitar riffs)
BILLY LAWRIE (song written by
Lawrie and Ringo Starr)
Rock and Roller
FREDDIE "FINGERS" LEE (Swedish)
Angry Young Man (Promised Land)
JERRY LEE LEWIS (song written by
Mack Vickery)
Rockin' My Life Away
JANNE LUCAS (Swedish)
Chuck Berry
KENNY LYNCH
Harlem Library

EDDIE MEDUZA (Swedish)
Norwegian Boogie
Sossialdemokraterna
THE MONARCHS IV
Surge (instrumental)
Weekend (instrumental)
COMER MONEY
Rambler (Berry guitar riffs)

JAMES MONTGOMERY BAND
I Can't Stop
TINY MORRIE
Bernadine

CARROL (WILD RED) PEGUES
Rhythm Feet
CHARLES PERRYWELL
Come Along With Me
PLASTIC BERTRAND (Belgium)
Ca Plane Pour Moi

TEDDY RANDAZZO
*Mother Goose Twist (Reelin' and
Rockin')*
JERRY REED
Hurrah for Chuck Berry (tribute)
AL ROBERTS JR.
Motorway Food (Johnny B. Goode)
*Someone Torn Out the Very Last
Page*
TOMMY ROE
Caveman
ROLLING STONES
Brown Sugar
*It's Only Rock & Roll (But I Like
It)*
Jumpin' Jack Flash
Starfucker
BOBBY RYDELL
Kissin' Time (Sweet Little Sixteen)
RYNO ROCKERS (Swedish)
*Pony Tail Girl (Sweet Little Six-
teen)*

SAVOY BROWN
Denim Demon
Shot in the Head (Berry riffs)
BOB SEGER
Get Out of Denver
Katmandu
RAY SHARPE
Monkey's Uncle
MACK SIMS (LITTLE MACK)
Drivin' Wheel
SLAUGHTER AND THE DOGS
Johnny T.
JOE STAMPLEY
Sheik of Chicago (tribute — best
ever!)
STEPPENWOLF
Berry Rides Again (tribute; also re-
corded by Norwegian artist Ole
Andersen)
ROD STEWART
Hot Legs
THE STRIKES
Rockin'
THE SUPER STOCKS

Thunder Road (Surfin' USA)
SCREAMIN' LORD SUTCH
 Go Berry Go
 London Rocker

KID THOMAS
 Wail Baby Wail
GEORGE THOROGOOD
 Back to Wentzville (tribute)
BR. THUE (Norwegian)
 Thue's Boogie (Guitar Boogie)
BOBBY LEE TRAMMEL
 I Love 'Em All (Johnny B. Goode)
 Sally Twist
THE TRASHMEN
 King of the Surf (Johnny B. Goode)
DAVE TRAVIS
 All Change

STEVIE RAY VAUGHN
 Love Struck Baby

THE VENTURES
 Go! (instrumental; tribute)
 No Trespassing (instrumental)
 Stop Action (instrumental)

MIKE WAGONER AND THE BOPS
 Basher No. 5
 Guitar Man
THE WAILERS
 Party Time USA (Surfin' USA)
SONEE WEST
 Rock-Ola Ruby (Berry riffs)
WILD ANGELS
 Midnight Rider (Promised Land)
JERRY WILLIAMS (Swedish)
 Shake Rattle and Roll (same arrangement as Chuck's version)
THE WOLFGANG (Danish)
 Sweet Little Maybeline

THE YARDBIRDS
 Jeff's Boogie (Guitar Boogie)
 Psycho Daisies

Songs with Berry-style titles; musically unrelated to Chuck Berry, however.

PETER BELLI (Danish)
 Roll Over Beatles

BOBBY HENDRICKS
 Molly B. Goode

MUNGO JERRY
 Johnny B. Badde

BRUCE SPRINGSTEEN
 Bye, Bye Johnny (title similarity only)
 I'm a Rocker (title similarity only)
 Promised Land (title similarity only)

WIZZARD
 Bend Over Beethoven

Many other recording artists use Berry-like guitar riffs in their songs, but are too numerous to mention here. Keith Richards, Dave Edmunds, and George Thorogood are well-known Berry imitators, as an example. Additionally, a number of sixties rock artists use Berry-derived stage names: Dave Berry, Jo Jo Gunne, Johnny B. Great, and The Rockin' Berries, to name a few.

CHUCK BERRY TRIBUTE SONGS (Summary)

CHRISTIE (English)	*Put Your Money Down*
ELEPHANTS MEMORY (American)	*Chuck and Bo*
HUMBLE PIE (English)	*Natural Born Bugie*
JANNE LUCAS (Swedish)	*Chuck Berry*
JERRY REED	*Hurrah for Chuck Berry*
JOE STAMPLEY (American)	*Sheik of Chicago*
STEPPENWOLF (American	*Berry Rides Again**
SCREAMIN' LORD SUTCH (English)	*Go Berry Go*
GEORGE THOROGOOD (American)	*Back to Wentzville*
THE VENTURES (American instr.)	*Go!*

*Berry Rides Again was also recorded by the Norwegian artist Ole Andersen.

MOTION PICTURE APPEARANCES & SOUNDTRACK ALBUMS

1956
"ROCK ROCK ROCK"
You Can't Catch Me (original Chess recording)
> The soundtrack album is Chess LP-1425, touted by Chess Records as the first rock music film soundtrack LP (but containing only Chess artists).

1957
"MR. ROCK AND ROLL"
Oh Baby Doll (original Chess recording)
> Berry's appearance seems to have been excluded in many copies of this film.

1958
"GO JOHNNY GO"
Memphis, Tennessee (partial)/*Johnny B. Goode*/*Little Queenie* (original Chess recordings)
> Berry also has a minor acting role in this movie.

1960
"JAZZ ON A SUMMER'S DAY"
Sweet Little Sixteen
> Documentary from the 1958 Newport Jazz Festival; Chuck is supported by the Jack Teagarden Band.

1964
"GATHER NO MOSS"
Sweet Little Sixteen/*Johnny B. Goode*/*Maybellene*
> Live on stage at the "TAMI Award Show," Santa Monica Civic Auditorium, October 29th, 1964. The movie was also known as "Teenage Command Performance" and "The TAMI Show."

1970
"SWEET TORONTO"
Rock and Roll Music/*School Day*/Medley: *Johnny B. Goode–Carol–Promised Land*/*Hoochie Coochie Man+*/*Sweet Little Sixteen*/*Reelin' and Rockin'*/*Johnny B. Goode*
> Live on stage at the Rock and Roll Revival Show, Toronto, Canada, 1969. Soundtrack album on Magnum Records (MR-703), **Chuck Berry Live in Concert** (2 LP set), issued 1978. Also released in West Germany as Bellaphon BLS-5573. The albums contain more songs than shown in the movie. See U.S. and U.K. album discographies for other LPs containing songs from the Revival.

1973
"LET THE GOOD TIMES ROLL"
School Day/*Sweet Little Sixteen*/*Reelin' and Rockin'*/*Johnny B. Goode* (plus instrumental jam with Bo Diddley)
> Live on stage at the New York Madison Square Garden Rock Revival, May 1972. Soundtrack album on Bell Records (DUBL-9002/3), but Berry's songs aren't included!

"THE LONDON ROCK & ROLL SHOW"
School Day/Memphis, Tennessee/Sweet Little Sixteen/Medley: *Mean Old World—Beer Drinkin' Woman+/Wee Wee Hours/*Medley: *Let It Rock—Roll 'Em Pete+—Carol—Little Queenie/Reelin' and Rockin'*
   Live on stage from Wembley, England, August, 1972.

1977
"AMERICAN HOT WAX"
Sweet Little Sixteen (original Chess recording only)/*Reelin' and Rockin'—Roll Over Beethoven* (medley, with footage of Chuck)
   A film about DJ Alan Freed arranging a Rock & Roll Anniversary Show at The Brooklyn Paramount Theatre in 1958. Double LP soundtrack album on A&M Records (SP-6500); one record contains live cuts, the other original 50s recordings.

1982
"CLASS REUNION"
It Wasn't Me/My Ding-A-Ling/Festival (as a medley)
   For about two minutes, Berry performs the above songs after being introduced as a special guest at the beginning of the class reunion party. He is backed by Jim Marsala on bass and two black musicians on drums and piano. (Berry is not on camera or heard for the entire two minutes.) Main title is sung by Gary U.S. Bonds; it's typical Berry music, but Berry is not credited.

OTHER MOVIE SOUNDTRACKS USING BERRY'S CHESS RECORDINGS
1971
"FRITZ THE CAT"
Johnny B. Goode
   Soundtrack album on Fantasy Records (U.S. and U.K.)

1973
"AMERICAN GRAFFITI"
Johnny B. Goode/Almost Grown
   Double album soundtrack on MCA Records (MCA-2-8001, U.S. and U.K.).
"HEAVY TRAFFIC"
Maybellene
   Soundtrack album on Fantasy Records (U.S. and U.K.)

1975
"RETURN TO MACON COUNTY"
Johnny B. Goode
   Soundtrack album on United Artists Records (U.S.).

1977
"CRUISIN' "
No Particular Place to Go

1979
"ROCK 'N' ROLL HIGH SCHOOL"
School Day
   Soundtrack album on Sire Records (SRK-6070, U.S. and U.K.).

MISCELLANEOUS LISTS

CHUCK BERRY'S FOREIGN TOURS

1958--1959: Australia
1960: Jamaica
1964: Germany and Great Britain
1965: Great Britain, Holland, Belgium, France (February and November), Germany, Sweden (October--November), Spain (TV show only)
1966: France (February 5--19)
1967: Great Britain and France
1969: Great Britain and France
1970: Sweden and Germany
1972: Great Britain (February, March, August), Switzerland, Germany
1973: Great Britain, France, Holland, Belgium, Denmark, Switzerland, Sweden, Germany, and Australia (November)
1974: Mexico (July)
1975: Great Britain, France, Holland, Germany
1976: Great Britain, Belgium, Mexico, Australia, Holland, New Zealand, Spain, Yugoslavia, Italy, Sweden, Denmark, Finland
1977: Great Britain, Holland, Sweden, Norway, Spain, Germany, Austria, Australia, France, Switzerland
1978: Great Britain, Germany, Norway, Denmark, Yugoslavia, Australia, France
1979: France (July), Germany, Great Britain, France
1980: Sweden, Norway
1981: Japan, France
1982: Japan
1983: France, Great Britain, Scandinavia, Bulgaria, Belgium

CHUCK'S TOP TEN EUROPEAN CONCERTS

1. Spanish TV show (1965)
2. West Germany, show with Jerry Lee Lewis (September 8--9, 1973)
3. Montreux Jazz and Blues Festival (1972)
4. French concerts at Paris' Olympia (November 2 and 4, 1965)
5. Live in Sweden (October, 1965)
6. England (July--August, 1973)
7. England (1964)
8. Paris (1983)
9. Germany (1979)
10. Oslo, Norway (1978)

CHUCK'S TOP TEN FAVORITE SONGS
(His own list from *New Musical Express*, 1964)

1. *Maybellene*
2. *School Day*
3. *Sweet Little Sixteen*
4. *Johnny B. Goode*
5. *Memphis, Tennessee*
6. *Go Johnny Go*
7. *Let It Rock*
8. *Back in the USA*
9. *Carol*
10. *Almost Grown*

CHUCK BERRY SONGS RELEASED
ON ELVIS PRESLEY BOOTLEG LPs

(From *Jailhouse Rock*, by Lee Cotten and Howard A. DeWitt, Pierian Press, 1983)

1. **The Hillbilly Cat Live** (Spring Fever Record Club SFLP 301, 2LPs, 1970)
   Song Recorded: *Johnny B. Goode*

2. **Live Experience in Vegas . . . February 1971** (Bonthold LP 2999, 1971)
   Song Recorded: *Johnny B. Goode*

3. **Rockin' with Elvis New Year's Eve Pittsburgh, PA Dec 31, 1976** (Spirit of America
   Records Record No. 7677, 2 LPs)
   Song Recorded: *Johnny B. Goode*

4. **To Know Him Is to Love Him** (Black Belt Records LP 1, 1978)
   Song Recorded: *Memphis, Tennessee*

CHUCK BERRY'S HIT RECORDS, 1955-1973

The following chart positions are from U.S. *Billboard*'s Hot 100 and U.S. *Billboard*'s Best Selling Rhythm & Blues Singles, and from England's British Hit Singles – Top 50. (*Billboard* did not publish R&B charts between 30/11-1963 & 23/1-1965.) Number combinations indicate: the highest position reached on the charts/the total number of weeks on the charts.

YEAR	U.S. HOT 100	U.S. R&B	U.K. TOP 50	SONG TITLE	U.S. RECORD NO.	U.K. RECORD NO.
1955	5/14	1/16		Maybellene	Chess 1604	
1955		8/8		Thirty Days	Chess 1610	
1956		11/5		No Money Down	Chess 1615	
1956	25/9	7/5		Roll Over Beethoven	Chess 1626	
1956		7/6		Too Much Monkey Business/Brown-Eyed Handsome Man	Chess 1635	
1957	5/26	1/13	24/2	School Day	Chess 1653	Columbia DB-3951
1957	57/7			Oh Baby Doll	Chess 1664	
1957	8/19	6/9		Rock & Roll Music	Chess 1671	
1958	2/16	1/11	16/5	Sweet Little Sixteen	Chess 1683	London HLM-8585
1958	8/15	5/12		Johnny B. Goode	Chess 1691	
1958	81/2			Beautiful Delilah	Chess 1697	
1958	18/10	12/6		Carol	Chess 1700	
1958	47/9	13/3		Sweet Little Rock and Roller	Chess 1709	
1958	83/5			Jo Jo Gunne	Chess 1709	
1958	69/3			Run Rudolph Run	Chess 1714	
1958	71/3			Merry Christmas Baby	Chess 1714	
1959	60/5			Anthony Boy	Chess 1716	
1959	32/13	3/13		Almost Grown	Chess 1722	
1959	80/4			Little Queenie	Chess 1722	
1959	37/8	16/8		Back in the USA	Chess 1729	
1960	42/6	18/3		Too Pooped to Pop	Chess 1747	
1960	64/8			Let It Rock	Chess 1747	

YEAR	U.S. HOT 100	U.S. R&B	U.K. TOP 50	SONG TITLE	U.S. RECORD NO.	U.K. RECORD NO.
1963			38/6	Go Go Go		Pye Int. 7N 25209
1963			6/13	Memphis, Tennessee/(Let It Rock)		Pye Int. 7N 25218
1963			36/6	Run Rudolph Run		Pye Int. 7N 25228
1964	23/10		27/6	Nadine	Chess 1883	Pye Int. 7N 25236
1964	10/11		3/12	No Particular Place to Go	Chess 1898	Pye Int. 7N 25242
1964	14/9		23/8	You Never Can Tell	Chess 1906	Pye Int. 7N 25257
1964	54/6			Little Marie	Chess 1912	
1964	41/7		26/6	Promised Land	Chess 1916	Pye Int. 7N 25285
1965	95/4			Dear Dad	Chess 1926	
1972	1/17		1/17	My Ding-A-Ling	Chess 2131	Chess 6145 019
1972	27/13			Reelin' and Rockin'	Chess 2136	
1973			18/7	Reelin' and Rockin'		Chess 6145 020

BIBLIOGRAPHICAL ESSAY

There is a wealth of information on Chuck Berry's career, but it is dispersed and sometimes difficult to gather. For that reason, it might be helpful to review the sources used here. The only other book devoted entirely to Chuck Berry is Krista Reese, *Chuck Berry: Mr. Rock N Roll* (New York, 1982). This is a quick look at Chuck's career, interesting but with a concentration on Chuck in the 1970s; it is somewhat error-prone and decidedly shallow on Chuck's earlier years. This in in part due to the paucity of research sources used, but probably as much a result of Ms. Reese's lack of familiarity with basic rock research.

Articles on Chuck Berry's Career

There are a number of excellent articles on Berry's musical contributions. The best are: Michael Lydon, *Rock Folk: Portraits from the Rock 'n' Roll Pantheon* (New York, 1971), pp. 1--24; Robert Christgau, "Chuck Berry," in *The Rolling Stone Illustrated History of Rock and Roll* (revised edition, New York, 1980), pp. 54--60; Ian Hoare, "Chuck Berry: Cruisin' and Playin' the Radio," *Let It Rock* (April, 1972), pp. 26--29; Stuart Colman, "Chuck Berry: Still Motorvatin'," *They Kept on Rockin'* (London, 1982), pp. 29--41; Elliot S. Cohen, "Rock History from A to Z: Chuck Berry," *Grooves* (n.p., n.d.), pp. 31--33; Ralph M. Newman, "The Chuck Berry Story: Long Live Rock and Roll," *Time Barrier* (no. 27), pp. 35--46; Tom Wheeler, "Chuck Berry in Outer Space, Johnny B. Goode Forever," *Guitar Player* (February, 1981), p. 14; and Billy Vera, "The Chess Sessions," *Time Barrier* (no. 27), pp. 48--49.

There are also excellent Chuck Berry facts, record listings, and general interpretive career information in Irwin Stambler, *Encyclopedia of Pop, Rock and Soul* (1974); R. Serge Denisoff's, *Solid Gold* (1975); and Dave Laing and Phil Hardy, eds., *Encyclopedia of Rock, 1955--1975* (London, 1977, 3 volumes). See also the first-rate article on Chess Records by Peter Guralnick in *Feel Like Going Home:*

Portraits in Blues and Rock N Roll (New York, 1971). Guralnick's article, "Chess Records: Before the Fall," is the most intelligent examination of the Chess influence ever written. For biographical information on Chuck see the encyclopedias by Lillian Roxon and Norman Nite. Generally, the encyclopedia treatments of Chuck's career, with the exception of the Laing and Hardy book, are not very interpretive, but they provide an excellent, if often misleading, starting point.

Conversations with Chuck Berry: Interviews

The most useful Chuck Berry interviews are: Patrick William Salvo, "A Conversation with Chuck Berry," *Rolling Stone* (November 23, 1972), pp. 35--42; Greil Marcus, "Roll Over Chuck Berry," (June 14, 1969), pp. 15--17; Dan Fries, "Chuck Berry: An Exclusive Interview," *Goldmine* (November, 1979), pp. 7--8; Fred Stuckey, "Exclusive Chuck Berry," *Rock Guitarist* (Saratoga, CA, 1974), pp. 16--19; Peter Knobler, "Sweet Little 16 Turns 32," *Crawdaddy* (April 16, 1972).

Interpretive and Academic Articles on Chuck Berry

The best interpretive and academic articles on Chuck's career are: Robert Christgau, "Chuck Berry's Back from the Blues," *Creem* (February, 1973); B. Lee Cooper, "Review of Chuck Berry's Golden Decade," *The History Teacher* (VII, February, 1975), pp. 300--301; B. Lee Cooper, "Audio Images in the City: Pop Culture in the Social Studies," *The Social Studies* (May/June, 1981), pp. 130--136; B. Lee Cooper, "Nothin' Outrun My V-8 Ford: Chuck Berry and the Automobile, 1955--1979," *JEMF Quarterly* (VII Spring, 1980), pp. 18--23; and Warren Belasco, "Motivatin' with Chuck Berry and Frederick Jackson Turner," (unpublished paper, American Studies Dept., University of Maryland, Baltimore, 1982), pp. 1--24.

On Chuck Berry's roots, see Charlie Gillet, "The Dark Age, 5--10 BC," *Let It Rock* (April, 1973), pp. 30--31; Malcolm Jones, "Records: The Classic Years," *Let It Rock* (April, 1973), pp. 32--33; and Philip Farr, "Records: The Later Years," *Let It Rock* (April, 1973), p. 33. An analysis of Berry's English recordings is well done by John Pidgeon, "Back in the UK," *Let It Rock* (April, 1973), p. 36. On Chuck Berry bootleg records see, Tony Martin, "Bootleg Basement," *Let It Rock* (April, 1973), p. 37.

Interesting looks at early Chuck Berry recordings and back-up musicians can be found in the following articles: Liz Eck and Duane Marburger, "Pre-Chess Chuck Berry," *Goldmine*, no. 76 (September, 1982), p. 25; Bob Angell, "The Man Who Hired Chuck Berry,"

Music and Sound Output (November-December, 1980), pp. 28--30, 38; Robert Christgau, *Any Old Way You Choose It: Rock and Other Pop Music, 1967--1973* (New York, 1969), pp. 61--66; and Charlie Gillett, *The Sound of the City: The Rise of Rock and Roll* (New York, 1970).

There are also some specialty articles important in analyzing Chuck's career; see, for example, Bob Greene, "Rock N Roll in Outer Space," (Sunday Punch Section) *San Francisco Chronicle*, December 7, 1980, p. 2; Richard Aquila, "Images of the American West in Rock Music," *Western Historical Quarterly*, XI (October, 1980), pp. 414--443; and Larry Ford, "Geographic Factors in the Origin, Evolution and Diffusion of Rock and Roll Music," *The Journal of Geography* LXX (November, 1971).

The literature on rock journalism is very extensive, and the following books were especially useful in this study: Richard Goldstein, *The Poetry of Rock and Roll* (New York, 1969); Greil Marcus, *Mystery Train: Images of America in Rock N Roll Music* (New York, 1975); Mike Jahn, *The Story of Rock* (New York, 1973); Steve Chapple and Reebe Garofalo, *Rock N Roll Is Here to Pay* (Chicago, 1977); Arnold Shaw, *Honkers and Shouters: The Golden Age of Rhythm and Blues* (New York, 1978); Gene Busnar, *It's Rock 'N' Roll: A Musical History of the Fabulous Fifties* (New York, 1979); Carl Belz, *The Story of Rock* (New York, 1969); Nat Henoff, "Something's Happening and You Don't Know What It Is, Do You, Mr. Jones?" in Jonathan Eisen, ed., *The Age of Rock: Sounds of the American Cultural Revolution* (New York, 1969), pp. 3--8; and Fred Worth, *Thirty Years of Rock 'N' Roll Trivia* (New York, 1980).

Books on Rock Groups Influenced by Chuck Berry

The literature on rock groups influenced by the sounds and songs of Chuck Berry is impressive, and it is important to analyze the best of these books. On the Beatles debt to Chuck Berry, see: Philip Norman, *Shout: The True Story of the Beatles* (London, 1981); Pete Brown and Steven Gaines, *The Love You Make: An Insider's Story of The Beatles* (New York, 1983); and also see Neville Stannard's book *The Beatles: The Long and Winding Road, A History of the Beatles on Record* (New York, 1982). There are also a number of books on John Lennon which offer some important insights into Chuck Berry's influence; see, for example: Anthony Fawcett, *John Lennon: One Day At a Time* (New York, revised edition, 1980); Malcolm Doney, *Lennon and McCartney* (London, 1981); David Stuart Ryan, *John Lennon's Secret* (London, 1982); Conrad Snell, *John Lennon: 4ever* (New York, 1981); and Jann Wenner, *Lennon Remembers* (San Francisco, 1971). There are also a number

277

of speciality books on the Beatles which aided this study; see, for example: Edward E. Davis, *The Beatles Book* (New York, 1968); James Sauceda, *The Literary Lennon: A Comedy of Letters, The First Study of All the Major and Minor Writings of John Lennon* (Ann Arbor, 1983); Brian Epstein, *A Cellarful of Noise* (Pierian Press reprint, Ann Arbor, 1984); and Jonathan Cott, et. al., *The Ballad of John and Yoko* (New York, 1982).

There were many other groups influenced by Chuck Berry; see, for example: John Platt, Chris Dreja, and Jim McCarty, *The Yardbirds* (London, 1983); David Leaf, *The Beach Boys and the California Myth* (New York, 1978); Byron Preiss, *The Beach Boys* (New York, 1979); John Tobler, *The Beach Boys* (Secaucus, New Jersey, 1978); David Dalton, *The Rolling Stones* (New York, 1972); Robert Palmer, *The Rolling Stones* (New York, 1983); and David Dalton, ed., *The Rolling Stones: The First Twenty Years* (New York, 1981).

There are many good books on individual musicians who were either influenced by Chuck Berry or built upon his contributions to rock music. For musicians directly influenced by Chuck, see, for example: Michael Gray, *The Art of Bob Dylan* (New York, 1972); Anthony Scaduto, *Bob Dylan* (New York, 1972); Betsy Bowden, *Performed Literature: Words and Music By Bob Dylan* (Bloomington, 1982); John Herdman, *Voice Without Restraint: Bob Dylan's Lyrics and Their Background* (New York, 1981); Carey Schofield, *Jagger* (London, 1983); Barbara Chadrone, *Keith Richards* (London, 1979); Anthony Scaduto, *Mick Jagger: Everybody's Lucifer* (New York, 1974); Marc Eliot, *Death of a Rebel: Phil Ochs and a Small Circle of Friends* (New York, 1979); Mandy Aftel, *Death of A Rolling Stone: The Brian Jones Story* (New York, 1982); Jerry Hopkins, *Hit and Run: The Jimi Hendrix Story* (New York, 1983); David Henderson, *'Scuse Me While I Kiss The Sky: The Life of Jimi Hendrix* (New York, Revised edition, 1981); and Howard A. DeWitt, *Van Morrison: The Mystic's Music* (Fremont, Ca., 1983).

Material on the Pioneer Rock Artists

The explosion in recent rock music literature has provided a great deal of material for this book. For the best books on the rock music pioneers, see, for example: Nick Tosches, *Unsung Heroes of Rock 'n' Roll* (New York, 1984); Myra Lewis and Murray Silver, *Great Balls of Fire: The Uncensored Story of Jerry Lee Lewis* (New York, 1982); John Swenson, *Bill Haley* (London, 1982); Nick Tosches, *Hellfire* (New York, 1982); John Goldrose, *Buddy Holly: His Life and Music* (Bowling Green, 1975); Britt Hagarty,

The Day The World Turned Blue: A Biography of Gene Vincent
(Vancouver, 1983); Robert Cain, *Whole Lotta Shakin' Going On*
(New York, 1981); Jerry Hopkins, *Elvis* (New York, 1971); Albert
Goldman, *Elvis* (New York, 1981); Bill Millar, *The Drifters* (London,
1971); Colin Escott and Martin Hawkins, *Sun Records* (New York,
Revised edition, 1980); Robert Palmer, *Baby That Was Rock n Roll:
The Legendary Leiber and Stoller* (New York, 1978); and Dave
Laing, *Buddy Holly* (New York, 1972).

Studies of Popular Culture in the 1950s

In order to understand the milieu Chuck grew up in during the
1950s, the following books are helpful; see, for example: Douglas
Miller and Marion Nowak, *The Fifties* (New York, 1975); Arnold
Shaw, *The Rockin 50s* (New York, 1974); Peter Guralnick, *Lost
Highway* (Boston, 1979); and Peter Guralnick, *Feel Like Going
Home* (New York, 1971); Jeff Greenfield, *No Peace, No Place*
(New York, 1973); Landon Y. Jones, *Great Expectations; America
and the Baby Boom Gemeration* (New York, 1980); Michael Rowe,
Chicago Breakdown (New York, Revised edition, 1979); Bengt and
Olsson, *Memphis Blues* (London, 1971); John Broven, *Rhythm and
Blues in New Orleans* (Gretna, La. , 1978); and Robert Palmer,
Deep Blues (New York, 1981).

Studies of Popular Culture in the 1960s

In order to understand the importance of folk music and the
fold-rock revival of the 1960s, see, for example: R. Serge Denisoff,
Great Day Coming: Folk Music and the American Left (Baltimore,
1971); Oscar Brand, *The Ballad Mongers* (New York, 1962); R.
Serge Denisoff, *Sing a Song of Social Significance* (Bowling Green,
1972); Jacques Vassal, *Electric Children: Roots and Branches of
Modern-Folk-Rock* (New York, 1976); Johnny Rogan, *Timeless
Flight: The Definitive Biography of The Byrds* (London, 1981);
and Bud Scoppa, *The Byrds* (New York, 1971).

One of the most overused and least understood terms in the
1960s is "counterculture." For descriptions of this cultural phenomenon, see, for example: Theodore Roszak, *The Making of the
Counter Culture* (New York, 1969); Charles A. Reich, *The Green-
ing of America* (New York, 1970); David Horowitz, Michael Lerner
and Chris Pyes, *Counterculture and Revolution* (New York, 1972);
Morris Dickstein, *Gates of Eden: American Culture in the Sixties*
(New York, 1977); Simon Frith, *Sound Effects: Youth, Leisure
and the Politics of Rock n Roll* (New York, 1981); Todd Gitlin,
The Whole World Is Watching: Mass Media in the Making and Un-

making of the New Left (Berkeley, 1980); Michael W. Miles, *The Radical Probe: The Logic of Student Rebellion (New York, 1973); Burton Wolfe, * The Hippies *(New York, 1968); Lewis Yablonsky, The Hippie Trip* (New York, 1968); Sherri Craven, *Hippies of the Haight* (St. Louis, 1972); and Toni Del Renzio, *The Flower Children* (London, 1968).

Literature on Rock Music in the 1970s and 1980s

There has been a wealth of material published on rock music in recent years. The following books were helpful in assessing Chuck Berry's recent career: Charles T. Brown, *The Art of Rock And Roll* (Englewood Cliffs, 1983); Dick Hebdige, *Subculture: The Meaning of Style* (London, 1979); Julie Burchill and Tony Parsons, *The Boy Looked At Johnny* (London, 1980); Miles Palmer, *New Wave Explosion: How Punk Became the 80s* (New York, 1981); Glenn A. Baker and Stuart Cope, *The New Music* (New York, 1981); B. Lee Cooper, *Images of American Society in Popular Music: A Guide To Reflective Teaching* (Chicago, 1982); Gary Herman, *Rock n Roll Babylon* (New York, 1982); Caroline Coon, *The New Wave Punk Rock Explosion* (New York, 1977); and Rex Weiner and Deanne Stillman, *Woodstock Census: The Nationwide Survey of the Sixties Generation* (New York, 1979).

Special References Tools

The following list of reference books were useful during the writing of this biography; see, for example: Michel Ruppli, *The Chess Labels: A Discography*, Vols I-II (Westport, 1983); Jon Pareles and Particia Romanowski, *The Rolling Stone Encyclopedia of Rock and Roll* (New York, 1983); Dave Marsh and John Swenson, *The Rolling Stone Record Guide* (New York, 1979); Brock Helander, *The Rock Who's Who* (New York, 1982); *The Rolling Stone Rock Almanac: The Chronicles of Rock and Roll* (New York, 1983); and Norman Nite, *Rock On*, Volumes I and II (New York, 1974 and 1978). There were also many other reference books used in this study, but the ones listed here are the most useful in terms of Chuck Berry's life.

INDEX

284

285

Howard DeWitt with Bo Diddley

Morten Reff with Chuck Berry

ABOUT THE AUTHOR

Howard A. DeWitt is Professor of History at Ohlone College, Fremont, California. For two decades he has been a proponent of teaching about American popular culture in the classroom. He has also been a concert promoter in Seattle, Washington. Professor DeWitt earned a Ph.D. at the University of Arizona in 1971, and he has taught at the University of California–Davis, the University of Arizona, Cochise College, and Chabot College. He is the author of eight books, and is a well known California historian. Two of De-Witt's books, *California Civilization: An Interpretation* and *Readings in California Civilization: Interpretative Issues*, are widely used in California colleges. He is also the author of *Jailhouse Rock: The Bootleg Records of Elvis Presley* (with Lee Cotten), and *Van Morrison: The Mystic's Music*. Professor DeWitt is presently working on a biography of Elvis Presley's early years, and has completed his *The Beatles: Untold Tales*, a study of the group's formative years.

CONTRIBUTORS

Morten Reff is Norway's foremost Chuck Berry expert. He is widely known for his discographic work on Chuck's career. Much of the material in the discography section of this book is the result of Mr. Reff's diligent and painstaking research. He lives in Drobak, Norway, and is active in a number of European societies and magazines dealing with rock music.